THE
AMERICAN
CRISIS
REVISITED

COMMON SENSE IN THE 21ST CENTURY

DAVE EVANS

Charleston, SC
www.PalmettoPublishing.com

The American Crisis – Revisited
Copyright © 2021 by Dave Evans

Hardcover ISBN: 978-1-63837-835-8
Paperback ISBN: 978-1-63837-836-5
eBook ISBN: 978-1-63837-837-2

DEDICATION

To Celine and Ian – with love, thanks, and the exhortation:
Never give up

CONTENTS

List of Maps/ Chart

List of Illustrations

PRELUDE,
INTRODUCING COMMON SENSE

"These are the times that try men's souls. The summer soldier and the sunshine patriot will, in this crisis, shrink from the service of his country; but he that stands it NOW, deserves the love and thanks of man and woman."

These 41 words electrified America.

With these opening lines, they formed the most memorable and impactful paragraph of *The American Crisis I*. And with its publication in December 1776, author Thomas Paine sought to re-energize flagging spirits during the darkest days of the American Revolution. The colonists were fighting to govern themselves because they believed their rights as colonial Englishmen – not yet Americans – had been denied. Despite glimmers of initial success after fighting began in April 1775, they suffered continual, gloomy reversals over the ensuing months. In response to the stirrings of revolution, the British government dispatched an army of over 30,000 men, well equipped, professionally led, and complete with a long history of victory. Beginning in August 1776, this army drove the ragtag colonials from one battlefield to the next. British officers scorned their foe by calling George Washington, commander of the Colonial Army, the "Old Fox." Hunting horns were used to taunt him, and the British enjoyed a fine chase.

The colonists valiantly tried to drive out the British, but no matter what they did, defeat followed. A two-pronged winter invasion of Canada failed in late 1775. Though Washington's tactics, troops, and cannons forced the British to evacuate Boston in March 1776, the Redcoats regrouped at Halifax, Canada, before landing outside New York City in July. By dint of their reinforced army, they won a number of victories over Washington in subsequent battles. His forces, now called the Continental Army after July's Declaration of Independence, relinquished New York City and New Jersey to the British as it retreated into Pennsylvania. Colonial leaders bickered as their army withered from the stress of battlefield setbacks, desertion, short-term militias departures, and inept leadership. Washington himself, far from being the godlike figure revered today, questioned in letters to close friends whether he was up to the task.

Paine's words are believed to have bolstered Washington's belief to per-severe, thereby playing a critical role in changing the entire direction of the campaign that would culminate in the creation of the United States of America. Paine himself, though already a famous writer, served as a com-mon soldier in Washington's depleted and dispirited army as it dwindled to fewer than 3,000 soldiers. Talk of surrender or simply heading home was spreading, not just around the campfires of this shrinking army, but throughout the colonies.

However, the brilliance of Washington never shone brighter than when facing these challenges. Despite his doubts, he never gave up. When Paine re-leased his second pamphlet, *The American Crisis I*, six days before Christmas in 1776, he signed it "Common Sense," thereby linking it to his earlier, stirring work. [1] Washington, moved by Paine's words, sought to spread its inspiration to the entire army. He mandated that the slim volume be read immediately to the beleaguered troops, many without shelter and clinging wretchedly to the warmth of their campfires and communications from their commander. [2]

Uplifted by Paine's writings, Washington led his army out of camp on Christmas night amid a snowstorm and freezing temperatures. Buoyed by *Common Sense*'s spirit, his army rowed across the ice-filled Delaware River,

---

1 Paine's first pamphlet was *Common Sense*. Published anonymously in January 1776, it helped awaken and unify a population leading to the Declaration of Independence on July 4, 1776. More detail at Appendix 1.

2 A series of 16 *American Crisis* pamphlets were published during the Revolution under the same pseudonym. The first was only a dozen pages long and featured the iconic opening, "These are the times that try men's souls..."

itself a major feat. His troops marched the rest of the night through the snow and wind. Some soldiers wore rags for footwear, with their bloody soles leaving a red trail back to the boats. Nearly 10 miles later, they reached the forward British outpost at Trenton just after dawn. Totally surprised, Britain's elite mercenary Hessians were overwhelmed; most surrendered or died. [3] Finally, the Continental Army achieved the victory it had so desperately needed, thereby reversing the course of the Revolution. The Old Fox had become the hunter.

No one had believed such a victory was possible. Militarily, the revolutionaries' cause had appeared lost, their army badly beaten, physically exhausted, and emotionally spent. Politically, colonial leaders had been scrambling to salvage their lives and property after fleeing the capital in Philadelphia. Economically, even the colonists' financial system had collapsed; British hard currency remained the only effective buying tool.

Yet, Paine, a 39-year-old immigrant who had left England only two years earlier, still believed. Heartened by Paine, Washington himself, a man whose pre-Revolution claims to fame included surrendering his command at the first battle of the French and Indian War and surviving the massacre of General Braddock's combined British-Colonial Army, would not give up. Believing in the justice of their cause, he saw his responsibility as leading the army by example. Creating something out of nothing proved to be Washington's genius – he not only built an army that defeated the forces of the British Empire, but later melded thirteen dissimilar colonies into the United States of America.

Sometimes in history, small events that are little noted by posterity, spark actions that result in momentous change. Paine's published words, twice, with *Common Sense* and *The American Crisis,* were two such events. Their impact on George Washington, Congress, and the people soon to be called Americans, are classic examples. It is impossible to confirm how profoundly Paine influenced Washington himself, but what is certain is that the timing of his publications could not have come at a more critical

---

3 The Hessians lost over 100 men killed or wounded with more than 900 captured. As many as 500 escaped before the encirclement fully closed, but the demoralized survivors spread shock among British ranks, resulting in other units pulling back from front line garrisons across New Jersey.

moment in American history. Washington's decisive actions immediately following '*Common Sense*'s release indicate that these words may have been the catalyzing factor in changing the course of the American Revolution. More such moments should be remembered. This study – an analogy – offers the opportunity to review several others, as well as a look at how the lessons of these moments may relate to today's troubles in the 21st Century.

George Washington, Abraham Lincoln, and Joan of Arc are now dusty names in history books. Few would consider them exciting or relevant today, let alone inspiring people to perform great deeds. Most people have heard of them; some may be able to recite popular, grade-school stories about them. However, others blame them for actions that they were not responsible for, but actively tried to overcome. In truth, they appear as individuals from different generations and widely varied circumstances, but who shared a number of values that distinguished them among their peers. Never was "Success" stamped on their forehead nor an easy path laid for them to achieve greatness. The challenges they faced were as considerable as any that exist today. They were often filled with self-doubt, anger, and depression. They frequently had little support or trust from those that they were attempting to help. And they shared similar, significant traits: strong character, the ability to accomplish far-reaching goals, and the resolute conviction to persist and lead effectively in the face of adversity. Often, their biggest difficulty was convincing their fellow countrymen to face the most crucial issues rather than the less important or more popular concerns.

These leaders chose to confront problems that others shunned. They willingly accepted responsibility and applied their abilities to the tasks at hand, thereby demonstrating true greatness. This study will examine these leaders in four sections. The first three sections address the common traits of Character, Statesmanship, and Faith, illustrating in separate chapters how George, Abe, and Joan coped and succeeded during "times that try men's souls." A final, fourth section will consider the primary three contemporary challenges of today in 2021 and speculate – with proposed solutions – how these three individuals might resolve them. The question is also asked if we have a leader of comparable character, statesmanship, and faith. If so, can he or she unify the country to engage and overcome today's challenges? For at least the past generation, the major challenges – or opportunities – of our times have been either ignored or just chatted about – with limited confrontation or action. It is time to reflect on history to assist us with the future. As these two men and woman have proven in centuries past, strong, just leaders can unify disparate populations and succeed against all odds.

May this first short prelude stimulate your interest to read further. Just as Paine's words electrified action amid a rebellious 1776, today they give us alarm that this century's trying times could also use some Common Sense. [4]

---

4 See Appendix 1 for more background on the initial *Common Sense* pamphlet, 1763 - 1776

SECTION 1 - CHARACTER

CHAPTER 1

GEORGE WASHINGTON'S YOUTH AND FIRST ADVENTURES, 1732 - 1758

Character. That word encompasses exactly what Paine's "summer soldiers and sunshine patriots" lacked. Fair-weather supporters were happy to be part of the crowd and excited to be seen doing something heroic so long as there were observers and accolades. For the most part they wanted what was best, as they saw it, for their particular colony (none yet thought of themselves as Americans). But once the heady, early days had ended and their commitment was tested, it turned into a different story. Adversity then became someone else's job. This was the situation in the United States of America in 1776, just as it is today – the hard work is someone else's job.

However, the desire to 'pass the buck', does not work when the world is falling apart.[1] About midway between the Revolution and today, Rudyard Kipling wrote a short poem titled, *If*.[2] All but the final three lines identify obstacles that life can throw in front of a person – not just a general or president, but anyone. A few lines of the poem do well to convey its message:

> "If you can keep your head when all about you
> Are losing theirs, and blaming it on you.
> If you can trust yourself when all men doubt you,
> But make allowance for their doubting, too."

---

1 "Passing the buck" is said to have originated in poker. When a player did not wish to deal, he passed the responsibility to the next player. The phrase was popularized by President Harry Truman who kept a desktop sign with the phrase, "The Buck Stops here" in the Oval office.

2 Circa 1895.

Kipling lists a dozen such obstacles and how one should react to them, then challenges the reader to "keep your virtue," while maintaining "the common touch." If one does, then "Yours is the Earth and everything that's in it. And – which is more – you'll be a Man." [3] Kipling's theme, like Paine's, is about character. How one reacts to adversity defines one as a person. It is all too easy to lose sight of that reality today.

George Washington epitomized the virtue of character. It is the unifying theme of his life.

Yet, he was not born with it, as the myths that surround him today imply. He developed it by self- education and by absorbing lessons learned from the hard knocks of the world. And his character development did not take a straight path, but rather by a winding trail, marked with stumbling blocks, causing a few steps backwards, yet many more steps forward. The result was an overall forward direction with a lifetime of character accumulated along the way.

Though born to an "established" family in Virginia, George had to grow up early as his father died when he was eleven. His older, half-brothers inherited most of the family wealth and he became responsible for caring for his mother and four younger siblings. He took advantage of the few minor opportunities available in his teens and benefited from a few slivers of patronage in the form of mentoring. [4] Although he received only rudimentary schooling, he educated himself through travel and hard work. [5] Washington surveyed lands in western Virginia and by age 21 was recognized across the middle Colonies as a leading expert on the "frontier." Progressing, he also gained the ability to work with various groups of diverse peoples, such as Native Americans, recent Scottish-Irish-Welsh-German immigrants of limited education and of many religious denominations, while maintaining the ability to mix with the original, upper-crust English settlers. These lessons proved invaluable during the years ahead.

---

3   Appendix 2, full version of the poem, *If*

4   Washington's half-brother, Lawrence encouraged the young George to spend long periods of time with him, introduced him to trained surveyors, and to his closest friend, George Fairfax. Fairfax' father, William was the manager for Lord Fairfax, the largest landowner in the colony of Virginia. George and George became close and lifelong friends.

5   Washington's only overseas trip was to Barbados at age 19 with his half-brother, Lawrence. He contacted smallpox there and nearly died, carrying lightly visible scars for life.

On October 30, 1753 he was handpicked by the King's Lieutenant Governor of Virginia, Robert Dinwiddie, [6] to lead a tiny expedition across a mountain range (Appalachians) that few had ever traversed to find a fort whose location was unknown. He was to deliver a message to the occupants, Britain's long-time enemies, the French, directing them to depart English land. Much of this area was the home of Native American tribes allied to the French; there were no British settlers. His "expedition" consisted of himself, a guide (Christopher Gist), a French interpreter (Jacob van Braam), and a few men hired to transport supplies on horseback. They began at the end of autumn and traversed unmapped territory without towns or trails, let alone roads. And it was unclear whether the local inhabitants would allow passage, turn the party around, or just kill them. [7] Washington was not paid, though his expenses were supposed to be covered. He saw it as an opportunity. Again, he was only 21 years old.

Just after departure, the late autumn weather turned into torrential rains, causing the rivers to flood. These conditions ended the possibility of traveling by canoe, in some cases the only practical method to transit the trackless wilderness. When the rains stopped, winter arrived early. The route became a mix of deep snows and ice, which again meant no river travel. As a result, the undaunted party traveled nearly the entire route by foot. Eventually, they even had to leave their packhorses at a trading post, carrying a bare minimum of supplies on their backs. Yet, amid this adversity, Washington convinced some of the local Natives to assist and guide Gist, van Braam, and himself to not just the nearest French outpost, [8] but to the unknown major fort beyond it – his ultimate destination.

Against the odds the bedraggled, weather-worn young Washington reached Fort Le Boeuf near Lake Erie in what is now northwest Pennsylvania. Mustering all the dignity he could, he told the French Commandant, Legardeur de Saint-Pierre, and his officers they had to leave the region

---

6 Dinwiddie had the powers of a de facto Governor as the appointed ones never left England.

7 At this time, western Pennsylvania/ eastern Ohio contained formal tribes and dispossessed, splinter groups of others that had been pushed west previously by the Iroquois Confederacy and settlers.

8 Near present day Pittsburgh.

by order of another sovereign's king 3,500 miles away and a governor 500 miles off.

There is no record of the Frenchmen's initial reaction. One wonders if they suppressed the shock and even laughter upon hearing Washington's preposterous order. Everyone present knew there were no British outposts nor settlers west of the Appalachians and that the land between was controlled by tribes friendly to the French. France had a string of trading posts and forts scattered throughout the Great Lakes and Mississippi-Ohio River Valleys dating back to 1634 and extending as far west as Fort La Baye (Green Bay, Wisconsin).

France's response was clear. They convinced the leaders of Washington's guides to stay behind, leaving Gist, van Braam, and Washington with only a few hunters to return through the snow and ice with France's written reply. In all likelihood, they never expected them to make it. Who could?

Washington and Gist did make it. After six days of arduous travel in extremely difficult conditions, they reached their packhorses and the hired men who had finally reached the first French outpost. From there they departed without any Native guides, but after four days of battling cold and stormy weather, Washington resolved to carry on with just Gist in order to make better time for delivery of the French response.

Then the truly demanding times began. Despite the bitter winter, the pair did make better time. They were fortunate to survive a "chance" meeting with a local Brave. He agreed to guide them on a shortcut, but near the end of the day's trek, turned around and fired his musket point-blank at Washington. Somehow, he missed. Catching the now disarmed Brave, Washington accepted his story that it was a misfire mistake and let him go unharmed, over the objections of Gist. Even under these severe conditions after nearly losing his life, this young man valued the dignity of life. Probably, he also suspected that the French had encouraged such an act. After following the Brave for a short time to determine if he had accomplices who might resume tracking the two of them, they headed in the opposite direction and travelled all night to ensure safety.

The next day they reached the banks of the Allegheny River. To their misfortune, the river was not frozen solid; the midstream was rushing, ice-filled water. The one hatchet between them served as their only tool to build a raft. When it was finally completed late in the day, they set out across the ice to the open water. The episode did not end well. The raft overturned. They had to swim for shore while avoiding ice chunks and weighted down by their clothes and what gear they could hold. Both survived and reached a small island. Soaked through, they tried to build shelter for the night. Totally wet and with temperatures well below freezing, few could have survived. But they did. Demonstrating how cold the night had been, the next morning the ice between the island and far-side riverbank had frozen solid. They walked across and by good fortune found a trader's cabin the next day.

The journey and its dangers were far from over. It was early January and winter had just begun. The Appalachians still had to be crossed. And the hazard of being captured or scalped by the Native warriors had not eased at all. Comparatively though, the worst was over. Their luck changed within a week on the trek east when they met a work party with packhorses. Now, east of the mountains and on horseback, Washington was able to ride the rest of the way.

While delivering the response from the French to Governor Dinwiddie, Washington also shared a clear, concise, and factual account of his mission, including the not-so-flattering inability to gain tribal support. Then, he went home. No fanfare. No hero's welcome. And no effort to share his story with any but those who had an official right to know. But this mission did not end quietly. Dinwiddie had the report released to the press throughout the Colonies and sent to the King in London. His report made Washington a famous man. [9]

To recap, Washington was 21 years old and had demonstrated that he understood the meaning of responsibility. He had dealt effectively with a wide range of people – the British leaders running the Colonies, colonists,

---

9 During Washington's early years of self-education, he developed and maintained a lifelong fascination with the ancient Greek/Roman philosophy of Stoicism. During his early years of reading, he gathered all the writings he could find from the founder, Zeno, to Caesar's contemporary, Cato the Younger, and the emperor, Marcus Aurelius, making notes on their teachings. Tenets that Washington endeavored to make central to his life included: Accept events as they are and work to better them. One's actions are more important than how one speaks. Virtue is the only good. Exhibit self-control and treat others fairly. Teamwork. Not only were his actions on his first adventure a demonstration of his adherence to his readings and notes, but these threads run throughout the remainder of Washington's life. Another aspect included the stoic exhortation to treat enslaved people leniently, as all people come from the same source.

frontiersmen, Native American people, and the representatives of an un-friendly foreign power. Clearly, he was persistent and uniquely qualified. Because of these remarkable attributes, it was unlikely that any other person in the Colonies – Colonial, British, or Native – could have completed this mission successfully.

This early tale of Washington was more than positive, even heroic. Yet, it was also just the beginning of his trials in the fires of adversity that would forge his strong character. Soon, he was about to meet challenges beyond individual adventure and danger -- trials that would test his leadership and political acumen as essential elements of his character development.

Success, particularly at a young age, can be a mixed blessing. There is no difference between the mid-18th century and any young celebrity today whose early promise sputters out before reaching his or her potential. So, it began with Washington. The story of his mission, the French response, and his expedition's exertions spread throughout the Colonies. It was clear that war was in the air, and each Colony chose how to prepare. Virginia, under Governor Dinwiddie was the first to act. He decided the colony needed protection on the frontier to be ready for a repeat of the bloody skirmishes experienced in previous Franco-British conflicts.

Deciding to raise a Virginia regiment to defend its western edges, Dinwiddie asked the now-famous 22-year-old Washington to be the new unit's second-in-command during the spring of 1754. Washington had no military experience nor schooling in the art of war. But he had proven to be a leader able to overcome incredible hardships to get a difficult job done. He accepted, but wisely requested a senior commander be assigned over him to ensure he could learn the requirements of the new role. Of course, the political leaders of the Colony assured him that would be the case.

Wars can often take unexpected turns, and show that whatever can go wrong will go wrong. This conflict, which became known in the Colonies as the French and Indian War, certainly proved that adage. Washington's new commander died unexpectedly a few weeks after his appointment. Washington had already led the initial contingent of volunteers out to the edge of the frontier, the same frontier he had ventured across the previous autumn. This act gave Governor Dinwiddie enough confidence in his young leader to allow Washington to remain in command, while providing him plenty of verbal support.

Unfortunately, wars are not won verbally. Washington, who held this command for over four years, came to realize that the challenges of an individual assignment were nothing compared to the responsibility of command. He learned, as his soldiers did, what was necessary to survive and how to defend the frontier. During these years, some challenges remained constant. There were never enough trained men. They seldom were paid, and when they were, it never covered all the missed paydays. There was never enough weaponry – muskets and rifles, powder and ball, or cannon. Supplies and shelter were always scarce, as were quality clothing, gear, and food. Though repeatedly promised the regiment's needs would be met, it never happened.

Subsistence was enough of a challenge by itself. But there was also a war happening and they were soon in the thick of it. The first "battle" of the war (actually a skirmish of a few dozen men each) was won by Washington with Native reinforcements in May 1754 on the west side of the Appalachians. He wrote afterwards, "I heard the bullets whistle. It was a charming sound." He would come to think differently of future battles.

Part of the learning began shortly thereafter. War had not yet officially been declared. The French had been ambushed. Afterwards, they claimed that their commander, Sieur de Jumonville, was carrying diplomatic documents to Governor Dinwiddie in response to Washington's trip the previous year. Everything about this affair was confused – the situation before battle, the inability of Washington and local allies to agree how to attack, and the results after shots were exchanged.

His next lesson was surrender. It taught him that his personal pride and his own mistakes were not as important as his duty to his soldiers. The French reacted strongly after the earlier skirmish by sending a large force against Washington's troops. He had selected a poor location to build a palisade, Fort Necessity, in the middle of a clearing, allowing his troops to be surrounded by the superior French force. His Native allies deserted after sensing the fort was indefensible. Colonial soldiers were unable to defend themselves when under fire. The French and their Native allies were able to fire from above and strike anywhere inside the stockade from the concealment of the dense forest. Washington lost a third of his men, killed or wounded. In less than a day he asked for terms to lay down their arms. These youthful lessons in character (humility/pride) and soldiering (the key military necessity of proper usage of terrain) were also ones he never forgot and rarely repeated.

The French accepted his request. More importantly, they made Washington sign a document of surrender. Van Braam, his translator from the Ft. Le Beouf expedition, purportedly explained the document before Washington signed it since he did not read French. It stated that de Jumonville had been "assassinated" because no state of war existed. The young commander either missed or ignored this critical word. Washington and most of his troops were released and allowed to return home because war had not officially begun.

After this return, Washington faced tough questions from the Governor and his Colony. Soon, the news had spread throughout the other Colonies. Many condemned him. Once the surrender document arrived in Europe it was widely disseminated and Washington and his actions were extensively criticized.

Yet as one looks at these affairs today, several aspects stand out. Without military training or experience and extremely youthful, Washington was woefully unprepared to lead a regiment of more than 400 soldiers. Due to his inexperience, he had been unable to convince his Native "allies" to assist, obtain the promised logistical support from his Colony, nor understand what the French were capable of doing. This result opened up the frontier to years of random terror and bloodshed. Internationally, Britain was blamed as the aggressor. Domestically, British aristocrats scorned the "Colonials" inability and ineptitude as military leaders (an attitude that would remain for the next 25 years).

However, those were not the sole results. At home, most considered Washington a hero for fighting a battle against the odds and preventing the enemy from advancing further. Also, he had demonstrated the ability to lead by example, with no concern for his own welfare, and the wisdom to know when it was time to save his men. In short, Washington learned, remembered, and did not repeat these kinds of errors again. All in all, good character development for young Washington.

Governor Dinwiddie, though far from pleased, nevertheless retained Washington as commander of the regiment. Washington returned to the troops and continued his efforts to secure sufficient men and supplies to do his job. Yet, if anything, he had even less support than before.

Later that year, 1754, three Colonies decided to conduct a joint attack against the new French fort at the Forks of the Ohio River (Ft. Duquesne, the current site of Pittsburgh). However, Washington was supposed to accept a lower rank, placing him under officers he had commanded earlier. His objections were ignored. Tactfully, he resigned from his position due to "ill health." He used this short break in service to rent an empty Virginia plantation from his half-brother's widow. He would inherit it when she died in 1761. Known as Mt. Vernon, it would be where Washington would settle and farm for the rest of his life.

Two months later, the Duquesne expedition was abandoned, amid news that a British general, Edward Braddock, was en route. He brought with him two British regiments, the authority to raise more Colonials, and the mission to seize Ft. Duquesne. Washington's intentions to farm evaporated, and he requested to be part of Braddock's staff as a volunteer aide. The offer was extended, gladly. Despite his youth and recent exploits, Washington had gained far more knowledge and experience in the region than anyone else in British North America. Braddock was more than happy to utilize it.

By joining Braddock's expedition, the untutored officer was able to observe and participate with professional soldiers for the first time. Up to this moment, Braddock's force was the largest group of trained professionals to ever appear in North America. Now, Washington had the opportunity to formally learn the art of warfare, fulfilling his goals from the previous year.

On the surface, success seemed all but assured. Like a Roman on campaign, Braddock built a road to support his mixed British and Colonial Army, the first valid line of communication across the Appalachian Mountains. The force seemed invincible, despite the fact they operated in the American wilderness as if it was open European countryside. Still, the main body of French and Native warriors fled before their advance. However, just outside Ft. Duquesne a small party, taking advantage of the thick forest, attacked Braddock's flanks along a narrow trail. The British had no flank support and panicked. They could not see the enemy who fought behind trees and outcrops. Their red uniforms made them prime targets, and the officers could not comprehend how to fight a seemingly disorganized enemy that appeared on every side. Braddock and his officers were unable to rally their troops.

Soon, Braddock was shot and mortally wounded, as were most of his officers. Washington, at Braddock's side for much of the day, ended up leading, organizing, and ordering a retreat of the surviving troops. His efforts certainly drew attention from the enemy. He had two horses killed that he was riding, his hat shot off, and a number of bullet holes through his clothing. However, the American Colonial, the 23-year-old volunteer, assumed the leaderless command, took control of a chaotic battle scene, and returned the remnants of the unit to safety. None of the remaining professional officers had stepped up.

This event, called the Braddock Massacre, marked the end of British efforts to win the war in the Ohio Valley for the next three years. The consequence was that the adjacent frontier erupted in violence as the Native tribes saw the opportunity to maintain their territories and drive the Colonists back from its edges.

There was another consequence. Washington's reputation soared throughout the Colonies. He received notes from many and praise from some of the surviving British officers. Others though, ignored his battlefield performance, including the future General Gage -- British Commander in Chief in 1775. Governor Dinwiddie asked Colonel Washington (rank now retained) to return to duty and command the expanded Virginia regiment of 1,000 men, and he accepted. An even lesser- known fact, but curious result of the Massacre, was that Braddock's personal orderly, Thomas Bishop, attached himself to Washington after the battle. He loyally served the future president for more than thirty years. It is worth noting as an early sign of the exceptional loyalty that bonded many men to Washington.

Resuming his command along the frontier posts, Washington returned to his previous regiment for three more long years. None of the challenges from his earlier months ever improved; promised resources never materialized. Despite recognition of Washington's skill and courage in battle with Braddock, the grievous defeat hung heavily on the restored commander and the remaining troops. They stayed on the defensive; no further offensive operations were undertaken until mid-1758. Indeed, the Braddock Massacre is still taught in military circles today as an example of how a lack of direct, hands-on leadership and failure to adapt to local conditions led to disaster. For Washington, the experience provided him insights into formal military operations along with confirmation that his own personal leadership made the critical difference between success and complete disaster. Likely, he also realized that he performed at his best when events proved be at their worst; he certainly would prove that characteristic again in the decades ahead.

As he would do throughout his career, Colonel Washington attained proficiency in the art of how to improvise. He held the frontier with meagre support and insufficient men or material to do the job properly. Yet, unlike the rest of the frontier colonies and despite repeated raids of small parties, Virginia never fell under serious attack. Virginians and their property were generally safeguarded, in large part due to Washington's efforts – and leadership.

Over the years, while sharing the day-to-day frontier hardships with his troops, and despite being younger than most of his soldiers and officers, Washington gained something that few commanders ever really win. He won the respect and the love of his men. He also showed he had learned from his earlier experiences. Some of his troops were trained to fight using conventional European tactics; others were organized and trained in small, unconventional units, fighting and moving as their indigenous foes did. Outside-the-box thinking was rare in that age, as it is today, and would prove critical in a war yet to be fought, the American Revolution.

Many examples can be found demonstrating the high regard that his soldiers held for the young Washington. Letters from the time illustrate this fact. Many soldiers continued to stay in contact with him after his service, again displaying this regard. The respect flowed both ways; the former commander helped many of his veterans over the years. [10] With time, Washington's renown as a respected Colonial commander, compared to the often-haughty British officers, spread throughout the Colonies. He

---

10   Three examples. Between 1768 – 1775, Washington hosted over 2,000 guests that stayed for at least dinner and often several nights at Mt Vernon; many were ex-comrades in arms. He was active in securing land grants in the Ohio country for his veterans via the Virginia legislature. One neighbor, ex-Captain Posey, was loaned more than 1000 pounds (over $200,000 USD in today's value) over a period of years for his farm, without the loan ever being repaid or farm foreclosed. Further, he educated and often housed Posey's children at Mt. Vernon.

became known as an experienced, reliable commander, someone worthy of high esteem.

Eventually, Washington became worn out. Frustrations continued to accumulate, as he could never outfit his soldiers properly. He disagreed with the direction the war was heading. His relationship with the governor became increasingly frayed, and hopes of being accepted into the British Army as a professional officer were repeatedly rebuffed.

It was again time to move on. Following the attack and destruction of Ft. Duquesne in 1758, Washington resigned at the end of the year and retired to Mt. Vernon to run his plantation – and marry.

Upon his resignation, Washington wrote a farewell message to his officers, delivered in person. He spoke of his thanks for their service and expressed appreciation for their warm words of praise. He considered it an honor to have commanded them and that they had given him the greatest happiness of his life. Their service and thanks were both his reward and his glory. [11]

The 26-year-old seasoned commander of 1758 had grown greatly since embarking on his first mission to the French as an untried twenty-one-year-old novice frontiersman. He had shown resilience and tenacity in the face of failure and much adversity. He had learned to bounce back and make the best of whatever situation he had encountered. He had become competent in leading men, learned the full extent of command responsibilities, and cared for them, all while performing whatever mission was assigned. His ability and willingness to mix with anyone had broadened, and he built further confidence by doing so. People realized they could depend on him, trusting him when he stated he would achieve something and looking to him for solutions.

If anyone bothered to look closely at this young man, they would also have seen he had an incredible thirst for knowledge. Self-educated and believing in the principles of the Enlightenment, he focused on one of its key principles: the ambition for renown and great deeds was positive if

---

11 Appendix 3 has Washington's complete farewell letter to his officers in response to their letter of appreciation to him, their commander.

and only if, one sought civic virtue rather than power or wealth. [12] Fame never changed his nature. At an early age, he had mastered surveying to gain financial independence as a teenager. Similarly, he had acquired the knack of being a competent soldier and officer. He would do this again as a farmer and as he gathered increasing responsibilities in his career. As he grew older, his ambitions grew consistent with obligations and volunteering. Initially, that obligation was as a neighbor and as a mentor for his ex-soldiers, but grew into representing fellow Virginians in the Virginia Assembly and eventually, serving his new nation. To sum up, in Washington's early years perhaps the most crucial skills he gained were perseverance and positive leadership, demonstrating an uncommon ability to inspire and impart his belief in those around him.

Washington's early background, growth, successes and failures guided his development. And without the failures, one must wonder if he would have achieved later success in winning the colonies' independence from Britain and unifying the country as its first president. Although the stories from his younger years are largely forgotten, they proved to be the foundation for what Washington became and the greatness he accomplished. The one thread that connects all of these tales is simple: character.

---

12 The Enlightenment was a European intellectual movement in the 17th and 18th centuries that focused on Man's ability to reason. It resulted with advances in science, philosophy, government, art, theology, and education. Washington's self-education concentrated on this recognition and goal to improve humanity's future.

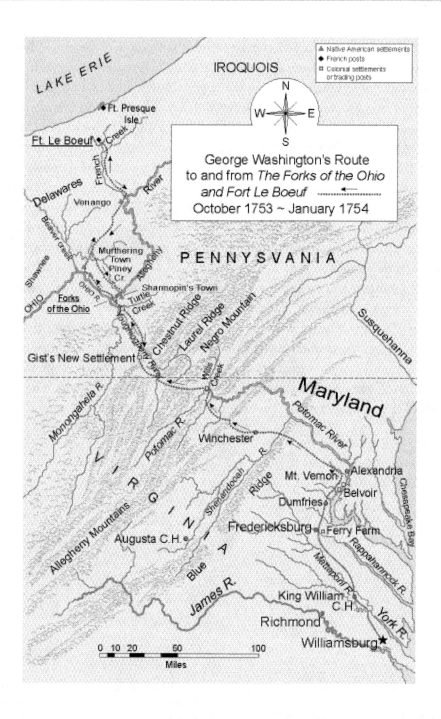

WASHINGTON'S JOURNEY: WILLIAMSBURG TO FORT LE BOEUF

GEORGE WASHINGTON IN 1772 WEARING HIS FRENCH AND INDIAN WAR UNIFORM. THIS CHARLES WILSON PEALE PAINTING IS THE EARLIEST KNOWN PORTRAIT OF WASHINGTON.

CHAPTER 2
ABRAHAM LINCOLN'S ROAD TO THE WHITE HOUSE, 1809 - 1860

Abraham Lincoln, like George Washington, began his life with hardship. Born in Kentucky in 1809 to struggling parents, young Abe grew up in a one-room log cabin on a small farm. Despite moving his family multiple times during his youth, Lincoln's father, Thomas, could never quite rise to any level above self-sufficiency. Problems with land titles in Kentucky pressured the family to move to the Indiana Territory and start over again when Abe was seven. His mother, who encouraged Abe's early learning and ambition, died at 34 when Abe was nine.

Young Abe's childhood challenges seemed only to serve as his inspiration. He became a voracious reader, walking miles to borrow the few books that existed on the Indiana frontier. He learned how to write, taught himself mathematics so he could understand accounting, and studied English to better express himself. Even at a young age, he was known as a good storyteller.

His formative years were less a childhood and more a series of apprenticeships. Like Washington, Abe grew to be a giant in his youth. His father exploited Abe's size and strength by hiring him out as a farm hand, which helped to sustain the family and secure Thomas' livelihood. As a teenager, in 1828 Abe took a flatboat down the Mississippi River to New Orleans to sell produce, witnessing large-scale slavery for the first time. One night with the boat moored to shore, Abe and his crew mate were attacked by a gang of cutthroats. They chased the gang off, but Abe was cut above his eye, resulting in a scar that stayed with him for the rest of his life. Drifting and poling down river for three months and 1,000 miles calls to mind Huck Finn's fictional trip on the Mississippi. The experience shaped Lincoln in ways comparable to the teenage Washington, whose surveying adventures took him to the edge of the Appalachian Mountains. However, in contrast to Washington, Abe paid his earnings to his father, as was the practice at the time, thus delaying his steeper climb out of financial hardship.

At age 21, Abe helped move his father and stepmother westward to un-tamed and unclaimed land in Illinois. With only simple axes, shovels, and bare hands, they built a home, fenced the open prairie, cleared ground for crops, and survived a ferocious winter with sparse food or heat. With his father settled, Abe joined a cousin and his stepbrother for a second flatboat trip to New Orleans (1831). While this trip provided no extraordinary ad-ventures, it did enable a clean break with his father, began a new chapter as an independent adult, and reinforced his belief that slavery was demeaning and unjust. [13]

Stories about Lincoln's youth began to circulate in the late 1850s and give evidence to his growing thirst for knowledge and a continuing quest for self-development. There is a tale of Abe walking 30 miles to a courthouse to hear and watch lawyers litigate a case. After observing politicians deliver speeches, he would mimic their words and gestures. He similarly observed itinerant preachers and peddlers hawking wares on the frontier. Though heavy drinking and smoking were commonplace, he decided that neither alcohol or tobacco suited his taste nor served his greater purpose. And always, he told stories, and he experimented on how best to attract folks' attention and convey his views to them.

Following his July 1831 return from New Orleans, Lincoln journeyed alone to New Salem, Illinois. There he worked as a shopkeeper on the edge of the frontier. The job offered him plenty of opportunities to see the world around him from new perspectives. His first taste of armed conflict came while serving as a militia "soldier" in what became known as the "Black Hawk War," April – July, 1832. His participation did not include combat but imparted some important lessons that proved vital for his long-term character development. He witnessed that officers often did not know what to do nor

---

13 Lincoln suffered an uncomfortable and somewhat distant relationship with his father. Later, when requested, he did assist his father and stepmother financially after he began to prosper.

how to cooperate. He learned that soldiers were a precious resource not to be wasted by endless, aimless marching. And he gained great appreciation for a leader's responsibility for taking care of his soldiers with adequate food, water, and rest. Indirectly, these lessons did influence him in his upcoming political career. He also learned that leaders must earn respect by their actions and that their success relied on planning with a purpose rather than reacting to situations at hand. And when care was taken for those under one's trust, the result was often a team far more capable of achievements than a group of individuals, no matter how talented. Abe never forgot these lessons, and they clearly helped shape his role as Commander-in-Chief thirty years later.

In short order, Lincoln won respect. He was elected to serve as an officer after his initial 30-day enlistment ended. Lincoln found, perhaps to his own surprise, that others looked up to him for more reasons than his six-feet, four-inch stature. While his varied experiences prepared young Lincoln for future endeavors, his work as a hired hand, shopkeeper, and short-term militia officer did not satisfy his early ambitions.

Prior to his militia service, Lincoln had already decided to run for the Illinois legislature in the August 1832 election; he was 23 years old. Though he finished a lowly eighth among thirteen candidates, he remained determined to seek election again. In the meantime, he learned surveying, which enabled him to support himself in the lean years spent gaining a foothold in politics. It is interesting to note that both Washington and Lincoln learned and applied this technical trade as they climbed the first rung of their respective career ladders. True to their surveying craft, both became future masters of studying the lay of the land, both topographically and politically, and creating order from disorder. Surveying provided them experience studying a complex problem and mapping out a step-by-step process to solve it - a skill that would certainly contribute to solving bigger problems later in life. To further advance his ambitions, Lincoln also began to study law in late 1832. With only enough income to live day to day, he studied law in every free moment at the shop, which doubled as a post office and where he literally burned the midnight oil after long days of surveying.

Incredibly, the multi-tasking shopkeeper, postmaster, surveyor, and law student added another role to his expanding employment portfolio: elected politician. Lincoln ran again for the Illinois state legislature in August

1834, finishing second in votes for his district and earning a position as a representative in November. He soon found that his income as a legislator for a few weeks of assembly each year was insufficient to support himself. Accordingly, he surveyed in between legislative sessions and continued to study law. True to public service, he also kept the postmaster role until May 1836. Following re-election in August of that year, he passed the equivalent of the Illinois bar exam, which allowed him to argue court cases beginning in September. He concluded his last surveying assignments in November.

After this relentless multi-role five-year "apprenticeship," the newly elected Lincoln decided to focus on only two paths: politics and law. Entering the legal profession and his second term in the legislature at age 27, he took his first significant steps in establishing himself with his chosen career as a lawyer and legislator. He had already advanced a long way from log cabin to the state capital. This whirlwind of activity, stirred with increasing responsibilities and success, offered a glimpse of Abe's future potential. His willingness to study and keenness to grow his knowledge only intensified in the years ahead. He intended to make a difference, and he quickly committed himself to the issues and challenges of his new state, just as he had done in all his earlier roles.

However, nothing that Abraham Lincoln ever started finished easily. His character was forged on the anvil of adversity. The following record of events clearly chronicles Lincoln's determination over three decades of repeated defeats and failures. It is a summary that outlines the continuous challenges he faced and surmounted.

Lincoln's Road to the White House

1. Failed in business, 1831
2. Defeated for State Legislature, 1832
3. Second failure in business, 1833
4. Fiancée died, 1835
5. Suffered nervous breakdown, 1836
6. Defeated for Speaker in Legislature, 1838
7. Defeated for State Elector, 1840
8. Defeated for U.S. Congress, 1843
9. Defeated for U.S. Congress, 1848
10. Defeated for U.S. Senate, 1855

11. Defeated for Vice President candidate, 1856
12. Defeated for U.S. Senate, 1858 (Lincoln – Douglas debates)
13. Elected U.S. President, 1860

Further, two of his children died at ages three (1850) and eleven (1862).

Yes, he saw some successes mixed with failure, such as his first election into politics at the Illinois state legislature in 1834, beginning his law practice in 1836, marriage in 1842, and an elected single term to the U.S. Congress (1847 - 1849). But no accomplishment beyond his marriage lasted for long. There was always a new mountain to scale or obstacle to overcome. And through it all in these early years, Abe clearly demonstrated persistence amid life's recurring defeats.

Or as Kipling continued in *If*,

> "If you can bear to hear the truth you've spoken
> Twisted by knaves to make a trap for fools,
> Or watch the things you gave your life to, broken,
> And stoop and build 'em up with worn-out tools"...

Kipling's message in *If* summons up Lincoln's grit and resilience, never broken by his life's failures, a quality that would define him for posterity.

Another pair of interesting stories about Lincoln concern his single term in Congress. They illustrate his tolerance and willingness to listen to all sides of an issue, while not allowing different political views to interfere with personal friendship.

Without previous association with other Congressmen before arriving in Washington, D.C., Lincoln befriended two other members of the Whig party during his 18-month term. One friend was Alexander Stephens of Georgia; the other was Robert Toombs, also of Georgia. Fourteen years later, Stephens would be elected as the Vice President of the Confederacy, and Toombs would be Secretary of State and later serve as a Confederate Army general. Although on the opposite side of the looming clash on slavery, Lincoln kept an open mind and did not allow differing views to divide his friendly relationships.

The second story is set during the 1848 presidential election. The country was at war with Mexico, and Zachary Taylor, a general and early hero of the

war, had been nominated by the Whig Party as its presidential candidate.
[14] Taylor came from a family of slave holders and had moved from Virginia
to Kentucky to Louisiana during his life. However, he favored a strong
Union, opposed secession, and believed that slavery should not be allowed
to extend into new territories (including land that had just been won from
Mexico). Lincoln campaigned for Taylor extensively throughout much of
the North on the belief that Taylor, although a slaveholder, was the best
candidate because of his opposition to extending slavery. And therefore,
Lincoln reasoned, Taylor's election would be the best way to maintain the
Union. Still 12 years before his own election, it would not be Lincoln's last
dilemma over the perennial crisis of slavery.

Despite being intensely practical, Lincoln never lost his idealism, even
in the murky world of politics. He remained committed to his two central
political beliefs that slavery was wrong and the Union must be preserved.
That era's political environment ensured these ideals would be challenged
regularly. Yet, he never lost his sense of humor. There are books written about
his storytelling and his ability to weave laughter into the fabric of many of
his lessons. One representative story occurred in mid-1863 amid unrelenting
pressure and the seemingly endless Civil War. At the time only one Union
general appeared capable of defeating rebel forces: General Grant. Hosting
a committee of congressmen and leading citizens amid discussions on how
to improve sagging Northern morale, the objection was raised about Grant's
history of drinking. Lincoln asked if any members of the committee could
name Grant's favorite whiskey. The puzzled members shook their heads,
negatively. Lincoln's response was to state that if he discovered the brand,
he would send EVERY general a barrel of the same whiskey.

He also gained a reputation for his willingness to help any visitor, friend
or stranger. He litigated a number of cases where he helped widows, folks
down on their luck, or even travelers requiring legal assistance. If he believed the accused was innocent, Abe would take the case, but only on the
condition of accepting a token fee if the case was won. He knew they these
citizens were too proud to accept charity, but not well-enough off to pay
the full fees normally required.

---

14 Mexican American War, 1846 – 48.

He earned the sobriquet, "Honest Abe," from his earliest days as a store-keeper in New Salem. In one instance, while in his law office in Springfield, several years after closing the New Salem Post Office, an agent of the postal service arrived, seeking a Mr. Abraham Lincoln, and advising that there had been a balance of $17 from when the office closed. He was there to collect. Lincoln rose from his chair, went to his trunk, dug through it, and pulled out a small package. It was the $17, which he turned over to the agent. He had kept the money awaiting resolution through all the succeeding years. Years later during the Civil War, his Union soldiers called him the same – and loved him for it. It was as unusual then, as it is now for a political figure to merit a title of Honesty.

Despite the hardships that challenged both Lincoln and Washington in their early lives, each saw their challenges as opportunities to elevate their station in life and realize their individual potential. They shared a number of common traits. Both were self-made and largely self-educated men. They both hungered for expanding their knowledge and shared lifelong passions for personal growth. They believed in a strong sense of justice and held firm stances between right and wrong. These core beliefs propelled their inner drive and guided them in difficult decision making for the remainder of their lives. And perhaps most important to the fate of our nation, neither man ever relented until he succeeded, despite every reason in the world to heed the cautions and complaints of "summer soldiers and sunshine patriots."

CHAPTER 3
JOAN OF ARC, BEGINNING HER MISSION, 1428 - 1429

O ur third historical figure bears little obvious resemblance to George and Abe, iconic American men of character of the 18th and 19th centuries. By contrast, she was an illiterate, French peasant girl, raised in Europe hundreds of years earlier, in an era and society when it was sinful for females to be educated outside of the home or to be involved in anything other than pro-creation and household chores. Nevertheless, as the Dark Ages neared their ending, she appeared as a streaking comet of hope enlightening all of France.

Jacques d'Arc and Isabelle Romée brought their daughter, Jehanne, into the world in about the year 1412, amid the Hundred Years War between England and France. Yet, despite the traditions of the time, Jehanne would leave her home as a teen, serve under the counsel of angels, rise to lead armies of men, rally her country to historic victories in battle, and establish France as a nation rather than a feudal kingdom. History came to know her as Joan of Arc; she called herself Jehanne la Pucelle. [15] And the life story of this teenage girl, though full of character, remains as mystifying today as it was to her contemporaries and stands unparalleled in recorded history.

---

15   Joan never used her father's surname of Arc/d'Arc; it was applied by posterity. A further complication is that surnames were not common at the time. Joan later testified that in her vil-lage it was common for girls to take their mother's surname. Yet, she used the name, Jehanne la Pucelle, Joan the Maid (Virgin, in original usage). Whether by coincidence or not, French legend foretold that a Virgin from Lorraine would one day save France. Joan's title for herself will be used throughout this work, as it has been the case historically.

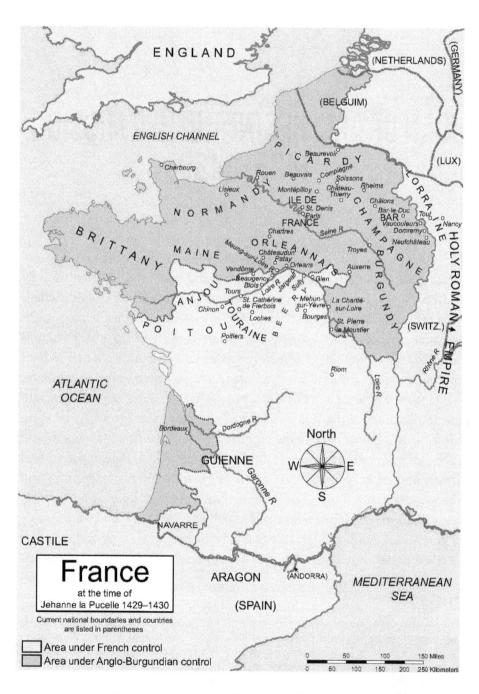

ENGLAND

(NETHERLANDS)

(GERMANY)

(BELGUIM)

ENGLISH CHANNEL

PICARDY

(LUX)

Cherbourg

Beaurevoir

Rouen   Beauvais   Compiegne

Soissons

Lisieux   Montépilloy   Château-   Rheims
                         Thiery

NORMANDY

ILE DE   Châlons

St. Denis   Bar-le-Duc
Paris   BAR   Toul

FRANCE   Seine R.   Vaucouleurs   Nancy

Chartres   Domremy

ORLEANNAIS   Neufchâteau

BRITTANY   MAINE   Meung-   Troyes
sur-Loire   Châteaudun
Patay

Vendôme   Orleans   Auxerre

Beaugency   Loire R.   Jargeau   Sully
Blois   Y   Gien

Tours   St. Catherine   R. Mehun-   La Charité-
de Fierbois   sur-Yèvre   sur-Loire

ANJOU   Chinon   Loches   Bourges   St. Pierre
                              le Moustier

POITOU   Poitiers   (SWITZ.)

TOURAINE

BERRY

BURGUNDY

CHAMPAGNE

LORRAINE

HOLY ROMAN EMPIRE

ATLANTIC
OCEAN

Riom

Loire R.

Rhône R.

Bordeaux   Dordogne R.

North

GUIENNE

W   E

Garonne R.

S

CASTILE

NAVARRE

France
at the time of
Jehanne la Pucelle 1429–1430

Current national boundaries and countries
are listed in parentheses

☐ Area under French control
▨ Area under Anglo-Burgundian control

ARAGON   (ANDORRA)   MEDITERRANEAN
                              SEA

(SPAIN)

0   50   100   150 Miles
0   50   100   150   200   250 Kilometers

A DIVIDED FRANCE AT THE TIME OF JEHANNE LA PUCELLE, 1429 – 1430

At the time of Joan's birth, the Hundred Years War had endured for 75 years. The roots of the war traced back almost 350 years to when the Duke of Normandy, ruler of a French province, won the English throne at the Battle of Hastings. Since 1066 the Duke and his successors as kings of England continued to hold French lands. Over the centuries, astute marriages to French nobles had expanded the Norman kings' holdings on the continent. In the 12th Century, Henry II gained an illustrious prize in his bride, Eleanor of Aquitaine, a duchess holding several provinces and one of the richest rulers in Europe. As a result, England controlled more French land and received more fief income than French kings. This stood as a constant source of friction between the two sovereigns.

By the early 1300s, despite somewhat diminished land holdings in France, English kings still retained significant French possessions, valued their local allegiances, and maintained a compelling desire to regain "their" lost lands. War broke out in 1337 and continued for decades with no end in sight. Following a decisive victory at the battle of Agincourt in 1415, England again controlled over half of France. (see 1429 map of France showing English and French possessions and current borders).

Accordingly, Joan grew up in a land that was battered by the brutal tides of war. Her village, Domrémy, was located in the Lorraine region of northeast France. Sitting vulnerably on the edge of the frontier between French and English-controlled lands, Domrémy had fallen under attack several times and had been ruined by fire at least once during her younger years.

Before she ever left her village, young Joan at around age 13 began hearing voices while performing family chores and shepherding their livestock. Up to that point, nothing had marked her as different from any of the other local girls.

Scared of what she believed she was hearing, terrified of voices that identified themselves as angels and saints, and wondering how this could be happening to her, she did what any normal person would do – she tried to ignore them. But the voices were heard more frequently, instead of going away, and they carried messages that the angels insisted be delivered.

She chose to confide first in the village priest. By itself, that was a frightening risk. Joan knew that the priest had the right to initiate an investigation by higher religious authorities. Those authorities would determine if the voices were angels – or devils. If the latter, that likely meant a trial would be conducted under church law, not secular law, and most likely would result in torture and being burned at the stake.

In that era, the Catholic Church, then the religious power across all of western Europe, was less tolerant than ever of religious differences. Jan Hus, a reformer who presaged the Reformation, had been burned at the stake during Joan's childhood. For the remainder of her life, the Church waged multiple Crusades, unsuccessfully, against Hus' followers. Even if Joan had been ignorant of Hus' history, she surely would have realized that an insignificant village girl was more likely to be persecuted than believed.

Few would care to face such a choice, let alone choose confession over silence. Joan did. The Domrémy priest listened, believed, and trusted her based on her lifelong devotion to God. He chose not to report her to his superiors and maintained her secret until after Joan left her village.

Sometime following her confession, Domrémy suffered another attack. It is unknown whether the foray was incidental or spurred her forward, but at age sixteen Joan decided she would deliver her messages. She asked her uncle to escort her to the local nobleman who maintained a garrison at the larger village of Vaucouleurs, a day's walk. The "castle" consisted of merely a tower with a small wall enclosing a courtyard. Fewer than 30 men-at-arms (soldiers) under the command of Robert de Baudricourt protected this regional fortress.

By all accounts, the visit did not go well. At best she would have been laughed away. More likely, the nobleman threatened her uncle with physical harm and she was threatened with being reported to the clergy. After all, why would angels choose to communicate through a peasant child rather than directly messaging an aristocrat or a person of royal blood?

She returned home, disappointed, disbelieved, and downcast. Who would – or could – believe her?

In today's world the concept of hearing voices is looked upon with skepticism – at best. In most societies this condition would likely be evaluated by medical professionals and if persistent, risk the patient's commitment to mental care. That assessment was certainly not the case in 15th century western Europe. In that era nearly everyone considered Joan's voices real – once she provided a "sign" and convinced her first believers that her messages were real and achievable. The only uncertainty was whether they came from Heaven or Hell?

The voices continued. France remained a battleground, contested by armies and "free companies" of mercenary brigands. Part of the French population questioned the legitimacy of their king. This stemmed from the previous king's decision to designate a new, English successor. In the aftermath of the calamitous French defeat at Agincourt in 1415 and further losses in the 1417 – 1420 campaigns, Charles VI of France permitted his daughter, Catherine, to marry the English King, Henry V. Charles further agreed that his new son-in-law would succeed him to the French throne. This decision disinherited the Dauphin Charles, his son and previously designated successor. [16] However, in 1422 the much younger Henry V predeceased Charles VI by two months. Henry's son, now Henry VI, was less than one year old at the time. He was to have become King of France when he reached majority at age eighteen. Most expectedly, the vast majority of the French peasantry bitterly resented the fate of having an English child as their next king. In contrast, a significant percentage of the French aristocracy supported Henry VI, as the English had proved to be the dominant power in France for several generations. (see French Royal family chart).

The younger Charles, ex-Dauphin and son of Charles VI, directly controlled only a tiny section of what was supposed to be the Kingdom of France. Much more of the land belonged to England. Independent nobles controlled the remainder and, generally, gave their loyalty to the stronger power. In this case, that power was England, which for over 90 years had not lost a major engagement. Considering England's string of victories and its dominant army of battle-hardened veterans with armor-penetrating longbows, why would any self-interested nobleman reject Charles VI's decision to anoint the English king as his successor, and cast his lot with the king's disinherited eldest son? Even his own mother chose not to support the Dauphin, which caused people to question whether Charles VI was actually his father. Moreover, the Dauphin – as a young man – lacked decisiveness, regal bearing, and any qualities to command respect and admiration.

---

16   The Dauphin is French royalty's equivalent to Great Britain's Prince of Wales – eldest son of the reigning King and heir apparent.

While this political turmoil engulfed the aristocrats, civil war raged across the French countryside, and the free companies pillaged and burned at will. Set in this context of conflict in early 1429, Joan's voices instructed her to attempt to accomplish a set of seemingly impossible tasks. First, she was to defeat the English army that was currently besieging Orleans, the only remaining French city of importance under control of the Dauphin. Next, she was to ensure the crowning of the Dauphin as the rightful King of France. [17] Finally, she believed that she was to expel the English completely from France within one year, parts of which they had occupied for over 400 years, and return the Dauphin's uncle, the Duke of Orleans, from his 14-year captivity in England.

Given France's decades of defeat, no one else in France or England, especially the Dauphin himself, could have believed that such a set of tasks could be achieved, let alone under the leadership of an illiterate peasant girl.

But Joan believed. And her strong belief, combined with the urging of her voices, compelled her to return to Vaucouleurs in January 1429, this time alone.

At this point, there is a need to digress and address the difference between Joan's upcoming accomplishments and what could be construed as a religious quest. In contrast to Washington and Lincoln, who both had years to gain experience, confidence, and education, Joan was thrust into her role with no preparation and no support except for her self-reliance and belief in her cause.

Joan's voices, or "counsels," as she often called them, never promised her personal salvation, reward, or even success. They simply advised her what needed to be done. France must be saved. To save France, Orleans must be relieved. Once Orleans was relieved, a French king could be consecrated and anointed. There was only one Frenchman who was legitimate to hold that crown, the Dauphin, not an Englishman. Once the Dauphin received the crown, the English could then be driven from the rest of France and his Uncle, the Duke of Orleans, returned to France. This was Joan's mission sequence. In all probability, it appeared to her as her own version "Common Sense."

---

17   French kings, since Clovis in 496 A.D., were crowned and anointed at Rheims, France. As Henry VI had not been crowned there, French peasants believed he had not been anointed by God.

French Royal Family
1380 to 1461

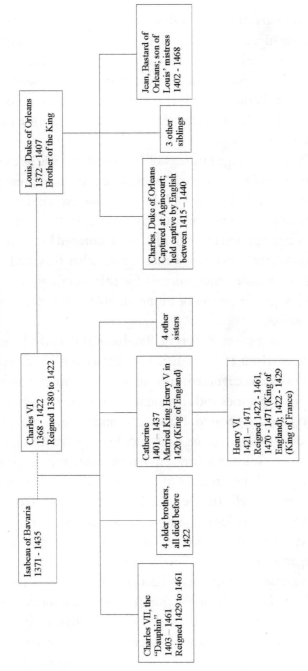

Note 1: Following the defeat of Agincourt in 1415, Charles VI of France and Henry V of England signed the Treaty of Troyes in 1420. The terms confirmed that Catherine was to wed Henry. Henry assumed regency of France and was confirmed heir of Charles VI, disinheriting Charles the Dauphin (later Charles VII).

Note 2: Two months before Charles VI death, the much younger Henry V died unexpectedly of disease, and his nine-month-old son inherited the English and French thrones.

The responsibility to fulfill this mission had not been attempted nor even accepted by the Dauphin, his nobles, and his warriors. This void created an opportunity that Joan would seize upon. Devout, trusting, adventuresome, and single-minded, Joan realized that success required her to out-think the most educated men in France, outwit the wiliest politicians, and out-fight the hardiest warriors. On top of all that, she would have to inspire a kingdom that had long ago given up hope.

She also realized the savage business of hand-to-hand warfare entailed injury, and that the equally savage business of politics entailed great prominence and influence – all to be accomplished in a narrow window of time and with no guarantee for her future. Further, Joan knew she would always be an outsider. Though uplifted by her faith and encouraged by her counsels, success would necessitate convincing others to do what they had already failed over many years. In essence, success for this seemingly impossible mission set would require a person of immeasurable character – and why her story is unparalleled

Rather than insisting to see Robert de Baudricourt directly, Joan urged his soldiers of the garrison to assist her. Of course, this generated only laughter and jeers, which she ignored. Instead, she concentrated on helping the soldiers in their daily duties and striving to set a positive example. After several days, the taunts disappeared. Robert's second in command, Jean de Metz, a grizzled, older veteran, came to respect Joan for her exemplary behavior among the men. When she insisted that the soldiers cease profanity, they did. And she gained their respect in the process. She did other things that influenced them as well. In one such instance, she asserted that the garrison's chickens would not lay eggs until she was allowed to meet Robert; while she waited, the chickens stopped laying. Witness to her prophecies and piety, the men began believing her. Now, it was time to convince Robert.

After weeks of numerous requests and denials, the nobleman reluctantly agreed to meet face to face with his inferior, the lowly peasant. In the hearing, Robert sought to bully, outwit, and embarrass Joan in front of his soldiers. Instead, her quiet demeanor and clear answers unnerved him. In their conversation, she made the outlandish request for an escort to travel to deliver messages to the Dauphin. And she boldly predicted the outcome of a battle that had not yet been reported. Pressured by his soldiers' support for her and guided by his own curiosity, he agreed to delay his answer until he had more information concerning the unknown battle. In the meantime, the chickens resumed their egg laying.

Shockingly -- and to the garrison's delight, several days later, a messenger confirmed Joan's account of the battle. In a time when news travelled no faster than a horse's gallop, such knowledge in advance was impossible – unless informed by God or the Devil. Prior to deciding whether or not to honor Joan's escort request, Robert's curé (chief priest of the parish of Valcouleurs) met with Joan, and by a series of interrogations, determined she was not representing the Devil.

The accurate prediction combined with the curé's affirmation convinced Robert to meet Joan's travel demands. He provided six soldiers, including Jean de Metz – all volunteers out of loyalty to Joan – to escort her across 300 miles of enemy territory. Weeks earlier, none would have even considered such a hopeless undertaking. (see map outlining the region of France that Joan was active – Domrémy/Vaucouleurs, Chinon, Orleans, Rheims, Compiegne).

She wore men's clothing and cut her hair for ease of travel and protection in case of capture. At the time it was considered a sin for a woman to wear male clothing, a certain aberration to God. Everyone in this era would have known this to be a hard and fast rule, not to be broken, ever. Before her departure, Robert gifted her a sword, another inconceivable act and a sign that Joan's tenacity and proper bearing had paid off at Vaucouleurs. Lastly, they rode horses. Joan had never ridden before, let alone on an extended journey at speed through enemy lands. The challenges of this expedition would be an initial test of her persistence, determination, and courage – all qualities that would serve her well in the future at surviving dangers and accomplishing quests. [18]

---

[18] In addition to the gifted sword, Joan had also been presented a warhorse, trained for combat, by the Duke of Lorraine. Previously, Domrémy had been part of his Duchy. Though currently, an ally of the English, rumors of the Maid from Lorraine galvanized the duke to hedge his position with both sides through his gift to his former subject, Joan. Civil war in France required complicated politics, even for the highest nobles.

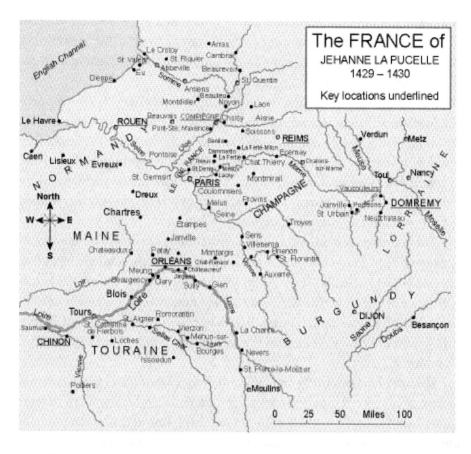

THE PART OF FRANCE THAT JEHANNE LA PUCELLE CONDUCTED HER MISSION.

Tales of Joan's exploits at Vaucouleurs began to echo across the land and also alerted the Dauphin's enemies. Her journey to the Dauphin's castle at Chinon transited 300 miles of enemy territory (English and their allies) in mid-winter, and necessitated the party travel by night and hide in forests by day. The enemy, on high alert for Joan, controlled all the towns and bridges. This meant the party had to avoid populated areas and must swim across frigid streams and rivers on horseback. Staying warm and dry on the trek would have been rare due to limited opportunities to build shelter or make fires. Yet, through it all, the farm-girl did not complain of these hardships. She mastered horsemanship enough to ride hard and fast, and she guided the soldiers to avoid detection as if she was the professional soldier and leader. The group arrived at Chinon with no issue, almost as if they had been protected by a guardian angel along the way. Their safe passage only reinforced the widespread rumors of the "miraculous maid" who had arrived to resurrect France.

By the time she arrived in Chinon, news of Joan had reached not only Charles, but also the English leaders. To the beleaguered French, she shined as a beacon of light; to the skeptical English, she presented a puzzle yet to be seen or solved. To Joan, she had come to lead an army to relieve Orleans, crown the Dauphin as King of France, and expel the English from French soil. Her tidings lost nothing in the telling and spread through both French- and English-controlled France like wildfire.

After several days of waiting, Charles allowed Joan to be presented to him at court. However, the meeting came with a test. Knowing that she had never met him and the probability of having seen his likeness was virtually nil, Charles disguised himself as a courtier and placed an imposter on his throne with his wife.

So, the scene was set for another of Joan's remarkable and unexplainable acts. An illiterate, 17-year-old girl dressed as a common (male) soldier, on her first trip beyond her destitute village, appeared at a majestic castle. [19] After climbing up its terraced steps, she arrived at the grand hall, where double doors were thrown open to reveal the entire royal court and accompanying courtiers, all decked out in their most magnificent clothes. Who would not have been overcome with bewilderment?

Joan was not.

By all reports, she strode confidently forward and stopped midway down the hall. Inexplicably, Joan realized that the man at the queen's side was not the Dauphin; she paused in a moment of confusion. Then, she exhibited presence of mind and gathered her wits, examining all the bystanders one by one. The royal court summoned her forward, but she ignored them, this teenager. Finally, she moved to an obscure bystander in a back row. As the front rows parted, Joan knelt down and simply stated: "Your Majesty."

Of course, it was Charles.

---

19 Unlike many castles of this era that lie in ruins today, this castle stands remarkably well-preserved in modern-day Chinon.

It is impossible to speculate how she could have known that the Dauphin would disguise himself at her introduction to the royal court, or how she could have identified the hidden royal from among the crowded hall. However, none of this royal majesty nor mischief phased Joan, this world unlike anything she had entered previously. After Charles addressed her, she calmly reported that she brought him important news.

Charles took her to a private room off to the side of the court. To this day, no one knows exactly what the two discussed, the royal Dauphin alone with the peasant girl. She never shared the details, nor did Charles, who was to live for another 30 years. [20]

However, as a result of their conversation, Charles agreed to provide troops to accompany her to Orleans, pending confirmation by Charles' religious advisors and theologians at Poitiers and Tours, again to verify that she was neither a fraud nor a devil. The investigation sent churchmen to Joan's home village and Vaucouleurs to check on her character, quizzing her about the voices, and examining her to confirm her virginity.

These examinations lasted six weeks, with the final report delivered publicly to the Dauphin and his advisors. The Archbishop of Rheims, the highest prelate (church official) in France and responsible for the clerical investigation, delivered the verdict: Joan was "of irreproachable life, a good Christian, and possessed the virtues of humility, honesty, and simplicity." These characteristics had been demonstrated consistently since her arrival at Vaucouleurs and as a girl growing up in Domrémy. Of course, the ultimate test would be the test of battle: allowing Joan to lead the army to Orleans to fight the undefeated English. In the meantime, during the weeks of investigation, she had won over a number of the leading men and women of France solely by her strength of character, frankness to one and all, and hard work at improving her horsemanship and sword skills. Among these new supporters was Yolande of Aragon, a widow and the mother-in-law of the Dauphin, who would arrange for the financial resources to raise Joan's future army.

---

20 Under extreme duress, Joan eventually described this meeting at her later trial. But it is highly likely that she invented details then as she had refused many times over two years to share details with anyone.

Following the announcement of the Archbishop's verdict, Chinon and its neighboring French provinces displayed a huge outpouring of emotion. Europe had not witnessed anything like it since the first Crusade 300 years earlier. Fundamentally, this wave of emotion transformed a 90-year-old political and familial dynastic war into a religious war, with the Dauphin's adherents on one side facing the English and their French allies on the other.

Like any inspiring and prominent historical figure, Joan immediately drew detractors.

Certainly, the English and those satisfied with the status quo in France would have been at the top of that list. Before Joan's departure from Poitiers, she had dictated a letter to the King of England (seven-year-old Henry VI) and the Duke of Bedford, regent of France (Henry VI's uncle). Some called the letter an act of callous arrogance, while others believed it showed gentle pity. Either way, she sent an extraordinary letter informing Bedford that she was bound for Orleans, offering the besieging English the opportunity to leave France immediately. If they did, the French would treat them with the best aspects of Christianity. If they did not, it would be to their great detriment. From Joan's viewpoint, the letter stated the facts without boasting.[21] But imagine the Regent of France, duke and uncle of the king, in receipt of a letter from a teenage, peasant girl dictating terms for the departure of his dominant armies. His view, one may safely surmise, would have been quite different.

Another aspect of the story bears repeating. Charles and his lords vied with each other to supply Joan the best equipment and horses. They prepared a standard (banner) exactly to her specifications, and even provided pages and attendants. However, she refused a new sword. Instead, she addressed a letter to the keepers of the shrine of St. Catherine. [22] In it she plainly advised the exact location of a buried sword, describing its condition, and directing that it be brought to her. One might suspect today – or then -- that a charlatan could have pulled off such a stunt. Yet, the sword was unknown to history. Unlike the Holy Grail or the Arthur epics, no legends or myths surrounded this sword. Under the circumstances, it is highly doubtful that a guileless

---

21 See Appendix 4 for the full transcript. Please note that 'Pity' was considered the highest quality of chivalry; this spirit and code flourished in the early 15th century.

22 Also known as St Catherine of Alexandria, she was a 4th Century virgin martyr.

innocent could have orchestrated a hoax of this magnitude. Nevertheless, the sword was found, cleaned, and presented to her. While the sword itself was superior, Joan's prediction was profound. And with the prediction, French fervor grew to an unprecedented level, in terms of religious intensity and as a rebirth of French pride.

The trajectory of Joan's story for the next few weeks was widely known. She set forth for Orleans outfitted in men's armor adjusted to her size, carrying her standard, and bearing the consecrated sword. Charles and the populace provided food and supplies for the besieged city, plus a small, well-outfitted escort, consisting of many of the Dauphin's best and most reputable knights. Along the journey beginning at Poitiers, small groups flocked to join, swelling and augmenting the escort to a considerable force. Although Joan did not have a specific, official position as a general or commander, she was the "envoy" of the Dauphin, and all clearly considered her as their leader.

Joan joined the assembling forces partway to Orleans at Blois. There, she first met the battle-hardened French veterans, whom she informed would drive the English from Orleans. Most laughed. She also ordered the enforcement of several new camp rules: swearing would be forbidden, all soldiers must confess to the church, and camp women would be removed. Over the next several days, the encampment radically changed, to the amazement of the officers. Joan led by example, participating in training drills, improving her riding skills, and visiting the men regularly across the camp. In a few weeks, she had transformed herself from a warfare novice into a warrior goddess. Her positive attitude and soaring confidence proved contagious, as pride and self-respect swelled through the ranks of France's underachieving forces.

Orleans was situated along the north bank of the Loire River. The French party approached from the south bank, as Blois was on that same side and English defenses were weaker on this opposite bank. Unaware of the geography, Joan was both surprised and furious; she had expected to meet the English outside Orleans' walls. The Orleans commander met them and bore the brunt of Joan's anger, not an auspicious beginning. Further, they were unable to cross the Loire as headwinds prevented their few boats from sailing. However, just after her arrival, the winds changed direction, allowing her and a small group to enter the city by sailing in-between the

surrounding English forts. The unexpected weather change further reinforced Joan's standing as a fortuitous leader, while imparting a calming
influence between the military leaders and the "envoy," Joan. The supplies
and escort troops had to be sent downriver to cross at a distant bridge. This
delay cost four days, but in the meantime, the entrance by Joan – now being hailed as the "Savior of France," had significantly bolstered the citizens'
morale. In fact, the inhabitants stirred themselves into a frenzy as Joan's
small band entered the city. The mass of people trying to touch La Pucelle
became so heavy that the soldiers had to clear the way. Everyone knew that
she had arrived to raise the siege of Orleans, in contrast to the lack of aid
over previous months. (see map # 4 -- Orleans siege)

But there was much more to accomplish. The English occupied a dozen
forts around the city to enforce their siege. These had been considered im-
pregnable during the previous months. Joan convinced the French leaders
to attack once the supplies and reinforcements arrived by land. The English,
inexplicably, did nothing to prevent Joan's escort or the separate provisions
from entering Orleans. Their inaction made no military sense. One may
wonder whether these tactical blunders were caused by English arrogance
or by being unnerved by the tales swirling about La Pucelle.

While awaiting the supplies, Joan sent two heralds to John Talbot, the
English commander at Orleans, to discuss the letter she had earlier sent to
Bedford. Against all the rules of chivalry, the English held one herald as cap-
tive. The other was sent back to convey a message that the captured herald
would be burned at the stake, a fate that awaited Joan once they captured
her, as the contemptuous besiegers undoubtedly expected. The English also
belittled her with slurs about her background.

THERE ARE NO KNOWN PORTRAITS OF JOAN OF ARC FROM HER LIFETIME;
PICTURED IS A REPRESENTATION OF HER ENTRANCE INTO ORLEANS,
MAY 8, 1429 BY JEAN-JACQUES SCHERRER, 1897.

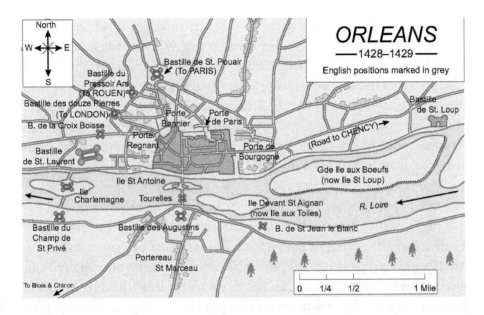

ORLEANS AND BESIEGING FORTS, 1429

After the supplies arrived and while standing on the open bridge between the walls of Orleans and the English citadel, Les Tourelles, within range of the dreaded English longbows, Joan again tried to convince the English to retire. Once more, they insulted her and made threats to burn her at the stake and abuse her before the burning. She responded with a simple shake of her head and then returned into Orleans, fully resolved that battle must decide the siege.

Despite the leadership and inspiration that Joan had already provided, the other French leaders chose not to inform their "envoy" of their imminent battle plan. After all, why would professional military officers feel the need to confer with a complete amateur in warfare? So, while Joan napped, they attacked the most isolated English outpost, Bastille de St. Loup.

Joan was awakened by her voices and informed there was a battle ongoing. After being armed by her page, she rode out in anger to join the French. Their assault had failed, and they were retreating in disorder again. She immediately exhorted the troops to re-form and led them forward herself. Despite the earlier failure to seize the fort, the warriors rallied and stormed it again, confusing the English by their unprecedented action. The French had never rallied! By her presence on the battlefield, Joan had rejuvenated the men. Victory had been stolen from retreat. With nowhere to go, the English fought hard, and many died in place. And with them, the aura of English invincibility died as well. Joan reacted to her first triumph with tears: the dead English had not been confessed and could not go to Heaven. She insisted that all the French be absolved by their priests for the killings – to the astonishment of the French leaders and the reverence of the men-at-arms.[23] Joan had successfully faced down and resolved another crisis. [24]

The Dauphin's Frenchmen were now fighting with a spirit the English had never seen. It must have been quiet in the other eleven English forts that night, as they contemplated their first battle defeat in generations. Like a tiny snowball starting its path downhill, Joan's first battle victory began, what would eventually become, an avalanche of increasing mass, power, and speed as it advanced across France and tore away the English self-confidence. Because the next day was the Feast of Ascension, a religious holiday, Joan requested, and the French commanders decided, not to fight. However, she sent another message to the English, this time tied to an arrow rather than delivered by messenger. She advised it was her third and last warning and requested the return of her herald. Once again, the English responded with laughter and insults. She burst into tears, not out of fear, but from the expectation that many brave men would soon die.

Unbelievably, the French commanders had not yet learned to include their muse in planning. Though willing to take advantage of her battlefield leadership, they again chose to omit her from a secret council of war. The council decided to conduct a feint against one fort on the north side of the river and direct the main attack against the principal English fort on the south side. Eventually, Joan was advised of the feint, but not the objective

23 Medieval armies comprised several groups of soldiers. Nobles held all the leadership positions and normally fought on horseback forming in groups around their liege lord. They trained to be individual experts at hand-to-hand combat, mounted or on foot, but did not usually fight as functional units.

24 As a general rule for medieval warfare, battles were few and far between. Most conflicts revolved around sieges or small raids rather than battle on open fields due to the brutality of combat and the cost to maintain armies. The primary goal was often not to win, but to capture nobles from the opposing side to sell for ransom to their families or lords. It was often warriors' main form of income, as pay only existed after towns were sacked. Joan's actions changed this practice; victory became the goal, not money.

for the main thrust. She paced around them angrily stating she knew they were not revealing the entire battle plan. One can only imagine the look of surprise on the faces of the haughty warlords as they realized they were incapable of concealing their plans and futile in outwitting this teenager on military tactics.

History offers contradictory accounts of exactly what transpired the next day. The planned feint may or may not have happened; there exist no reports of this maneuver, nor of Joan's involvement in it. The French did construct a floating pontoon bridge across the Loire as a way to reach the most isolated English fort, Bastille de St. Jean le Blanc, on the far bank. For reasons unknown, the English decided to consolidate their defenses rather than contest the crossing and relinquished this outpost without a fight. Were they intimidated? It is impossible to explain; their retreat was another action contrary to the English army's standard, aggressive practices. Joan's whereabouts at the time were unknown, though it was likely that only foot soldiers crossed the river initially, to be followed later by mounted troops. After briefly occupying St Jean, the French attack of the main English fort, Les Augustins, had been repulsed, and troops were retiring back towards St. Jean. The English were pursuing the retreating French in the open field between the two forts by the time Joan's presence was first recorded.

Again, as occurred two days earlier, Joan rallied the French. Disregarding the war captains' orders, Joan and one rogue war captain, L'Hire, attacked by themselves the overexuberant, pursuing English in an act of incredible bravery – or recklessness. The upshot was an immediate rush of French troops inspired by Joan and L'Hire. The English panicked and attempted a chaotic retreat. But the French seized control of the entrance before the English could close the fort's gates, and gained control of Les Augustins. This capture exhilarated French troops, but their leaders must have suffered mixed emotions. Their battle plans had proved hollow, and each battle had been reversed and won by the brave efforts of a novice. Who was the professional now?

That night must have been interesting in both camps. Despite losing three forts, the English army remained the approximate size of the French. Plus, the English retained the advantages of strong defensive fortifications, while the French had none of the heavy siege engines typically used to reduce a medieval fortress. Every tactical advantage lay with the English. The interesting part would have been the English realization that after two defeats, their certainty of victory in battle was now very much open to question. That evening's French war council recognized the English advantages and decided to retire back to Orleans for reinforcements. Joan missed the start of this council, as she had been wounded in the foot that day by a caltrop. [25] While this meeting took place, Joan was likely having her wound tended. Apparently, it was no more than an inconvenience, and she joined the council after the decision to retire had just been made. When advised, Joan informed the war captains that their council was not as powerful as her higher counsel – meaning from God's messengers (council and counsel have the same word stem in French, conseil). They would attack, blood would flow, and Joan prophesized that she herself would bleed from a chest wound.

Plans changed.

The English citadel, Les Tourelles (the Turrets), was situated on the bridge between Les Augustins and Orleans. Its south wall rested on the river bank with part of the Loire flowing through it, which necessitated a second drawbridge. Les Tourelles was heavily fortified. Without siege engines, the French had only scaling ladders to employ against the walls, and their courage as armor against longbows' arrows. They should have had no chance.

Despite being a forlorn hope, at least in the war captains' minds, they attacked early in the morning. [26] They were beaten back. Over and over, they furiously stormed the walls. Ladders were flung back. Men who successfully scaled walls were beaten down from the parapets, shot in the moat, or smashed by boulders dropped from the wall. Yet, they returned. At midday, Joan was shot by an arrow in the left breast. Protected from further injury by soldiers using their bodies and shields, she was carried away. Believing her dead, the French were distraught and the English reinvigorated. But she lived. The arrow had been driven six inches deep; Joan pulled it out herself and accepted medical care, though refusing soldiers' good-luck talismans as

---

25 A caltrop is a spiked metal weapon deployed on the ground to injure foot soldiers and horses. Its spines, like a sea urchin, are arranged in a way that, even if tipped over, at least one spike points upward.

26 Forlorn Hope. Military term to describe a group of volunteers leading an expected suicide attack against the enemy strongpoint.

against church teaching. The odds were that she passed out and stayed unconscious for several hours. Observers there must have been in disbelief; one just does not simply pull out an arrow lodged so deeply in one's own chest.

In the meantime, the battle continued to rage.

A dozen hours of unavailing struggle would have been exhausting, and the French Commander, called off the futile assaults. [27] The English, every bit as exhausted, must have heaved huge collective sighs of relief, as they began to relax and regain confidence. They had held.

It was at this moment that Joan regained consciousness, another fortuitous coincidence. She begged the commander to delay his decision and rest the troops a moment, while she stepped outside to pray. Word must have streaked through the French ranks that Joan was not dead, but had risen again. Fortified by prayer, despite an injured foot and a hole in her chest, her voice rang strong. Her clarion call to the troops to regroup and return to the fray was enough to once again revitalize them.

Certainly, the English heard the unexpected tumult of the refreshed enemy and wondered what had happened. As the restored French army dashed forward again, the reanimated Joan would have been clearly visible to the English. Joan's men swept all before them. The English had nowhere to escape and fought desperately on both sides of Les Tourelles, but without hope. Between fire and sword, all was lost, and the garrison wiped out. Joan's herald had not been burned and was rescued.

The seizure of Les Tourelles broke the siege. Joan had surmounted her next crisis and fulfilled her first promise to the Dauphin.

Her initial prophecy had come true. The seventeen-year-old peasant girl's personal example had repeatedly led the French forces to victory. In less than one week, Joan had secured France's first significant triumph against England, overcoming more than 90 years of uninterrupted loss and defeat.

How had this "good Christian of humility, honesty, and simplicity" convinced cynical politicians, disbelieving churchmen, hardened soldiers, and the common folk that she could steer France to a rebirth?

---

27 The French commander, named Jean, was the illegitimate son of the Duke of Orleans, but raised by him as a son and as a cousin to the King. Unusual as it may sound to our ears today, he was officially known as the Bastard of Orleans at this time, which was a sign of respect and honor. He had been fighting the English and their allies since he was 16 (born in 1402).

These events would have been even more difficult to believe in the paternalistic 15th century than they are today. But they happened. Initiative, integrity, self-confidence, sound judgement, and bulldog persistence have been hallmarks of all the great captains of history. Yet, they had years of preparation and experience before emerging to win their achievements. Joan's exploits, as outlined, began in January at Vaucouleurs; Les Tourelles fell on May 7 – to the unschooled teenager. France had completed an about-face in less than four months and for only one reason – Joan. She encapsulated each of these attributes of character and combined them with her representation of the best attributes of chivalry: devotion to God, compassion, courage, and loyalty. Yet, her greatest gift of all was to convince France that the French could do the impossible – and succeed in tasks they dared not even dream about prior to her arrival. Her confidence, faith, and belief were infectious and irresistible, carrying her nation on her back to its first victories in decades.

Clearly, as events later proved, the people of France wanted to believe a miracle could happen. But though such wishes are frequent throughout history, they are almost as frequently unanswered. Perhaps, these desires were answered in 1429 because Joan embodied so much that France's (and England's) leaders did not possess - character. She was the living embodiment of what the vast majority desired in a leader. For a short period, this young girl persuaded all that her messages could be accomplished exactly as she stated. They followed her, or in the case of the English - recoiled from her, for a while longer. Joan wasted no time in celebrating; the relief of Orleans was only step 1. Crowning the Dauphin at Rheims was next, and she would begin this quest on the following day. [28]

---

28 More than any other individual in medieval Europe, Joan's story was documented in detail by numerous witnesses and by her own sworn accounts. These formal statements were done by the Dauphin's church and legal representatives at Poitiers, two years later at her trial for heresy at Rouen, and 24 years later at sessions inaugurated by the Pope to review her actions and legitimacy. Accordingly, stories like the chicken and eggs, prediction concerning the Battle of the Herrings while at Valcouleurs, the sword at the shrine of St Catherine, and her battle actions were all documented by eyewitnesses.

SECTION 2 - STATESMANSHIP

CHAPTER 4

WASHINGTON, FIRST U.S. PRESIDENCY, 1789 - 1796: THE MODEL OF STATESMANSHIP

As the preceding three chapters have shown, George Washington, Abraham Lincoln, and Joan of Arc shone as beacons of character in their respective eras. However, many more stories illuminate their admirable qualities, allowing this new section to examine their outstanding statesmanship.

The anecdote at the beginning of the book related Washington's experiences at age 21. This next tale takes us 35 years beyond that point. But first, there is a need to account for his intervening years.

After delivering Governor Dinwiddie's message to the French, Washington continued to serve the State of Virginia. For four more years during the French and Indian War, he commanded the state's regiment in defense of its borders. And then at age 26 he "retired" and returned to private life, already well respected across the Colonies as a military leader.

Shortly thereafter, he married Martha Custis, a widow, and dedicated himself to running their combined estates. Martha's estates consisted of over 20,000 acres with a property and cash value in excess of $5 million US dollars (today's value), moderately larger than George's estates. Over the next 17 years, Washington became known as both an enterprising and innovative farmer. He shrewdly grew the estate by purchasing lands in what was called the "Ohio country" (now parts of West Virginia, Ohio, and western Pennsylvania), sections of which he personally surveyed. And he demonstrated agricultural innovation by converting his land from the soil-depleting, slave-intensive tobacco farming to mixed crops of wheat and corn. He used the savings in labor and time to invest in new endeavors such as developing a water mill, grinding grain, fishing, breeding animals, making his own tools, and weaving cloth. These efforts functioned commercially, as they were also available for neighbors' use, minimizing imports from Britain, and allowing his workforce to earn extra funds as well. Always the multi-tasker, he also made time to serve in the Virginia legislature's House of Burgesses, more as a patient observer than prime actor in the growing rift with Great Britain.

By spring of 1775, this rift was fracturing relations between the colonies and their King because of colonial refusal to accept taxation without representation in British Parliament. And relations broke wide open into armed conflict when a small British force sent to seize arms from the Massachusetts colonial militia encountered resistance at Lexington and Concord. Almost concurrently, colonial representatives had assembled at a pre-planned meeting of the 2nd Continental Congress in Philadelphia. Emboldened by the news of the Massachusetts skirmishes, the business of the colonies' second Congress focused on how best to respond to the British Crown. They decided to petition King George III to respect their rights as Englishmen, yet at the same time saw the wisdom of organizing a colonial resistance. They appointed one of their members, an exceptionally tall man wearing the Virginia militia uniform, to lead the Colonial Army forming in New England. George Washington would once again be answering the call to duty. [29]

Over the next eight years, from the first skirmishes of 1775 until finalizing a peace treaty in 1783, Washington led the Continental Army to victory. During these years, the Colonists issued a Declaration of Independence, evacuated their capital, and suffered defeats on nearly every field of battle – except the ones that mattered most. In the process they shed their identity as Colonists and became Americans. Key victories, which inspired the

---

29 By chartering an army on June 14, 1775 – more than a year before declaring independence – Congress with forethought gave birth to the U.S. Army more than a full year before establishing the nation. Washington became the first mustered service member, and his handpicked staff enlisted as the next five.

colonies to persist, were won at Boston, Trenton/ Princeton, Saratoga, and Cowpens. Although the culminating victory was secured on the field of battle at Yorktown, the Army's resilience, courage, and character enabled it to survive and win the War of Independence. This persistence and growing success convinced the majority of citizens of the justice of their cause and their ability to administer themselves – exactly as Thomas Paine had outlined in *Common Sense.* These were attributes, military and civilian, borrowed from its commander, General Washington, always leading by example and bearing the full weight of his new nation every step of the way.

Yet, with victory came choices. How was this new nation to be governed? The solution, following several years of bitter disagreements, was a compromise that established a Republic with three branches of government: legislative, executive, and judicial. [30] The legislature was defined as a Congress consisting of two separate chambers, one representing each state's legislature and another selected based on each state's population. It was responsible for drafting legislation and passing it into law. The executive branch, led by an elected President, was tasked to administer the federal government and enforce laws. The judicial branch was established under a Supreme Court. These three branches were deliberately interconnected; the written Constitution provided each with powers to check and balance the other two, while serving as a guideline for division of powers. This framework has served our nation well for 234 years, while inspiring countless other countries of the principles of self-government. [31]

Despite the years of acrimonious debate in Congress during and after the Revolution, only one choice existed among the opposing factions, states,

---

30 Washington served as president and presided over The Constitutional Convention of 1787. Representatives of all 13 states had insisted that he was the only choice for president forcing him to return to service, despite his 1783 retirement. Deadlocked on a process to establish a representative Congress, the Convention's Roger Sherman of Connecticut proposed a compromise to placate both large and small states. He recommended a Congress consisting of two houses, one based on a state's population and the other with all states having equal representation. Accepted by the delegates, this legislative solution became known as the Great Compromise of 1787.

31 Underscoring the durability of the Constitution, it has been amended only 27 times in 234 years. The first ten amendments were ratified in 1791, with the remaining 17 approved over the next 229 years. Nearly all countries in Europe, South America, Asia, and Africa that have established representative governments have been influenced by the U.S. Constitution or have borrowed it as a framework.

and citizens to lead the United States as the first president. In the 1788-89 election each state cast its votes for a single man – Washington. Again. Despite his efforts to maintain the retirement he sought following the War of Independence and the Constitutional Convention, his requests were not heeded. [32]

No reputable political leaders would serve unless he returned to service as their executive leader. George reluctantly accepted. He believed that he was obligated to lead again, committed to growing the new nation as a Republic and calming any strife remaining from the Great Compromise of 1787.

The hard work began after he took the oath of office. The Constitution existed, and the new government's structure was set – generally. The document read ambiguously enough, by intention, implying that in practice a good deal would be open to subjective interpretation. There remained opposition to some of its provisions, and major, unsettled issues lingered unresolved. The two most notable, which continued to divide the country for decades, were states versus federal rights and the accommodation of slavery. No reference books nor legal and governing precedents existed at the time. And in fact, the Bill of Rights codifying the Constitution's first 10 Amendments had not yet been ratified when Washington assumed office.

One of the Constitution's foundational concepts was rooted in the belief that the president could lead the government by exercising impartial judgement in the best interests of the country. And, informed by the recent struggle to break from England, Constitutional checks and balances ensured that no president could ever act as tyrannically as George III. Not coincidentally, leading figures of the Revolution and the pre-Constitutional government had been educated in the concepts of the European Enlightenment and the Roman Classics. These taught that the ideal leader served and sacrificed for the public good, led rationally, and believed that humanity continually progressed forward towards greater freedom and knowledge. As the Declaration

---

32 On December 23, 1783, following the signing of the peace treaty ending the American Revolution and marking the departure of British troops from New York City, Washington resigned his commission as Commander-in-Chief. He handed his resignation paper directly to the President of Congress, which was in session. He stated verbally and in writing: "I here offer my Commission, and take my leave of all the employments of public life." He intended to demonstrate publicly the authority of the civilian government over the military and to show that his retirement meant the military would not mix with politics.

of Independence stated, men instituted governments to secure their rights of "Life, Liberty, and the pursuit of Happiness."

Consequently, every decision by the first president set a precedent for future interpretation of this unique governmental framework – the American Constitution. This was George Washington's primary contribution. This defined his statesmanship. Like a parent, he knew that every decision he made would have cascading and far-reaching effects beyond any single issue, impacting many generations to come. No other U.S. president has had to bear this singular weight of responsibility, as is the case with other elected leaders of new democracies. Washington, however, set the first successful example.

In a young America, Washington faced a number of unique and complex challenges over the first presidency. [33] Today's issues and those of the Civil War era – another time when the country's survival appeared at risk – pale in comparison to the challenges he faced, both domestically and internationally. With brilliant statesmanship, Washington steered a balance that gave the young nation consistently positive direction. Quite naturally, the president could not please everyone all the time. But despite his detractors and critics, Washington maintained the support of all three governmental branches along with the respect and admiration of the vast majority of the people.

He also governed as a true visionary. The Constitution does not require the establishment of executive departments or subordinate executives; all executive authority is vested solely in the president. But Washington envisioned an executive branch at the national level beyond his personal span of control. Therefore, he selected a group of advisors and made them responsible for key elements of the executive branch of the government. It came to be called the Cabinet and was composed of several Founding Fathers – the most notable and impactful men in the country. The first cabinet included Thomas Jefferson, the future president and the primary author of the Declaration of Independence; John Jay, the key negotiator in the treaty that ended the Revolutionary War and soon to become the first Supreme Court Chief Justice; and Alexander Hamilton, responsible for establishing

---

33 Washington served two four-year terms as president, 1789 – 1797, setting another precedent that remained until Franklin Delano Roosevelt sought a third term in 1940 on the eve of U.S. entry into World War II.

the financial self-sufficiency of the national government. [34] James Madison, another future president, combined with Hamilton and Jay in writing the Federalist Papers, which ensured ratification of the Constitution. He also served as a leader in Congress and key adviser to the president.

The president made this Cabinet work as a team. He expected them to serve as his primary advisers and to discuss all sides of an issue, verbally or in writing. Following thorough debate and consideration, Washington would then make decisions – as he put it, based on "obeying the dictates of my conscience" – and expect all parties to carry them out. He also expected Cabinet duties to include collaboration with Congress in order to keep the Legislature informed and to secure its support. Washington deliberated over even the simplest matters, such as how he would be formally addressed as chief executive. He chose "Mr. President," rejecting a long list of proposed royal salutations by Congress. [35] He wanted to be treated merely as an elected official, assuring fellow Americans that he and his Cabinet were citizens first. [36]

Washington led by example, exactly as he had as a military leader. No matter what the issue, he always placed the interests of the country first. In public and private, formal and informal, when ill, weary or angry, he never made things personal. He never bullied others. He never joined a political party and did not use his position to promote himself. He remained selfless, represented all Americans and treated them graciously, including those who were enslaved. And he made sure he interacted with his fellow citizens on a regular basis. After Congressional sessions adjourned for the season, Washington travelled, covering all states during his years in office. He committed to meeting groups of citizens at official functions, which were organized prior to his departure from the Capital. During his travel back

---

34 Hamilton is renowned enough to this day that one of Broadway's longest running plays immortalized him again more than 200 years after his death. The popular musical also celebrates his bonds to his mentor, Washington.

35 Among the titles proposed: Highness, Electoral Highness, Excellency, and Majesty.

36 In contrast, British Ministers of the Crown were titled "The Honorable" and controlled the system of patronage, which meant responsibility for all appointed government roles and salaries. Abuse was rife in this system, and these positions exalted the holders above all others outside of the immediate royal family. Washington strived to distance the United States from this system as far as possible.

to the Capital, he wandered off the beaten roads with minimal escort and a relaxed schedule, lodging at common taverns to ensure he encountered citizens casually across the countryside. He acted the same as he had on the frontier 35 years earlier. People approached him because they knew he listened and took action whenever possible. The contradiction with America's former colonial masters could not have been more stark.

As president, as he had done his entire life, he dined or met with anyone: visitors, officials, and representatives from all walks of life and offering all points of view. Martha and he hosted weekly formal "levees" and countless informal gatherings. He encouraged others to give their opinions and share their experiences – as he listened. His persona was not – as he is perceived today – as the monumental Mt. Rushmore figure standing above and apart from others. But rather he appeared as someone very approachable and open to mentoring those eager to learn. He did not carry grudges, not even toward recent enemies in Britain. Nor was he overly generous to recent allies, the French and Spanish. Ever the balanced statesman, Washington throughout his life, he treated friends, allies, and former enemies with equal respect and graciousness, just as he did in his personal and professional relationships.

And yet, though far less apparent than in his youth, Washington retained a fiery temper. He could lash out when dissatisfied or disappointed. Still, it was noted throughout his life that following an altercation, he would take steps to make amends. He practiced common courtesy. Despite the fame that his successes had brought him, he endeavored to treat everybody as he expected to be treated. Arrogance did not exist in George Washington, a rare trait then and today -- for someone of such notoriety, power, and prominence. [37]

The America of his presidency faced a huge array of problems, both foreign and domestic. Many of these challenges had the potential by themselves to overwhelm the agrarian and lightly populated Republic and its novice government.

---

[37] Washington was constantly besieged by admirers wherever he went by both domestic and foreign visitors, who called him the "greatest" in the world.

In foreign affairs, the French Revolution commenced less than three months after the start of Washington's presidency. [38] During the American revolution against Britain, conservative, propertied leaders held power and authority in America. By contrast, France soon spiraled into rule by fanatical extremists that thrust France, most of Europe, and self-governing nations around the world into warfare and chaos. Washington's own Cabinet was split dramatically between supporters of both sides. Yet amid this global disharmony, Washington orchestrated the signing of the Jay Treaty, effectively ending residual enmity towards Britain, while maintaining a neutral stance towards conflicts erupting in other corners of the world. [39]

Perhaps just as importantly, he impressed his presidential successors to maintain this U.S. policy of neutrality for the new nation's formative years ahead.

Another foreign affair, largely forgotten in the mists of time, concerned the marauding and elusive Barbary Pirates, who ruthlessly seized American merchant vessels, while operating from semi-independent kingdoms along the North African coast. These corsairs prospered by seizing cargos and selling wealthy prisoners for ransom. They enslaved other captives from vessels and from raids along the southern European coasts, selling them throughout the Arab world, where slavery thrived. To counter this threat, Washington executed two actions: the reconstitution of the U.S. Navy to protect American ships, as well as a concerted effort to eliminate the piracy through diplomatic means – without war. [40]

Turning to domestic affairs, the westward push by pioneers brought probable conflict with the Native Americans living on the western side of the Appalachian Mountains. Initially, Washington attempted to apply the lessons he had learned as a young man in the region – seeking to have both

---

38 The French Revolution transitioned from a political discussion to violence with the storming of the Bastille prison on July 14, 1789.

39 The first of the revolutions or wars to break out after France's call for "Liberty, Equality, and Fraternity" was the 1791 revolt by Haiti against their colonial masters -- France. The new French republic ironically did not accept this act of liberty, resulting in a brutal suppression. Haiti's proximity to U.S. shores concerned an America with no navy and small army.

40 Congress auctioned off the Continental Navy's last warship in 1785; it re-authorized the Navy in 1794 with the first warship launched in 1797. The Barbary kingdoms signed treaties with the United States, requiring tribute be paid annually to the pirates until the Navy could protect U.S. interests at sea.

sides live together peacefully. He pursued efforts to ensure treaties protected both sides, smoking peace pipes, encouraging and entertaining tribal visits, and striving to integrate their way of life with the small farmsteads of the incoming settlers. All the while he demonstrated respect for them equal to that of U.S. citizens. His efforts succeeded for a few generations with the powerful Iroquois (northern New York) and tribes in most areas west of Georgia and the Carolinas. However, partly incited by the British, hostilities broke out in the Ohio Valley in 1789 after the Governor of the Northwest Territory, Arthur St. Clair, failed to implement an updated, fair treaty. [41] Washington dispatched troops to disband the tribal coalition. The first two expeditions failed disastrously. For the third, he recalled one of his best Revolutionary War generals out of retirement, "Mad Anthony" Wayne. He not only defeated the alliance of tribes decisively, but ended warfare in the Ohio Country and extinguished further British influence. This action in essence confirmed that which the treaty ending the American Revolution had specified -- this land belonged to the United States of America. Wayne's victory at the Battle of Fallen Timbers launched the beginning of large-scale settlement of the Midwest and allowed American expansion in that era without conflict.

Though external incidents often garner the main news headlines, the critical part of establishing and running a successful government is the management of domestic matters. This remains as true today as it was for Washington. The key domestic decision he confronted as first president was about how the nation would be run. From one perspective, the nation could be governed in a decentralized manner by the individual states, a view supported by Jefferson and Madison. From the opposing perspective, the nation could be governed by a strong, central government, as advocated by Hamilton and Vice President John Adams. The first group came to be called the Democratic Republicans and wanted the national government to exercise as little federal power as possible beyond those specified in the Constitution (mainly covering war and foreign affairs). Their primary goal was to prevent

---

41 By failing to evacuate forts on American soil and inciting tumult, British actions in the Northwest Territory stood in clear violation of the Treaty of Paris, which ended the Revolutionary War. The two largest tribes impacted by St. Clair's failed treaty were the Miami and Shawnee; they led the resistance for the next six years.

the federal government from being self-supporting by having states control revenue (taxes). In contrast, Hamilton led the group that came to be called the Federalists, who believed that the national government needed to control its own purse strings and have the authority to set and maintain national goals, rather than each state or territory choosing its own direction.

Since the first Continental Congress in 1774 this topic had been debated widely among Congressmen and across the former colonies. After the Declaration of Independence, Congress decided to employ a decentralized approach during the war. Washington endured under this system and saw firsthand how the army suffered due to lack of sustainable resources. Without a guaranteed source of national revenue, soldiers went without pay and war supplies, and decisions were not made within reasonable timelines. In short, the states placed their shallow interests over the nation's deeper needs. The result was a grossly under-resourced and oftentimes chaotic, national-level war effort.

No official written records exist of the detailed negotiations on the Compromise of 1790. It followed a face-to-face meeting between Jefferson, Hamilton, and Madison. Hamilton received support in getting his federal financial system through Congress. In exchange, he agreed to move the U.S. capital from New York City to Philadelphia and then to land between Maryland and Virginia, occupying an undeveloped, rural area rather than in an existing city or town. [42]

Consequently, this compromise enhanced the United States' ability to work as a nation rather than as an association of semi-independent (and quarrelsome) states. There is no record of how much influence or even effort that Washington personally exercised to arrive at this compromise. However, the process used was the same one Washington had employed during the Revolution -- give quality leaders the authority and responsibility to make vital decisions. Then back them.

Following this agreement, Hamilton, as Secretary of the Treasury, assumed all states' unpaid debts accumulated since the American Revolution.

---

42 Initially unnamed, the Federal City would become known as Washington D.C. Hamilton championed urban development and manufacturing; he preferred a financial center as capital. Jefferson and Madison championed agriculture, distrusted wealth, and insisted on a location in the countryside.

With that huge and unprecedented first federal step, he then focused on raising sufficient revenue to pay off the debts while maintaining a balanced budget. Begun by Secretary Hamilton and continued to World War I, preserving zero national debt became a cornerstone of U.S. domestic policy.

This financial compromise triggered another vital precedent for Washington. Part of Hamilton's plan included the establishment of a Bank of the United States, which required passage of a law by Congress authorizing approval, since the Constitution did not define such an institution. Rather than seeking a new law, Washington utilized "implied presidential powers," using his broad executive powers instead of relying strictly on powers enumerated in the Constitution. Washington's interpretation and decision stands as the first clear-cut case of implied executive powers, marking a key moment in U.S. history and solving an early pivotal national issue. This action initiating implied powers provided – and still provides -- the opportunity for the government to utilize flexibility when necessary, while maintaining democracy and monitoring this power by the checks and balances of the Constitution. The previous support Hamilton secured from Madison with the Compromise proved crucial to ensuring Congress' acceptance of the banking decision – and Washington's precedent-setting use of implied powers.

The event that came to be called the "Whiskey Rebellion" provided an early test of how a young nation's new national authorities could work. Settlers on the edge of the frontier earned their living as subsistence farmers. And many supplemented their meager farming income by distilling whiskey. After the Compromise of 1790, whiskey became a taxable commodity. Still stung by excessive British taxation, this first national tax proved hugely unpopular and strongly opposed.

Revenue collectors were beaten or chased away. Taxes went unpaid. Local militias were asked to assist, but they refused to take action against their neighbors. It appeared that presidential leadership would be required to again solve an emerging national issue. Washington responded by mobilizing distant state militias, as the national army totaled less than 1,000 men and had been committed already into the Ohio country. He offered to lead the forces himself, marking the first and only time in U.S. history when the Commander in Chief commanded military forces in the field. Once formed and organized, Washington deployed the troops under "Light Horse" Harry Lee, one of the leading Revolutionary War's officers, to protect tax agents, collect the taxes, and arrest the worst and most brutal ringleaders. [43] This mission succeeded; courts convened trials and passed down sentences. And in a smart move to soothe lingering animosities, Washington exercised executive clemency towards those sentenced to death. Peace had been restored, and of even greater long-term significance, the authority of the national government to enforce its laws had been confirmed.

It is necessary at this point of the story to digress slightly to give more background on two critical issues that Washington confronted in his presidency: slavery and religious tolerance. Like today, both issues divided the nation and required strong national leadership and statesmanship to address.

Slavery. The very word stirred deep emotions of anger, frustrations, bitterness, and extreme convictions in every American. Sentiments were nearly as strong during Washington's presidency as they were 70 years later at the onset of the Civil War. [44] And of course, these sentiments continue today as our nation struggles with the fact that past efforts and idealism have not yet secured equality by and for all individuals.

Any attempt to explain Washington's involvement with slavery are complex – well beyond the scope of this account. There were no easy answers in his time. Like the head of every large Virginia farm of this period, Washington owned slaves. [45] During his presidency, Congress passed a number of laws strengthening the institution of slavery as a means for slave-holding states (8 of 13) to sustain their agrarian economies and culture.

---

43 Ironically, Lee was to be the father of Robert E. Lee, the senior commander of the most violent revolt in US history.

44 These sentiments did not have the strength to prevent union, but did result in deletions from the Declaration of Independence and silence in the Constitution and Bill of Rights. As will be explained in more detail later, representatives realized that the current economic model of the slave-holding states appeared to be in decline, and as such, expected the issue to sort itself out over time.

45 Slavery and word choices. The reader will have noticed the word, "slave" used multiple times in chapters discussing America's efforts to confront institutional slavery and the enslaved people who served in bondage. To better capture the sense of the historical period and the language in use at the time, the author has chosen to use the word, "slave" at appropriate points in the early chapters. In recognition of changes in modern usage, and out of respect for descendants of the enslaved, word choice will switch to, "enslaved people" or "former enslaved people" in Chapter 8 passages that discuss the Emancipation Proclamation and beyond.

As president, Washington signed these measures into law. He rationalized that by signing these laws he was preserving the formative United States' fragile unity. He further believed that the slavery dilemma would be resolved peacefully over time.

Today, some people judge our Founding Fathers against modern perspectives and current cultural mores and find them, deficient and lacking. The morals of other ages are quite different from today. So, comparisons translate, unsurprisingly, harshly. By this metric, we often see the leaders of the newly formed United States of America condemned for their flaws or for presumably evil intentions. However, one has to attempt to stand in the full context of the historic period and understand its cultural fabric and perspective before casting aspersions.

Since the dawn of time and the earliest days of human coexistence and formation of civilizations, slavery has existed and even flourished. Historical records from more than 5,000 years confirm slavery as a long-standing inhumanity among people, crossing all civilizations, all religions, and all continents. And the late 18th century proved to be no exception -- worldwide. Before Washington and others can be criticized as slaveowners – with their monuments toppled and achievements taken from our history books – they should be remembered as our Founding Fathers -- the first leaders in the world attempting to change the enduring and entrenched reality of slavery, both legally and morally, for an entire nation. Change did not come overnight. It would come only decades later, following a four-year civil war, deaths of hundreds of thousands of Americans, and a Constitutional amendment abolishing slavery in the U.S. Still, today, the vigilance of good people around the globe is needed to prevent and eliminate the scourge of human trafficking and unlawful servitude that exists in many dark corners of the world. We would do well to understand a broader scope of history and channel our righteous indignation against these remaining dark corners.

And like it was for the rest of the world, the full story on slavery for Washington and the United States was not that simple. From his first interactions with Native Americans in Virginia's unsettled Shenandoah Valley, Washington learned to respect diversity and ignore the derisive slurs heard on the frontier. He learned from his life's experiences to accept and work with anyone, whatever their background, as long as they demonstrated ability and showed a willingness to work for improvement. As a planter years before the Revolution (1766), he converted from farming tobacco to mixed-grain crops, primarily corn and wheat, long before his peers had made this shift. The former required large amounts of labor -- slaves and indentured servants performing backbreaking work. [46] Tobacco also, depleted the soil. The latter required far less labor and was less taxing on the land and on the workers' exertions. By 1772, Washington had ceased buying slaves. In 1774, he co-authored the "Fairfax Resolutions," a paper calling for an end to the slave trade and advocating for an "entire stop forever put to such wicked, cruel, and unnatural trade." In themselves, these actions did not make major strides in abolishing slavery, but taken in context, they illustrate incremental and meaningful steps taken by a man who clearly stood for change.

In short, despite growing up in a culture and economic system dominated by "King Tobacco" and its inherent reliance on slave and indentured servant labor, Washington learned from personal experience that self-reliance was the key to success – whether one was British or Colonial, native or settler, free or slave. With his own slaves, Washington provided them training for trades, ensured families were kept together, and sought to avoid invoking harsh punishments allowed by law. In the context of the times, he exhibited a high form of respect and provided opportunities to better themselves. In fact, Washington encouraged his slaves and servants to save their hard-earned trade money in order to purchase their freedom.

During the drafting of the Declaration of Independence, the entire issue of slavery could have been resolved once and for all. The original draft of the document included phrases that were partially struck from the final version, such as "that all men are created equal *and independent*," and "endowed by their Creator *with equal rights*."[47] Another full paragraph condemning slavery also was struck from the original draft. These omitted words had been drafted by another slaveholder and future president, Thomas Jefferson.

---

46 Indentured servitude was common practice in 18th century America, allowing poor immigrants from mainly Ireland, Wales, Scotland, and the Rhine River valley to move to the Colonies. Individuals would perform labor at minimal wages in order to be released from their bond and as payment for the cost of their voyage. A multi-year contract was normal with seven years being most customary. As many as 50% of the immigrants arriving in the Colonies during this timeframe were indentured servants. The American Revolution largely put an end to this system.

47 The italicized words were removed in the final version of the Declaration.

Yet, in the necessity of securing unanimous support, the Founding Fathers removed this anti-slavery language in order to gain agreement with the slaveholding states. Most educated people, North and South, believed that slavery would die off soon on its own. Leading indicators of the day showed slavery in decline for much of the South, both in total number of states and in terms of economic dependency. The willingness to compromise, combined with confidence in the demise of slavery, found its basis in the tenets of the Enlightenment – that freedom, knowledge, and pursuit of happiness would lead to universal progress. In time, it would happen. [48] Though first, continued progress demanded compromise.

Washington's own views on slavery continued to evolve during the Revolutionary War, partly due to the fervor brought to his armies by writings like the Declaration of Independence and *Common Sense*. In a sense, liberty was on everyone's lips. A percentage of the Army consisted of Black men, both free and slave, who had as much at stake as anyone else. [49] These revolutionaries, Black and White, believed the Declaration's premise that all men were created equal, and they were willing to fight to make it happen. In contrast to his years of Virginia residence, as Army commander Washington lived with a number of people outside of his culture and upbringing. His staff, aides, and leading generals included people from all the colonies and across Europe; they held a wide range of outlooks. Colleagues like Hamilton and the Marquis de Lafayette had substantially different life experiences, and together they shared viewpoints and held spirited discussions during their daily staff meals. The subject of slavery often arose when an incident highlighted both the abilities of Blacks and the inequality of their treatment.

48 Little did anyone know then, but the invention of the cotton gin in 1794, would make another labor-intensive crop, cotton, more profitable and cause plantations employing slavery to expand rather than die out. Ironically, large-scale tobacco farming was decreasing due to soil depletion, as Washington had realized decades earlier.

49 Black men constituted approximately 5% of the total number of soldiers who served. A much higher percentage (estimated up to 25%) served in the professional Continental (national) units than in the state militias. The general rule for a slave who served as a substitute in the place of another would be the granting of freedom after one year of service. Though the Revolution did not introduce a national draft for manpower, Congress required each state to furnish men for the Continental Army. States filled quotas and accepted slaves and indentured servants as substitutes when volunteers were insufficient. Further information outlining their views and fervor are found in Section 3, Chapter 1. Continental army units operated as fully integrated formations, which would not happen again until 1948 when President Truman reinstituted full integration.

The ultimate statesman and learner, Washington welcomed these differing perspectives, and they made deep impressions that would influence future decisions.

One perspective of Washington's that is unknown is his view of the plight of his own slaveholdings in 1781. At least 21 of his own slaves took flight and fled to freedom in the wake of the British invasion of Virginia. He felt that he treated his slaves better than other plantation owners, and therefore he may have pondered the meaning and motivation behind their escape. Perhaps he realized that slaves believed, much as America's revolutionaries did, that freedom from tyranny was worth the risk of one's life.

By the end of the war in 1783, Washington certainly realized that even in the worst of situations, people with far fewer opportunities and less education still could succeed as their own masters and strive for even greater achievements. He recognized a self-reliance in others that matched his own. In overcoming steep obstacles, the Colonials had demonstrated commitment and persistence. Harnessing and encouraging this widely shared, early American-spirit, the Colonies persisted and won a relentless eight-year war – inspired in large measure by Washington's own persistent leadership and personal example.

To refine the perspective further, again consider Washington's own early education, which was based on the concepts of the Enlightenment. The efforts of Washington's soldiers, his colleagues in government, and he, himself, brought progress and drove change. He believed that the new republic, having won independence and adopted a splendid Constitution, would continue to move forward, based on the framing values, ideals, and principles tied to the Enlightenment.

As president, Washington could not enact change by himself; he needed the cooperation of others to attain his goals. The support of Congress in both roles, as army commander and president, proved essential. Six of the original thirteen states held significant populations of slaves and economic systems that depended upon them. Plus, two others (New York and New Jersey) still allowed slavery. [50] Washington reasoned that he needed to create policy,

---

50 In addition to the fact that eight of the original states permitted slavery, three other states entered the union during his presidency. Tennessee and Kentucky allowed slavery; Vermont did not. In total 62% of the population lived in states permitting slavery, according to the 1790 census.

cultivate coalitions, and enforce existing laws if the nation was to remain united in peace. As president, he faced a Hobson's choice regarding slavery. [51] His personal beliefs – and past actions – contrasted with his public oath and responsibilities to uphold the Constitution and execute the laws of the United States. As outlined earlier, today's debate on Washington and other Founding Fathers centers on whether or not they could have done more in their roles to resolve slavery. In framing this debate, it is important to note that any judgment in the modern era must account for the differences in culture and societal norms that prevailed over 200 years ago. [52]

In comparison to being a political leader requiring cooperation and compromise, as a military commander Washington had more opportunity to consistently demonstrate his personal beliefs. Simply put, during the Revolution, he had the authority to organize the army as he saw fit. He worked with the tools he had available – integrating units, clear and fair standards, ensuring accountability, and providing opportunity among others. Note that the vast majority of Washington's professional soldiers, the Continentals, consisted of poor Whites, freed Blacks, indentured servants, and slaves. Few others served after 1776. Earning loyalty from their commander all too often proved their only reward for their service. And their service perpetually meant unpaid wages, poor food, and inadequate supplies. Yet, it also included the unwavering loyalty of their commander, who they witnessed sharing all their privations. A number of books dating back to 1851 outline Black soldiers' contributions to the American Revolution. They fought in every campaign and battle and formed an integral part of

---

51 Hob (or Hobb) is archaic slang for the devil; the term means one has 2 terrible choices. GW had a no-win set of options during his presidency.

52 In contrast to 1790, at the eve of the Civil War, 15 of 33 states authorized slavery, less than half the states. Four of those 15 chose to remain in the Union when war broke out. Comparably, over 60% of the population lived in free states, while one third of the residents from slave states lived in bondage. Washington, his successors, and Congressional leaders had incrementally shifted the country from majority allowing slavery to majority free, despite the economic boom of King Cotton.

the Continental Army. [53] The views and recollections shared by Washington's soldiers, Blacks as well as others, gave emphasis to his reputation for leadership, respect, and his ability to delegate responsibility – traits always valued by soldiers.

Washington's enlightened treatment of Blacks continued to the end of his life. His will stipulated that upon death, his personal slaves were forbidden from being sold and freed upon his wife's death (many of his slaves were married to hers). The one exception, Billie Lee, his personal manservant from before the Revolution until his death, gained freedom immediately and lived until 1828. To sum up, such decisions and actions reveal Washington's leadership by example, no matter how rare or outside of society's norms he ventured. He chose to follow his conscience.

The second major issue of Washington's presidency appears as one that can often be taken for granted today: religious freedom and the toleration to exercise one's own faith. Like slavery, American politicians had long realized that this issue seemed intractable and at an unfathomable impasse. Several of the original Colonies had been founded primarily by people who had been unable to worship freely in Britain or western Europe. Other than in Jamestown, Virginia, from the 17th century and well into the 18th century the majority of immigrants journeyed to the Colonies first and foremost for religious freedom. Organized groups seeking the latitude to practice their sect's faith included the Puritans in Massachusetts (the first "Pilgrims"), Catholics in Maryland (English/Irish), and Quakers in Pennsylvania (William Penn's followers). A number of other groups and individuals, less organized, also immigrated for the same reason: Presbyterians (Scots), Methodists (Welsh), Swedish Protestants (Lutheran sects), Baptists (Dutch), Mennonites (Dutch/German/Swiss), Huguenots (French), the Amish (Swiss/German), along with various others. Members of the Jewish faith also arrived searching for religious and civil toleration. Further, many from the mainstream Church of England (Anglicans) chose to come as well in order to lessen the oversight

---

53 William Cooper Nell's 1855 book, *The Colored Patriots of the American Revolution* followed a shorter work by him in 1851. He was an African American and wrote the first history book about American Blacks based on written documentation from first-hand accounts through pension requests from veterans. Harriet Beecher Stowe, famed abolitionist and author, wrote his introduction.

from their stifling church administration. By the time of Washington's birth, the settlement of the Colonies had resulted in a far more religiously diverse territory than any country in Europe.

Despite its religious diversity and the fact that many original settlers had fled Europe for religious freedom, the Colonies – ironically – did not see widespread toleration along its eastern seaboard. As a teenager surveying Virginia, Washington met a variety of settlers on the frontier from diverse backgrounds, religions, and ethnicities. The Washington family raised their son as an Anglican, as were most of the plantation owners in Virginia at the time. However, on the frontier, people practiced a number of different religious customs and spoke languages unfamiliar in the original Colonial settlements. His reaction during his first meetings with such folks may well have been surprise. However, on subsequent travels, he quickly adapted to accept and fit in with any and all. Washington became known widely on the border as a person to be trusted by fellow frontiersmen regardless of their background or origin. Yet this open-mindedness was an exception in the 1750s, and change in attitudes still had not occurred by the 1780s.

When America elected President Washington, most state laws protected their majority religion or discriminated against others; some had both. Nearly three years later, the passage of the Bill of Rights and its 1st Amendment guaranteed freedom of religion. At the point of passage, the Constitution now confirmed this right. However, like other civil rights that have been protected by law but not fulfilled in practice, toleration required much more effort to gain public acceptance. Several key Founding Fathers made extensive and vigorous attempts to convince their fellow citizens to accept religious toleration, both in word and deed (the 1st Amendment). These leaders persistently endeavored to not only roll back the existing discriminatory state laws, but also made a concerted public effort to change attitudes matching the spirit of the amendment. As a specific example of this effort, Washington sent a letter to the Hebrew Congregation of Newport, Rhode Island, on August 18, 1790, following a widely publicized visit to its parish. He emphasized the importance of toleration by stating that religious liberty was "the exercise of inherent natural rights." Similarly, and with greater legislative impact, Thomas Jefferson drafted, introduced, and sponsored the Virginia Statute for Religious Freedom. This 1786 law pre-dated the Bill of Rights, and it served as a template for the 1st Amendment. Noting his pride in this accomplishment, Jefferson's tombstone cites this Statute while ignoring his time as president. Some of these other respected voices included Alexander Hamilton, future presidents Adams and Madison, Benjamin Franklin, and Thomas Paine. Their goal of matching religious diversity with religious toleration resulted in a shared heritage that contributed to unifying Americans as one people during the country's nascent years. [54]

Beginning with Washington's youthful adventures on the frontier, his personal faith both mellowed and matured based on his life experiences. Working and sharing ordeals with this diverse cast of characters, he realized early that toleration was not only the fair-minded situation to accept, but plain common sense. In addition to the many sects and faiths of the frontier settlers, he encountered Native Americans and their view of the spiritual world. He would also have come across freed Blacks and observed that some openly practiced their former West African religions. Based on these experiences and observations, he developed into a Deist. Referring back to the early fathers of the Christian Church and later refined in the writings of St. Thomas Aquinas (1200s), the Deist concept gained significant followers during the Enlightenment years (late 1600s to early 1800s). It predicated two main premises: God exists, and God gave man the ability to reason. The responsibility for everything else remained with the individual. No statements or assertions insisted that any one religion was right or others wrong. Toleration followed as a simple step from that viewpoint. As noted previously, many founding fathers adhered to these premises, which explained why they pressed to widen toleration and encourage unity.

The Declaration of Independence offers evidence of the philosophy of Deism with the well-known phrases "all men are created equal" and "life, liberty, and the pursuit of happiness." The original Bill of Rights cites these freedoms as basic rights. The ability to reason means toleration. As president, Washington helped ensure these written principles became the way of life

---

54 Keep in mind that in the 18th century the vast majority of the population shared strong religious convictions. Yet, few, if any, other locations allowed full religious freedom. For 250 years Europe had been engulfed in civil and international wars concerning religious beliefs. The United States offered a haven for all, though it encountered bumps along its historical path before and after these events.

for U.S. citizens. And despite populist movements (Know Nothings of the 1840s-50s being the most prominent), the United States has generally shone as a beacon for religious toleration. Clearly, the actions of the first president and other Founding Fathers secured this Constitutional right, and by their strong personal leadership, made progress in making religious toleration a social norm.

Washington planned – and hoped – to serve only one term as president. He wanted to retire and return to his wife and farming. In preparation for this, he asked James Madison to assist him in preparing a farewell address prior to the election of 1792. Unfortunately, despite his best efforts and hopes, all was not well with the United States. The French Revolution had surged, still cresting to its peak, while inflicting extreme violence against its own citizens. It had sparked a worldwide war that threatened to directly involve the United States. Foreign navies impressed American citizens on the open seas, [55] and the Barbary Pirates continued to prey on American shipping. Though the Battle of Fallen Timbers had been won in August 1792, it was too early to determine if the western frontier would remain secured. The Whiskey Rebellion had started and not yet peaked; two more years would elapse before it was fully resolved. Major challenges abounded in every direction around the new nation. However, the biggest threat to the fledgling government involved Washington's key advisors: Jefferson, Madison, Hamilton, and indirectly Adams did not get along and had formed two rival political parties. The increasing vehemence of their attacks on one another threatened to undo all the good work of his first years as president and, potentially, send the new nation into an anarchic spiral similar to the one consuming France.

Probably because of all this turmoil, leaders of both parties urged Washington to seek re-election. None had confidence that either party or any other person could sustain a unified, functioning United States and its government. Reluctantly, Washington filed his farewell address away and agreed to serve four more years. As in the first election, he was re-elected

---

55 Impressment involved kidnapping sailors at sea to augment foreign, primarily British and French, ships' crews. The Europeans, like the Barbary Pirates, targeted American merchant ships because they were insufficiently armed but still crewed by competent sailors.

unanimously, the only President who achieved support from all electors of every state. [56]

In Washington's second term the country continued to confront ongoing challenges from his first four years, and presented plenty of new ones – including more political infighting. Yet, well before 1796, Washington had resolved to retire. Realizing that if the United States was to survive, he knew it needed an orderly change of government by the president voluntarily leaving office. None of his advisors, let alone the rest of the government or population in general, agreed at the time. Still, he determined, again, to lead by example. As Harry Lee eulogized at Washington's funeral, he was "First in war, first in peace, and first in the hearts of his countrymen."

Washington earned that accolade because of his conviction – and actions -- that the Republic could only survive by similar selfless acts. Accordingly, he pulled out his unused 1792 farewell address, which Madison had helped prepare, and sought help with revisions from the opposite side of the political spectrum -- Alexander Hamilton. The point was to indicate that Washington valued both political vantage points.

Rather than delivering a speech, Washington dictated his parting thoughts to Hamilton in September 1796. They were published in the American Daily Advertiser, the closest thing to a national newspaper at that time. Other newspapers rapidly reprinted them, spreading his words and thoughts across the country. By printing early, over two months before the election, potential candidates and voters had plenty of time to digest the contents prior to the upcoming election. [57]

He did not use this address to call attention to his achievements or demonize his opponents. Washington began his message by reminding his fellow countrymen what they had earned. He continued with advice, warnings, and his views on what was necessary to maintain America's progress.

---

56 For the first four American presidential elections, each elector submitted two votes. In 1792, 100% gave one vote to Washington; the balance went to a number of others with John Adams again winning the second highest amount. Based on the rules at this time, he became Vice-President for the second time.

57 Washington's Farewell Address has held this title ever since its first release. However, he actually entitled it, "The Address of Gen. Washington to the People of America on His Declining the Presidency of the United States." He had it written as a letter; it was never meant to be given as a speech.

He did not mention any other politician, let alone an endorsement. He maintained his neutrality to the end.

To recite Washington's Farewell Address aloud takes about ten minutes.[58] Though much of it discusses the issues and events of the time, the central points apply as much today as they did then. Like Paine's pamphlets, *Common Sense* and *The American Crisis*, Washington's farewell mixes basic beliefs, hard-earned wisdom, courtesies, and encouragements that would seem hardly believable if spoken by a modern-day politician.

The opening words "Friends and Citizens" immediately strike the reader. Another noteworthy phrase states the president's "grateful respect for their past kindness." In these opening paragraphs Washington's words illustrate how he saw himself as a true servant of his "beloved country," ... a "dutiful citizen" who offered his countrymen "service," serving with "zeal for your future interest," and "sacrifice." He further states that the situation with internal and external events has cooled sufficiently to elect a new citizen to "administer the executive government."

He apologizes for his "fallible judgement" and "inferiority of my qualifications" for the position. Humbly. He expresses his gratitude for the country's "steadfast confidence" and describes the constancy of its "support" as the pillar that made the achievements he presided over possible. He frames the Constitution as the source of guidance and higher judgement, "which is the work of your hands" and needs to be "sacredly maintained." None of his comments give credit to himself, only graciously to his fellow citizens.

These initial paragraphs act as his preamble. He even mentions he could stop at that point of the address. But he continues on, believing in his obligation as a "parting friend" with "no personal motive" to offer recommendations based on his "reflections" and "observations."

Washington's first main point stands out as the address' lengthiest exhortation. He emphasizes that "unity of government" is the main strength and key requirement for preserving America's independence. He adds that unity in many undertakings will not be easy. There will be "internal and

---

58 The complete Farewell Address is in Appendix 5 (per the Avalon version from Yale). Quotation marks indicate actual words or phrases taken verbatim from the text of the address. In addition, the effort has been made to incorporate as many other of Washington's actual words from the address while summarizing his thoughts.

external" opponents who do everything possible to weaken or break unity. They will do so, "often covertly and insidiously." The president points out that failure to make every effort to protect our government would likely cause it to fail. He further states that all Americans, whether, "citizens, by birth or choice" have this responsibility. Washington reminds the country of the causes for unity, rather than citing examples of differences. With their shared history of common cause, Americans have "fought and triumphed together."

Understanding his era, yet anticipating the future, Washington also discusses the different interests of North and South, East and West, and how these could divide the country. He encourages citizens to recognize that each region brings its own strengths, but also to realize the synergy of a union -- together the total, combined regions stand strongest. His answer to when patriotic bonds are tested: trust in experience rather than speculation. He advises caution when people attempt to misrepresent others in order to dramatize issues or differences. This caution also applies to foreign affairs, emphasizing that we should not rely on foreign alliances to further U.S. liberties and interests. He stresses that Americans must trust and respect the **Constitution** as indisputable proof of permanency for the Republic. [59]

As the address continues, Washington returns to warnings. Beware of people, he advises, claiming "popular ends," as they can bring "cunning, ambitious, and unprincipled men"... "to subvert the power of the people and usurp for themselves the reins of government." He adds that it is necessary to resist those who oppose the acknowledged authority of the government and that intransigence can be manifested as excess political party spirit. He declares that this spirit to band as a group "is inseparable" from human nature. However, when the spirit animating one group becomes excessive, it presents the worst danger to "public councils" and "administration." These spirits must therefore be discouraged and restrained lest, "it opens the door to foreign influence and corruption."

Bear in mind that these are Washington's near-verbatim words as spoken to Hamilton and written in 1796. Consider how warnings from more than two centuries ago remain valid to the central challenges facing the United

---

[59] "Constitution" is highlighted three times in the original version by underlining it where Washington focuses attention on his critical points.

States government today. These warnings provide the principal impetus for this study, ever mindful that today's citizens should remember and heed these sensible and fatherly concerns of our first president and Father of our Country.

Washington's repetitive message always returns to the same answer -- rely on the Constitution. The checks and balances included in it serve to restrain excess and maintain moderation. Otherwise, it is far too easy for despotism to follow. When the **Constitution** (again, highlighted) fails to provide answers, it can be corrected by an amendment that the people confirm. [60] Left unsaid, but clearly implied is that no one individual is above the Constitution and the laws that are derived from it.

Following these warnings, Washington provides counsel on what should enable the United States to fulfill its potential. He makes observations on the characteristics that strengthen organizations, whether political, military, or commercial.

The first of these observations reveals an attribute of Washington's own character. He affirms that, "religion and morality are indispensable supports," for political prosperity. Together, they contribute to citizens' sense of duty, obligation, integrity, and respect, as well as both "public and private felicity." [61] Patriotism untethered by moral behavior could subvert the country.

Washington says that educational institutions should be promoted to encourage the "diffusion of knowledge." The more enlightened that citizens became, the stronger the government. Taken by itself, this statement appears to be simple common sense. Yet consider that in 1796, elementary schooling was haphazard. No more than a dozen universities existed in the country, and only minute percentages of women or slaves learned anything more

---

60 As mentioned previously, there have been 27 Amendments to the Constitution. The right to amend is outlined in Article V of the Constitution. The process requires either both houses of Congress to pass a proposed amendment with two-thirds of votes in favor, or two-thirds of states' legislatures voting to call a Constitutional Convention. To date, Congress has initiated all 27 Amendments. Following Congressional approval, three fourths of the states (38 of 50) require passage of the resolution allowing ratification. The president and Supreme Court are not part of this process.

61 Washington discounts the idea that morality can exist without religion, asking "Where is the security for property, for reputation, for life, if the sense of religious obligation desert (sworn) oaths?" And remember, that Washington's definition of religion included embracing all faiths and extending tolerance to all faiths.

than basic reading and writing. Clearly, the concept of expanded institutional education was visionary. By these words, Washington is encouraging universal education – decades before it actually happened.

"Cherish public credit." The paragraph where Washington discusses this point should be mandatory reading for all students, citizens, and legislators at every level of government. It is difficult to conceive that our elected officials today follow any credo but the exact opposite of this admonition. In his Farewell Address, he employs the following phrases stressing public credit as a critical pillar of good governance: "very important source of strength and security,"... "sparingly as possible" to avoid waste, "cultivating peace" rather than the expenses of war, while remembering "to prepare for danger" to prevent even greater expenses, avoiding "accumulation of debt," and "by vigorous exertion in time of peace to discharge the debts which unavoidable wars may have occasioned." Finally, this paragraph concludes with the exhortation to "not ungenerously throw upon posterity the burden which we ourselves ought to bear." [62] Washington insists that while it is the responsibility of elected officials to manage governmental affairs, it is essential that public opinion guides them. And his final comment addresses taxes: that to pay off debt, one needs revenue, and to obtain revenue, there must be taxes, as inconvenient and unpleasant as those are.

Regarding international relations, the outgoing president advises that the country "observe good faith and justice to all nations; cultivate peace and harmony". He believes that our free and enlightened nation will one day be "a great nation" capable of giving to mankind the "too novel example" of a people with magnanimity, "exalted justice, and benevolence." He expects temporary disadvantages but projects that in the long-term "such a plan will richly repay." A review of American history shows that our nation has stood as a guiding, aspirational symbol of freedom for the rest of the world to emulate. Ninety years after Washington wrote his address, France gifted the U.S. with the Statue of Liberty and its message of hope to all "yearning

---

62 The current United States' debt exceeds $28 trillion or over $85,000 per every American including children. In the twelve months ending June 2020, the federal government spent $3 trillion more than it collected in revenue and another nearly $1 trillion in July 2020 following COVID spending.

to breathe free." [63] Following the end of World War II in 1945, the establishment of the United Nations, and the Marshall Plan/ Operation Blacklist, the vast majority of the world held a similar view of the U.S. [64] As recently as 1989 when public citizens tore down the Iron Curtain across Eastern Europe and Chinese students stood in Beijing's Tiananmen Square face-to-face with tanks, the example of the U.S. provided a similar inspiration. Can one say the same today?

Washington recommends the U.S. take actions to keep its own affairs in order. He again warns with a simple concept about foreign countries. Show no special affections or animosities toward individual countries; either can lead America astray from its duty and interests. Washington makes this point clearly: "Against the insidious wiles of foreign influence (I conjure you to believe me, fellow citizens), the jealousy of a free people ought to be constantly awake." With these words, he urges that the country's dealings abroad remain impartial and wary.

Washington believes that "the great rule of conduct" in foreign relations means expanding commercial efforts as much as possible, while minimizing political connections. At different times in our history, this viewpoint has been branded "Isolationism." Yet, that view misses the first part of the great rule: "extending our commercial relations." His point: it is impossible to hide behind a wall and not interact with the rest of the world. To their own ends, some have twisted the meaning of Washington's complete message, just as he prophesied.

Washington states that if the United States could sustain this rule (and policy), it would soon be able to stand alone and, "defy material injury from external annoyance." Commercial growth and prosperity guarantee

---

63 In 1883, poet Emma Lazarus wrote a sonnet to help raise funds for the pedestal of the Statue of Liberty. A bronze plaque with the poem was added to the statue's base in 1903. It reads in part:
    Give me your tired, your poor
    Your huddled masses yearning to breathe free,
    The wretched refuse of your teeming shore,
    Send these, the homeless, tempest-tost to me,
    I lift my lamp beside the golden door!

64 Marshall Plan. The US committed $12 billion to assist the rebuild of western Europe between 1948 - 1952; more detail in Chapter 10 and Appendix 13. Nearly concurrently, Operation Blacklist, the codename for the occupation, initiation of democracy, and the beginning of the economic "miracle" of Japan, made similar contributions in east Asia.

that others will "not lightly hazard" giving the U.S. provocation (unlike the previous 30 years of America's history). Focusing on the country's needs and not risking entanglement in long term alliances continues as a necessary corollary to this warning. Securing a "respectable defensive posture" maintains this insurance when the rest of the world proves incapable of avoiding "ambition, rivalship, interest, humor, or caprice." Belligerent nations exist, and others will cause collisions with our country. Yet, he advises "that honesty is always the best policy." Coupling honesty with efforts to preserve harmony, maintaining liberal trade with all nations, and investing in the necessary insurance of defensive preparations should allow the U.S. to keep the respect of others. Concurrently, such steps provide the opportunity to avoid their mishaps.

In concluding his address, Washington refers to it as the "counsels of an old and affectionate friend." To borrow a phrase from Winston Churchill, the president's words "in a dark, cold winter, ... warmed the cockles" of his countrymen's hearts. [65] Washington's words then and today should inspire every American with the belief that the country symbolizes freedom and hope for the entire world. He was indeed an, "old and affectionate friend."

Washington "dares not hope" that his words will make a lasting impression, but does hope that they "may be" of partial benefit to moderate party extremists, foreign influence, or pretending patriots. Without doubt, Washington believes these are America's primary threats. He aspires that the United States be different from all other nations in history by controlling these passions. He explains why he had initiated the policy of U.S. neutrality in the European wars after gaining the full support of Congress and why he persevered to stay this course. His goal was to give America time to develop in order to be in "command of its own fortunes."

Finally, he concludes by apologizing. He accepts that he has made, unconsciously, many unintentional errors. He asks two things. First, he appeals to the "Almighty" to avert or mitigate his errors. Secondly, he asks the indulgence of his countrymen for these same mistakes. His final words

---

65 Speaking on December 18, 1939, Secretary of the Admiralty Churchill addressed the sinking of a powerful German naval vessel shortly before total war was unleashed on Western Europe (and he became Prime Minister of the British Empire). His phrasing includes a play on words, using 'cockles' for both its maritime meaning and as a metaphor for warmth and comfort to the heart.

express his intent in joining his fellow-citizens at home to enjoy the benefits of "good laws under a free government" after the "mutual cares, labors, and dangers" they have shared together.

His signature rests at the bottom.

Looking at the address today, one comes away with two definite observations. First, the educated people of the late 18th century practiced an oratory style and employed a vocabulary far beyond that in general use today (particularly, among public figures). Secondly, Washington keeps his message simple and clear: work together and the United States can overcome any challenges. Again, like with *Common Sense*, he speaks in a positive, inclusive manner with straightforward meanings to appeal to all citizens.

Hard as it may be to imagine today, the U.S. Senate still reads this address annually on the anniversary of Washington's birth, maintaining a tradition for more than 100 years (the House ended the practice in 1984). Our foremost Founding Father's words have served as a guideline for good governance for centuries. And they ring as fully relevant today as they were in 1796, however, sadly, they do not appear to be much in practice.

GEORGE WASHINGTON AS PRESIDENT, 1796. THIS GILBERT STUART
PAINTING IS KNOWN AS THE "LANSDOWNE" PORTRAIT.

CHAPTER 5

LINCOLN'S STEPS TO HIS INAUGURATION, NOVEMBER 1860 - MARCH 1861

O ur first president assumed the role as chief executive with no precedent. The unamended Constitution served as his only governmental framework. George Washington set the precedents in both foreign and domestic affairs, presided over the first modifications to the Constitution (the Bill of Rights), and passed on to his successor a fairly established and prospering administration.

In the years following President Washington, the young nation faced wars, recessions, and recurring excitement from overzealous political passions. But despite this string of crises, the Office of the U.S. President grew in prestige and influence, just as young America grew from a small, weak group of ex-colonies into a powerful and maturing nation. However, one crisis from Washington's era remained unresolved for the next 60 years: slavery.

At the presidential election of 1860, the country, for the first and only time, saw four major political parties running for office. [66] All of them projected to either win or exert enough influence with the future government

66 Of the 4 main political parties, results recorded as follows: Republican Party (Abraham Lincoln) with 39.8% of votes, 18 states carried, and 180 electoral votes. Southern Democratic Party (John C Breckinridge) with 18.1% of votes, 11 states carried, and 72 electoral votes. Democratic Party (Stephen Douglas) with 29.5% of votes, 1 state carried, and 12 electoral votes. Constitutional Union Party (John Bell) with 12.6% of votes, 3 states carried, and 39 electoral votes.

to rouse a significant percentage of American voters to support them. Conversely, this situation pointed exactly to what Washington warned about in his Farewell Address. Party extremists thundered all manners of threats if not elected, and so-called patriotism failed to focus on the nation, rather than to various sections of the country.

More than 80% of eligible voters cast their ballots in the 1860 election (by comparison, in 2016 it was 55%). 33 states comprised the nation. The losing three parties won over 60% of the votes and carried 15 states (sharing part of New Jersey with a split vote), but the winning candidate, Abraham Lincoln of the Republican party, decisively beat them at the Electoral College. Lincoln won only in non-slave-holding states (commonly called the North); he failed to win any electoral votes in the slaveholding states (commonly called the South).

No U.S. president has ever been elected with less of a mandate. The election proved that the country remained polarized by slavery and radically divided by geography and economic systems. And furthermore, only a minority of the population supported the new president and his party. To make matters worse, Lincoln had run without national name recognition and with only limited party backing. With his own caucus, Lincoln had received the Republican nomination because various political leaders, many of whom belittled him as nothing more than a country bumpkin, believed he could be easily controlled. And abroad, he held no support from any of the country's main trading partners, including the largest, Great Britain, still the leading world empire despite its defeat in the Revolutionary War.

Compounding Lincoln's pre-inaugural problems was the fact that seven states of the South seceded from the country and declared themselves an independent nation as the Confederate States of America between the November election and his inauguration in March. [67] During his first 100 days in office another four states seceded. Four others remained in the Union, but experienced intra-state divisions based on slavery. Americans feared that secession would cause civil war. And these fears became reality only five weeks after Lincoln's inauguration when the Confederacy attacked the federal island of Fort Sumter in the harbor outside Charleston, South

---

67   Ratified in 1932, the 20th Amendment adjusted the start date for the newly elected president from March to January 20th.

Carolina. The Civil War had begun, and the new president faced bigger problems than his lack of an election mandate.

George Washington's warnings had failed to inspire responsible leaders to prevent or resolve the upcoming cataclysm. His Farewell Address and his service were still revered by all, but his personal example and pleas to unite the country had not been followed by subsequent leaders. The Compromises of 1787 and 1790, under Washington's guidance, had enabled the country to establish itself on common ground and with a unified purpose. Accordingly, the chief executives and Congresses moved the country forward with some measure of effectiveness and efficiency.

In later years, and in sharp contrast, the Compromises of 1820 and 1850 proved to be only band-aids. The results were not working compromises, due to the failure by elected officials to follow up and reinvigorate the entire United States.

Rather than build on the success – and opportunity – that the Compromise of 1850 offered to reunify the country, Lincoln's predecessors, James Buchanan and Franklin Pierce, made little effort. [68] Tragically, extremists on both sides, pro-slavery and abolitionists, sprang up and operated with violence and impunity to usurp the agreement – and the opportunity. A de facto civil war broke out during 1854 in Kansas between pro-slavery and anti-slavery factions. And the federal government chose not to be involved, manifesting the ineffectiveness of Pierce's administration. With similar disinterest and lack of leadership, Buchanan also chose not to attempt to reconcile the "bleeding" Kansas issue. In addition, he presided over a recession and the fateful Dred Scott Supreme Court decision, which profiled his inability to work with Congress in reaching a practical legislative solution for all parts of the country. This case stated that Blacks could not become citizens and ruled that limitations on slavery in new territories were unconstitutional.

---

68 The Compromise of 1850 generated a set of five laws that outlined the organization and boundaries of the new territories and the state of Texas following the Mexican War. It declared that popular sovereignty for each territory would decide if it would be slave or free. The Compromise also tightened the fugitive slave law and ended the slave trade in Washington D.C.

In short, both of Lincoln's presidential predecessors contented themselves to be silent. Most notably, lame-duck Buchanan remained inactive while the first states seceded in the four months following the election of 1860.

President-elect Lincoln inherited the disintegration of the nation. Unity of government did not exist, and regional differences were escalating out of control. Another of Washington's admonitions – to leverage regional differences as a collective strength – had not been heeded either. Politicians had ignored warnings on excessive party influence and continued to pretend their patriotism. Americans had forgotten the incredible accomplishments of their shared national history. The few rational and brave leaders speaking out on national unity were drowned out by the rising public chaos and cacophony.[69] The ancient Greek saying, "Whom the Gods will destroy, they first make mad" (crazy) gave every appearance of coming to life in Lincoln's America. [70]

The governing precedents established and developed over the course of 70 years meant nothing now. Despite thriving as a longtime lawyer and defender of the Constitution, the new president realized he had no guidelines nor experience to draw on when dealing with secession or civil war. Differing from Washington, Lincoln enjoyed no national reputation of national service, held no acclaim as a military leader, nor any relationships with leading political figures who could have helped him in transition.

Lincoln entered this office as an outsider, the first president born west of the Appalachians and often scorned because of it. At six-foot-four-inches, he towered over the average man of his era (five-foot-seven-inches), and still stands as the tallest U.S. president in history (see photo of Lincoln at Antietam). His personal appearance – uncommon height, gangly physique, and cavernous look – gave rise to ridicule, which grew even more severe since his election. His penchant for answering questions indirectly by telling stories elicited first impressions as an unsophisticated hayseed. The

---

69 A mix of able and dynamic leaders attempted to rally support for unification and common-sense compromises on slavery throughout the middle of the 1800s. Among others, they included Henry Clay (Kentucky, slave holding state), Daniel Webster (New Hampshire, free state), Stephen Douglas (Illinois, free state that was also in the "West"), and Sam Houston (Texas, hero of Texas' War of Independence, and a western slave state). However, none could build the necessary support from either citizens or members of Congress to ease escalating passions.

70 Sophocles, the classical Athenian playwright, used this line in his tragedy, *Antigone*, early 400s B.C. His words – and meaning -- have carried down through the ages.

political cartoons of the time reviled him with a harsh caricature based on his looks. On top of all of this, Lincoln's wife, Mary Todd Lincoln, grew anxious in the public eye, was sensitive to perceived slights, and was not a primary contributor to her husband's efforts, despite their close relationship. Of course, this stood in stark contrast to Martha Custis Washington, who complimented her husband by accenting his strengths and assisting him greatly in both public and private gatherings.

In short, neither the nation nor Lincoln appeared postured for survival as America faced its greatest crisis in its 72-year history.

Yet, he – and the U.S. – did survive.

Survival did not happen because a heroic and famous general surfaced to lead the country to a quick and bloodless victory. The existing general-in-chief, Winfield Scott, had earned renown as a hero and famous general of the Mexican War. However, in 1860 with his first war nearly 50 years earlier, he had grown into a large shadow of himself – old, tired, and weighing over 300 pounds. His choice as his successor was Army Colonel Robert E. Lee, who had distinguished himself for more than 30 years as an innovative soldier and leader, including a tour of duty as Scott's key staff officer in the Mexican Campaign. But Lee, ever loyal to his home state of Virginia, declined the promotion. Instead, he assumed a command in the Confederate forces, eventually rising to become their master general against the Union – in contrast to his father's service under President Washington in helping to preserve the Union.

Survival did not happen because of any impactful foreign intervention either. None of our international friends, which we had so carefully cultivated over decades, rushed to assist the U.S. In fact, other countries considered the North as competition, due to its industries, and the South as a more valuable trading partner, due to its raw materials and commodities. Actually, America's so-called friends made more of an effort, albeit indirectly, to keep the sides separated than united. Another Washington warning had come to pass.

Lastly, survival did not happen because of any political intervention. No one stepped up from Congress to attempt a reconciliation, though plenty of aimless talk and ineffective conferences rambled onward. Prior to Lincoln's arrival in the capital, none of the senior politicians of any party, Republicans or otherwise, offered to assist. The one exception was Stephen Douglas, his longtime rival in Illinois. Unfortunately, Douglas had already contracted a terminal illness, and he passed away shortly after Lincoln's inauguration. To sum up, Lincoln had plenty of advisors willing to guide him or tell him what to do, yet altruistic support did not exist – outside of the dying Douglas.

One example perfectly demonstrated Lincoln's isolation and lonely last steps en route to the White House. Warned of a possible assassination attempt, he arrived in D.C. days before his inauguration just before dawn, without fanfare and without friends, in disguise, accompanied only by a pair of bodyguards, and a nearly empty railway station. This unheralded arrival was a sad precedent, never before or after occasioned, that discredited the dignity of the chief executive while forecasting the isolation Lincoln would endure in the years ahead.

ABRAHAM LINCOLN (TOP HAT) AT THE BATTLEFIELD OF ANTIETAM WITH HIS GENERALS. PHOTO BY ALEXANDER GARDNER ON OCTOBER 3, 1862.

To use his own words, truly, the new president had arrived in "a house divided." And the summer soldiers and the sunshine patriots were nowhere to be seen.

Survival of our nation occurred because President Abraham Lincoln chose to face this crisis alone and unafraid. His earlier years had prepared him well for such an undertaking: a self-made man, scarred by a lifetime of defeats yet strengthened by a relentless willpower to overcome.

Like any reasonable person, Lincoln never desired this situation. Yet, he plunged immediately into the challenges and applied his considerable skills and persistence to begin to build solutions. He was determined to use both the authorities and the symbolism of his new office to reconcile the country's divisions and restore its unity.

The day he won the election Lincoln started to assemble support for his administration with one goal in mind: uniting the country. He set to work right away. He sought advice from trusted advisors, local friends and responsible Illinois politicians who had assisted him at the state level in the past. However, he initiated and actioned his main efforts himself. Based on his life experiences, he believed passionately in what are referred to today as the "5 Ps for success and planning" -- prior preparation prevents poor performance. Lincoln spared no effort to ensure he was ready to assume his office and its burdensome responsibilities on inauguration day.

Lincoln first focused his attention on the assembly of the Cabinet. In past elections of the previous half century or so, each new president rewarded his most loyal followers with a Cabinet post. Patronage had become a key aspect of 19th century American politics – and a terrible blight on national unity. The existing custom of allowing only party affiliates to serve as the nation's top federal administrators had created narrow outlooks and disharmony rather than rewarding merit and maintaining the unity that Washington had stated was essential. Lincoln was determined to form a national government of very capable leaders who represented the entirety of the nation, from different parts and parties of the country – shades of Washington. Intentionally, several of them happened to be main rivals within his own party.

Two weeks after the election, he met his vice president-elect, Hannibal Hamlin, a former Democrat-turned-Republican from Maine. Likely, they had never met before, as neither had any memory of it. But Lincoln explained his plan and strategies to him, reviewed potential personalities, and asked Hamlin to pick a fellow New Englander for Secretary of the Navy. Hamlin chose Gideon Wells, an editor from Connecticut, politician, and a former Andrew Jackson Democrat. [71] The point for the meeting and reason for nominating Wells was to publicly demonstrate Lincoln's willingness to work with whomever was required. It began the process of building a national unity government. The example clearly showed that his spoken goal of unity was reality, rather than following the previous process in which chief executives had only rewarded their direct supporters. This first position, a relatively minor one, went to a New Englander to symbolize that the midwestern president-elect would choose a voice from a different section of the country. Astutely, the choice also showed to the South that the strongly abolitionist leaders from New England would not have a dominating role in the Cabinet.

They further discussed New York Governor William Seward, Lincoln's main rival for the Republican nomination, whom Lincoln had unexpectedly beaten. Seward was also a key national figure and former senator. In 1860, New York was the most populous state in the country with 30% more population than any other state. Consequently, Lincoln and Hamlin recognized that the new administration must gain Seward's and New York's wholehearted support and therefore concluded that Seward should be offered the position of Secretary of State. From this point on, Hamlin returned to Maine until the inauguration, while Lincoln proceeded with Cabinet selections according to their plan.

For a number of practical reasons, including a distinguished history of high competence, Edward Bates was next on Lincoln's list. He came from a noted family of Virginia but then spent most of his life in Missouri as a lawyer and Whig politician. Like Seward, he had also run for the

---

71 Between the late 1820s and 1860, political parties in the United States underwent a transformation. The Democratic Republican Party split; part becoming the Democratic Party that focused on a strong presidency, populist base, and minimal federal control of citizens. Andrew Jackson represented them as the new party's first president beginning in 1828. The Federalist Party began to break up earlier with the Whig Party emerging later as the main rival to the Democrats. It focused on the primacy of Congress, encouraged industry, and the growth of a middle class. William Henry Harrison served as the Whig Party's first president in 1840. Additionally, a number of short-lived parties came and went after one or two elections, while exerting significant influence and power as the country also transformed. They included the National Republican, Anti-Masonic, Liberty, Free Soil, Know Nothings (formally called the Native American Party) among others before the rise of the Republican Party to challenge the Democratic Party in the 1850s.

Republican nomination but failed to gain sufficient backing. Securing Bates for the Cabinet meant an endorsement from a slave holding state, as well as the first-ever Cabinet member from a state west of the Mississippi River. The "Show Me" state's representative judiciously agreed to be nominated as Attorney General.

Like all politicians, Lincoln had to take into account agreements by his political promoters that carried over from the presidential nomination process. He also realized the compromises that such actions required. The Cabinet position offered to Caleb Smith demonstrated such a compromise. Raised in Ohio, Smith had attended school and practiced law there before moving to Indiana. Publishing a newspaper, serving in the Indiana legislature, and later elected to Congress for Indiana, Smith brought a strong legal and political background to the Cabinet. He represented the upper Midwest and became Secretary of the Interior after the Senate approved his nomination.

Prior to the next selection, Lincoln had to see a visitor who insisted on meeting him face to face. The visitor was Thurlow Weed, the powerbroker of New York politics and mastermind behind two previous presidents, William Henry Harrison in 1840 and Zachary Taylor in 1848. Further, he helped establish the Republican Party and advocated in 1856 for its first presidential nominee, John C. Fremont. Seward and Weed formed a strong political alliance and maintained a close personal friendship for decades. Weed also published an Albany-based newspaper, extending his influence well beyond state boundaries. Nobody recorded exactly the Lincoln-Tweed conversation, however, it probably linked Seward's Secretary of State selection with Weed's subsequent support of Lincoln throughout his presidency.

The Secretary of Treasury position proved to be one of the most challenging for Lincoln to fill, and it required him to draw on his courtroom craftiness to snare his target, Salmon P. Chase. The ambitious Chase had helped found the Republican Party and had run for the Republican nomination, like Seward and Bates. A native of Ohio, the third most populous state, he had previously served as a U.S. Senator, just completed four years as governor, followed by reelection to the Senate. Famous for his strong anti-slavery stance and defense in court for escaped slaves, Chase had argued cases as high as the Supreme Court. Rather than asking Chase to take the position, Lincoln told him that he was considering him for Secretary of the Treasury and asked if he would accept it if offered. Chase gave a noncommittal response, but immediately urged his supporters to put pressure on Lincoln for the Treasury nomination. The chase was over … Salmon Chase had been hooked.

A far easier selection was Montgomery Blair. Already well known by Lincoln, he readily accepted the offer as Postmaster General, a key post in the days before modern forms of communication. Blair, born and raised in Kentucky, graduated from West Point, practiced law in Missouri and Maryland (three slavery states), and had already served in legal roles under several administrations. His father, Francis P. Blair, remained active in politics and for 40 years had served as a close friend and adviser to presidents dating back to Andrew Jackson and crossing all political parties. Like Weed, Francis P. published a major newspaper, the *Washington Globe*. Further, Montgomery's brother, Francis Jr, tirelessly campaigned to keep slave holding states in the union and later proved to be a capable Civil War general. Lincoln listened and took advice from all three members of the influential Blair family.

Lincoln considered his toughest Cabinet selection to be Secretary of War. Keeping in mind that General Scott, America's most illustrious military officer of the past half century still commanded as the senior general, Lincoln knew that this Cabinet member would be more effective as a collaborator rather than as an authority figure over Scott. Politically, Lincoln required support from Republican campaign rival, Simon Cameron. He led politics in the second most populous state, Pennsylvania, served twice as a U.S. Senator, and made a fortune as a businessman. Further, he held a reputation that he controlled the Pennsylvania political world from his back pocket. Swallowing a bitter pill, "Honest Abe" decided he had to nominate him for the post to ensure national unity, despite Cameron's dubious character. Lincoln recognized Cameron's broad political background as an ex-Democrat, ex-Know Nothing, and Republican, and valued the support his Cabinet inclusion would bring to his presidency.

As mentioned earlier, while these Cabinet deliberations progressed between November and February, seven Southern states seceded from the Union beginning on December 20th. These states formally formed the

Confederacy on Feb 4th while another eight slavery states remained in the Union, but with questions looming on their future intentions. Meanwhile, mindful of his minority mandate, Lincoln's intent was to form an executive branch representative of diverse geographies and differing political parties. This approach contrasted with the customary practice of exploiting political spoils and filling positions with party supporters. He believed such an approach would increase stakeholders in his future government and could mitigate secession efforts in the remaining slave holding states. Unity and diversity were essential preconditions to start the process of restoring the Union and rebuilding a nation of all 33 states. Despite the rapid changes and uncertainty provoked by secession during these few weeks, Lincoln created a Cabinet of seven members, consisting of two noted Southerners (Bates and Blair), one abolitionist (Chase), and four Democrat or Republican moderates (Wells, Seward, Smith, and Cameron) covering every part of the country – except his own state and those that had seceded. In other words, he had created a national unity government within the political system as it existed in early 1861. The last time American citizens witnessed this type of unifying effort, a true statesman had occupied the presidency: George Washington.

In Lincoln's view, this opportunity to form his Cabinet was the best option available to reunite the United States. Like Washington, he feared neither others' abilities nor their ambitions. He wanted the best he could muster, and he hoped that he could rally as many Americans as possible to this concept of a unified, party-blind government symbolizing all of the people. With secession in progress and no fathomable end in sight, he realized he had no choice but to hit the ground running. In the same way a military leader would prepare an operations plan or a tradesman would organize his tools for a project, Lincoln knew he must complete his preparations before taking the oath of office on Inauguration Day. A unified and diverse Cabinet represented the most likely way to gain support from the political and business leaders of the country, while also broadening the representation for all citizens. He ensured that he would arrive ready.

During this time, as he had throughout the election period, Lincoln chose not to speak publicly. As speeches had long been the standard means for politicians to garner support and votes, this decision showed that Lincoln resolved to set a unique course for his upcoming administration. When pressed for an explanation on his relative silence, he regularly responded that his views were well known and had not changed. The only exception was a short statement, "Let us at all times remember that all American citizens are brothers of a common country." Again, his sparse words gave emphasis to his sole priority: national unity. He preferred that his past record speak for himself rather than risk inflaming overzealous extremists with new speeches.

With that said, Lincoln had already built his reputation for his ability to articulate clearly. His message had long been simple and frank: the essential necessity for America's survival required national unity. Prior to the start of the Lincoln - Douglas debates in 1858, Lincoln delivered a speech that defined his beliefs. During the contest for that year's Senate election in Illinois, these debates generated extensive coverage. Despite losing, he gained a widespread audience as the speech and the debates were nationally reported and discussed well beyond Illinois' borders. Referred to as the "House Divided" speech, Lincoln stated that "A house divided against itself cannot stand. I believe this government cannot endure permanently half slave and half free." The concept was straightforward, easy to visualize, and paraphrased from the Bible (Mark 3: 25) – a familiar reference in 19th century America.

Similarly, Lincoln held a firm public stance on slavery, which he staunchly opposed and readily viewed as the critical crux of troubles threatening the country. Recalling his youthful flatboat days floating down the Mississippi to New Orleans, he had personally witnessed the injustice of the institution. Politically, though, he recognized the institution existed as a part of American society and could not change for the sake of national unity ... the same issue faced by Washington in 1787 at the Constitutional Convention. Accordingly, he adopted a public position that he opposed the extension of slavery rather than its abolition, as the "radical" Republicans proclaimed. Hence, his reluctance to speak publicly after the 1860 election and maintaining his short public statement that "all American citizens are brothers of a common country" line, rather than risk fanning the emotional flames that raising the slavery issue would bring,

Lincoln clearly reiterated this stance in his first public speech outside of Illinois, in February, 1860 (before the Republican nomination process

began). Labeled the Cooper Union speech and given in New York City --
Seward's stronghold (and, ironically organized by Chase's Republican supporters), the event announced Lincoln's appearance on the national stage.
His speech began poorly. His physical appearance, rumpled clothes (long
train ride from Illinois), high-pitched voice, and midwestern accent did
not impress his sophisticated New York audience, the elite of the political
establishment. Rather than discuss (or attack) other politicians or parties,
he concentrated on the Founding Fathers who had written and approved
the Declaration of Independence and the Constitution. Clearly, he had done
his research using quotes and records to illustrate his two main points. His
first point emphasized that the words "slave," "slavery," or "property" were
not used in either document. However, the line, "All men are created equal"
perfectly conveyed the Founding Fathers' intentions. Secondly, he pointed
out that they knew slavery was morally wrong, but in order to get both
documents ratified, that belief could not be declared in writing. Lincoln
stressed that the Republican Party now carried that same banner as the
Founding Fathers. Though positioned against slavery, they must temporar-
ily accept its existence, while resisting its extension to new territories. By its
powerful content, the speech generated popular support among citizens and
editorial support from newspapers. Though he made no mention of it, the
speech marked his first serious effort to raise his profile outside Illinois and
launched his effort to gain the Republican nomination for the presidency.
Indeed, a lofty goal rising well above his log cabin and shopkeeping origins.

When a figure became famous in the 1800s unauthorized biographies
appeared. Few were commissioned, but many were still published. It happened during 1860 with Lincoln. However, knowing how this social plague
worked, he decided to use it as part of his strategy. Following an interview,
he authorized a writer, John Scripps, an editor with the *Chicago Tribune*, to
write a biography. The book was entitled, *Life of Abraham Lincoln*, and made
quite short (32 pages) and inexpensive (5 cents). With it, he took advantage
of the system to release it to the Penny Press (low-cost books/ papers that
could be released in huge quantities – and easy to read). Comparable to his
speeches, he focused on the common threads connecting Americans, obstacles overcome together, and his ordinary background. Nearly any American

could relate to these shared characteristics – and his efforts to lift himself and the country along with him.

Truly, Lincoln stood as a man of the people. Consequently, he never had to act the part. Citizens could relate to his early life. The log cabin birth and youth as a farm worker, flat boating voyager, and famous "rail splitter" all contributed to his common-man reputation. His work as a shopkeeper, militiaman, and surveyor on the untamed frontier provided additional threads to the Lincoln life tapestry. All had continued that fabric of life experience and character development upon which he based his legal and legislative careers. This is also when the nickname "Honest Abe" came to personify him. His ability to tell stories and relate any incident to a homespun tale, which contained both humor and a teaching point, were another part of his renown. Lastly, he was very comfortable with his past. And without effort, he could recall a personal anecdote from his past and relate it to any situation and any individual or group, casual or formal, to reinforce the focal point he was making in regards to their concerns and conversation.

Perhaps the most famous story to illustrate Abe's relatability occurred in October 1860. Lincoln had received a letter from a young girl, Grace Bedell, in New York asking him to grow a beard. He had been smooth-shaven his entire life up until that time. Based on the girl's request, he began to grow one. Today, no one can picture Abraham Lincoln without his beard. To complete the story, he made a stop in the girl's hometown of Westfield, N.Y. while traveling to Washington, D.C., for his inauguration. He asked her to join him on the train station platform where he gave the 11-year-old Grace a very public kiss on the cheek. Of course, such a story lit up the telegraph wires. It also warmed people to this now-bearded man with the hidden chin, but with no hidden pretensions.

Today, as it was then, it is impossible to know how much, if at all, Lincoln stage-managed his reputation. Negatives can always be voiced by naysayers. However, Lincoln modeled consistency. He devoted his time regularly and generously to one and all. Often, he worked for no or limited pay, and he sat as comfortably with a group of farmers as well as members of high society. Ignoring the oddities of his appearance and the impressions he often gave as a rustic, he more than made up for it by shrewdness and hard work. This consistency that he had long demonstrated throughout his life carried over to the extensive preparations he made prior to his arrival for the inauguration. He resolved to make his start as seamless as practical. He clearly realized that once he took the oath, anything could occur, and he meant to be as prepared as possible with workable options. This history and these actions indicate anything but a pretender or a person more focused on his image than achievement. He was the real deal – and so he proved as president.

Lincoln's February 11th departure from Springfield, Illinois to Washington, D.C. completed the parting from the familiar, comfortable phase of his life amid a relatively controllable environment. He was set to begin a new life amid the uncontrollable maelstrom at the center of the U.S. government. At the railway station, he gave a brief, unplanned speech among a crowd of friends, neighbors, and reporters. As Washington had done in his Farewell Address, Lincoln thanked his hometown crowd for their 25 years of unwavering support. He stated that he believed that the "task" before him was "greater than" the challenges facing George Washington. And without divine help, he feared he could not succeed. With it, he could not fail. He concluded his remarks by asking that they trust in "Him" ("that Divine Being") so "that all will yet be well."

Rather than traveling directly from his home to the capital, he and his family meandered by train through many cities of the Midwest and East, totaling 23 separate stops. At each station he delivered a short speech about national unity and met all the local dignitaries, including young Grace. In many ways, Lincoln used this trip to relax, knowing it was the calm before the storm. He had already written his final draft inaugural speech and managed to keep it secret. The travel time allowed him to both review the preparations already completed and contemplate the actions he would take prior to entering the White House. He realized that in order to face the crisis threatening the country, he had to seize the initiative as soon as he had authority to act on it. Certainly, with his experiences and knowledge, he also used the frequent stops to gauge how much support really existed for unity. His "task" as cited in his farewell speech at Springfield could only succeed with the full backing of the mainstream citizenry of the North. The crowds and his approachable interactions with them during the journey gave him confidence to act on their behalf in the weeks and months ahead.

Lincoln arrived in Washington, D.C., before dawn on February 23rd under the unheralded conditions and circumstances described earlier. With the two-day train trip becoming a twelve-day, confidence-building tour, Lincoln wasted no time in getting started. First, he met Seward for breakfast. Then, Seward and he visited then-President Buchanan and his Cabinet, followed by meeting Illinois representatives and the defeated Presidential candidate, Stephen Douglas. The day wrapped up with dinner at Seward's house, followed by more meetings with Buchanan's Cabinet members and his own soon-to-be Cabinet. He also held a short conference with General Scott allowing him to understand the status of the army. Lincoln was determined not to let any dust gather. Those events marked a busy first day in his new hometown.

This pace continued up until the Inauguration on March 4th. Lincoln made every effort to meet and talk with as many influential people as possible, especially those Southerners from the eight slave-holding states remaining in the Union. Some of these elected Southern representatives and government officials were still in the capital or lived nearby. He listened, cajoled, and encouraged members of the government to help convince these people that the United States still existed. The opportunity also existed that these eight slave-holding border states could remain in the Union. To this end, Lincoln made commitments in these face-to-face meetings that his administration would not overturn existing laws nor deny enforcement of them, while protecting all citizens' rights. He would leave no leaf unturned if it provided an opportunity to maintain national unity – again, his fundamental objective.

As an aside, another aspect of his role as chief executive required attention, though not his priority focus. Concurrent to his unification effort, he also had to deal with the time-consuming and energy-draining system of "patronage." Looking all the way back to Thomas Jefferson's administration, the president himself had become responsible as the hiring authority for all federal office supervisors under the executive branch. Such positions included post offices, customs inspectors, and every federal office throughout the country and in Washington, D.C. Thousands of jobs existed, all ripe for political influence and corruption, and placed a huge demand on any new president's time. Wherever he went he had to face this never-ending wave of eager office seekers, all while attempting to figure out how to save the Union and prevent further secessions. The distractions never relented. However, he succeeded in keeping his focus on his priority, while using the distractions as an opportunity for short breaks, oftentimes filled with humor and homespun stories. Odd as it may sound, these encounters enabled him to establish some early rapport with his soon-to-be Cabinet and senior government officials. Likely, they began to see Lincoln's wit and shrewdness, while realizing he was far from the political simpleton and shy Midwesterner they had expected.

As mentioned, Lincoln had completed his draft inaugural address and kept it to himself up to this point. Upon arrival at the capital, he asked his former rival and Secretary of State designee, William Seward, to review and comment. Seward did contribute, several times softening the tone to the South and helping to adjust the ending. [72] Thus initiated their working relationship. Lincoln used the address to set the public tone for how he would deal with the crisis dominating America. All of his work since November had laid the foundation for this speech. The address introduced all of his planned future actions, plus it issued a final plea for full national unity. And on a personal level, by his interactions with Seward he demonstrated that he welcomed input and embraced inclusiveness, symbolic of his strategic approach to the nation.

The morning of the inauguration ceremony dawned with pleasant spring weather, but as the day advanced, it changed to cold and bleak, quite matching the mood of the country. Washington, D.C.'s normal population of 75,000 had swelled another third with visitors filling the streets and hotels. By the time that President Buchanan rode in an open carriage to pick up President-elect Lincoln at his hotel, a crowd of over 10,000 swarmed about the east side of the unfinished Capitol building. A small squadron of the local police escorted the carriage the short distance through the crowds along Pennsylvania Avenue. Standing at the Capitol, a sharp-eyed observer would have noted sharpshooters positioned on both wings of the Capitol, as well as along nearby buildings. General Scott took no chances. Upon

---

72 The complete Inaugural Address is at Appendix 6.

arrival, Lincoln was introduced by his close friend, Senator Edward Baker of Oregon to polite, but quiet applause. [73]

Lincoln delivered a relatively short address, especially compared to the long-winded norms of the era. The speech focused on Lincoln's recurring primary theme of preserving the complete Union. He began by reassuring the country that he would uphold the Constitution and its existing laws. Further, he would protect the "property, peace, and security" of all sections of the Union. [74] He restated several points made over the past years, remarking that neither he nor his party had made a call to abolish slavery, but rather he would work within the status quo. He referenced specific laws passed by Congress concerning escaped fugitives and the security of freed slaves. As chief executive it fell on him to enforce these laws, just as his 15 predecessors had done for the past 72 years.

Like his "House Divided" speech, Lincoln made a simple argument for preserving the Union by tracing the nation's evolution from individual colonies to the United States of America. In that evolution, there had always been a binding contract, beginning with the first Congress (1774), reinforced by the Declaration of Independence (1776), formalized by the Articles of Confederation (1778), and concluding with the Constitution (1787). All states had agreed to this timeless contract, and rescission required all parties to agree. Therefore, since the contract remained intact, the Constitution stood as the highest law of the land, and the United States should stand unbroken.

Consequently, acts of violence against this contract meant either insurrection or revolution. Lincoln saw and understood his duty as president to execute its laws faithfully. The oath of office he would take after this address reinforced this commitment. This statement about acts of violence was not

---

73 Work on the second dome of the Capitol building began in 1854. Work completed in early 1866. Senator Baker, originally from Illinois, had been one of Lincoln's oldest friends since their early Illinois legislative days together before he headed west. Lincoln's second son, Edward Baker Lincoln, was named after him. Appointed a colonel at the advent of the Civil War, Baker was killed at a minor skirmish at Ball's Bluff in October 1861. His body was laid in state at the White House.

74 Property, based on current laws, included slaves. In March 1861, Lincoln's purpose was utterly focused on maintaining the Union. This statement plainly illustrates his intent to accept slavery as it was at this point in time.

a threat; it defined the purpose of his role as chief executive in accordance with his oath and the Constitution. He held no intention to inflict bloodshed or violence unless compelled to do so in defense of the Constitution and all that it stood for. He stated emphatically that there would be no invasion, as long as the ability to maintain federal property and collect revenues was not impeded.

Lincoln pressed on by declaring that he was speaking to lovers of the union, not to those "who seek to destroy" it. He asked what rights had been denied? The government's enforcement of the law had protected the rights of minorities and individuals as much as possible. In contrast, the idea of secession epitomized the essence of anarchy. If part of the country rejected the will of the majority, it meant the country, this democratic country, faced only the options of continued anarchy or despotism.

Lincoln returned to his central point by defining the dispute as one side believing slavery was right and ought to be extended; the other side did not. Again, Lincoln drove straight to the heart of the matter. The federal government had literally been established by compromise. Checks and balances codified in the Constitution required the government to work together in order to successfully resolve disputes. He cited two examples of this form of compromise: the fugitive slave law and the banned foreign slave trade. [75] Though both difficult issues, inclusive solutions had been developed, demonstrating the process worked, the majority of the time. Granted, some individuals chose to disobey or not enforce laws periodically. But the process still worked because measures existed to deal with infractions. And it would work better if the country stayed together rather than trying to resolve disputes as two irreconcilable governments. Contiguous geography prevented a divorce of physical separation. Friends could make laws together better than foreigners could negotiate treaties. And those laws, when made by friends, could be amended through the process spelled out by the Constitution. As president, he certainly recognized that Constitutional process, and he would administer change if resolved by the people through the amendment process.

He affirmed that he had "patient confidence in the ultimate justice of the people." He asked if "any better or equal hope" existed anywhere? As

---

75 The last slave ship that entered U.S. waters was the Clotilda in 1860. Rediscovered again in 2019, it had been scuttled following delivery of its "cargo."

Washington answered this same question in his Farewell Address, Lincoln proclaimed the same by emphasizing his trust for the judgement of the American people.

Lincoln remarked that as long as the people retained "their virtue and vigilance, no administration" by wickedness or folly could "seriously injure the government" in four short years. Lincoln's predecessors procrastinated on addressing slavery and failed to work with other parties. Now, the crisis of potential civil war was upon them. Despite all the many and clear lessons of history available to any responsible leader, too often the same mistakes repeated themselves. Lincoln implied that he would not be making the same mistake of procrastination, but rather would be leading from the front to confront the crisis.

Lincoln summarized his address by asking people to "think calmly and *well*", not to rush, and to remember that no good object can be frustrated by taking time. The crisis could be overcome if his countrymen remained intelligent, patriotic, Christian, and faithful. To his dissatisfied fellow countrymen, he affirmed that the momentous issue of civil war sat in their hands, not his. The government would not assail them. However, if they insisted on aggression to destroy the government, his inaugural oath, "registered in heaven", had him swear to "preserve, protect, and defend" – the U.S. Constitution – and in effect, preserve the Union.

He concluded his address by asserting that "we are not enemies, but friends." Bonds stretched back through battlefields, graves, and happy hearts. His final request was to ask all to remember this shared past and to allow the "better angels" of their nature to lead them.

Upon completion of his short oration, Chief Justice Taney administered the Oath of Office, and Abraham Lincoln assumed the role as 16th President of the United States. The responsibility to resolve the Union's crisis now fully sat on his shoulders. To a point never before seen in American politics, crowds of citizens also eagerly awaited this moment. Newspaper offices around the country were overflowing with people anticipating the first words to arrive off the telegraph wires. Presses rapidly printed broadsheets and later complete papers of his speech with the analysis of what his words might mean for the country. Even as far away as Saint Joseph, Missouri, riders stood impatiently outside the telegraph office for his speech. Upon printing, the Pony Express galloped into action spreading Lincoln's words across the western territories all the way to California in only seven days for nearly 1500 miles of riding. The country, North and South, East and West all realized this inauguration marked a momentous occasion that would affect everybody.

Though perhaps not as dramatic as Caesar ordering his army to cross the Rubicon River commencing the final act of the Roman Republic's civil wars, Lincoln outlined a clear path for the entire nation. He made a final attempt to persuade his fellow countrymen to follow their shared history by offering peace and reconciliation rather than face civil war – a fate that caused the Romans to lose their Republic. The country just needed to reunite. All would be welcomed back, and the administration would work within the existing Constitution and laws, which protected equally all sections of the country. However, if attacked, the government would resist. All was simple; all was clear.

Unfortunately, it was not so simple and clear for the South. The seceded states chose not to listen to his plea. In fact, many of their newspapers mocked him. Five weeks after the inauguration, Fort Sumter, federal property, suffered an attack by the South, and Lincoln did exactly as he promised. He called for 75,000 volunteers to suppress the states that had attacked the property of the United States and to fulfill his Constitutional responsibility to "preserve, protect, and defend it." The Civil War had begun.

The events that followed progress as another story. Worthy of review is what this new president had already achieved as a statesman. In contrast to his predecessors, Lincoln accepted he had the duty to use the authority of his elected office. He would exercise his powers under the Constitution to resolve this decades-old crisis with Congress' aid. Consequently, he began to muster the support necessary to restore the union by including a wide range of all Americans. Nothing was off the cuff; everything planned in advance as much as possible to be prepared for as many contingencies that he surmised would unfold. Despite expecting the worst, he made every honorable attempt to heal the crisis before violence could erupt. He used language that was meant to heal and unite not only to his supporters, but to those opposed to him. Lastly Lincoln – fervently – believed that the United States consisted of one country composed of many parts, but that its greatest strength was the sum of these parts. His readiness to serve in this incredibly challenging role and confront head-on the dual issue that faced the country is probably unequalled in U.S. history. Maintaining the Union while reluctantly accepting slavery had long proved to be America's gordian knot; even Washington had been unable to resolve. Lincoln entered his presidency with open eyes, and he continued to stride forward, confidently, while inspiring other fellow Americans to share his vision of reunifying the United States.

Like Thomas Paine, Lincoln had endeavored to use common sense in his approach to preserving the Union. He made deliberate plans, fostered inclusion, and laid a solid groundwork to resolve the nation's long-festering issue of slavery, now complicated by secession. He exhibited leadership that had been absent at the presidential level for far too long. No blames were cast, no threats were made, no bullying was delivered. Lincoln's singular focus was toward addressing the nation's issues. All that mattered was the willingness to work together.

CHAPTER 6
JOAN AND CROWNING A KING, MAY - JULY 1429

If today it seems incomprehensible that a 17-year-old would lead an army in driving away a previously undefeated foe, it was more unbelievable nearly 600 years ago. Joan next sought to re-establish the House of Valois' rule over France. One might say she convinced reluctant French political and religious leaders to support this next step of her quest, but frankly, she worked more by force of character than by persuasion.

Once again, if her actions – and results – are hard to believe now, they were even more so then. Yet, Joan did raise the siege of Orleans, exactly as she predicted could happen. As at Orleans, the next campaign did not unfold smoothly. Even up to the final hours prior to success, few in the French hierarchy believed it would happen.

To understand when this next step began, one needs to start at Orleans. It was Sunday, May 8, 1429. The previous day, following a day-long struggle, French forces had destroyed the English citadel of Les Tourelles. It marked the fourth English fort conquered in three successful battles over four days. The English mystique of invincibility was well and truly broken.

But as proud English soldiers, Talbot and his men remained anything but quitters, even then. They still had plenty of men-at-arms and controlled seven forts. At dawn this morning, their full army filed out and arranged themselves in order of battle to fight on the open fields. They held in place to offer combat.

Joan's retainers awakened her and partially armed her for battle (wearing a padded chainmail coat rather than full armor; her wounds would have made steel plates quite uncomfortable). In the meantime, she advised the captains to wait. This time they listened. The French forces arrayed themselves opposite Talbot's men. They must have been eager to launch themselves in attack again, while the English hesitated about engaging in another conflict with this man-eating Maid. [76]

Instead, Joan had the French celebrate Mass, ignoring the opposing army. The English watched, confused. Whether it was because they had never before seen such behavior (an army celebrating Mass) or they simply feared this woman, who they believed in league with the Devil, they reacted by beating a hasty retreat. Joan instructed her captains to let them go. It was Sunday; the "rules of war" did not permit attacks on this day, though it is unlikely anyone in the French leadership would have ever previously observed this convention. [77] It is probable that if the French had attacked, the English would have broken ranks and been destroyed. Their morale had melted away. Militarily, annihilation of the enemy would have been the typical soldier's goal. It made perfect sense to either destroy the hated, arrogant invaders or to acquire prisoners for ransom. But Joan was not a typical soldier. Her voices had said to relieve Orleans. Done. Next in line was the coronation of the Dauphin, not the destruction of others. Particularly, since she had already told the English that if they left, she would let them retire unmolested. And she did.

At this point she left the army at Orleans. She rode hard with her small group of attendants to Tours, a good 70 miles away – plagued by her bad foot and chest wounds. They arrived in less than two days, which would have been challenging to do even under the best of conditions. No account

---

76 As mentioned earlier, the name that Joan went by was "la Pucelle," translating as Maid, Maiden, Virgin. Religiously, in this era, it was firmly believed that a Maid could not be tempted by the Devil. Accordingly, the name/ title she carried had a huge symbolic value as well, meaning that she did represent God as his messenger.

77 Going back as far as the 10th century, the Catholic Church attempted to control warfare by instituting a series of rules that came to be called the Peace of God and the Truce of God. The Truce of God forbid battle on Sunday and church feast days. As a general statement, these rules were ignored during the Hundred Years War, though in this case, Joan had the French army adhere to it.

survived of how Joan managed to both bear the pain and recover. However, accounts clearly record that she immediately went to the Dauphin and pushed him to commit to being crowned at the city of Reims.

The highest church official in France had historically invested every King of France at Reims cathedral. This tradition began with the baptism of Clovis nearly 1000 years earlier and renewed with the crowning of Pepin (legitimizing the first of the Carolingian dynasty) in the 8th century. In Joan's eyes, and those of the French people, Reims was the only place where God ordained a French king.

Joan was eager for the coronation for at least two reasons. As she made clear to the Dauphin and others, her voices strongly urged her to have him crowned. Secondly, she already believed that her time to complete her quests had a deadline. Later narratives chronicle that she stated she barely had one year to do her work as a messenger. Consequently, she hastened in all her actions, and she hounded the Dauphin to commit immediately upon her arrival at Tours, just as she had done at their first meeting at Chinon.

The French Dauphin, like his military leaders earlier, realized that it was sensible to take advantage of the English withdrawal. But opinions diverged on how best to do so. Some leaders recommended clearing the English strong-points along the rest of the Loire River. In fact, most of the Orleans army had already begun this campaign, albeit without success. This may have been because Joan's absence enabled the English to regain their composure. Others insisted on securing Normandy, which controlled entry into Paris by the Seine River, or even to attack Paris itself. None had confidence to back Joan's demand to confirm the Dauphin as King of France. After all, the English and their Burgundian allies controlled nearly the entire route to Reims, which was a good 225 miles from Tours. Only three months earlier, no opponent of the English in their right mind would have dreamed of crossing such a huge expanse of enemy lands.

The Dauphin did not welcome Joan's request. Long considered not only indecisive and unmilitary, the Dauphin was perceived to be bullied by his advisors. They adamantly attempted to convince Charles not to risk everything based on the word of this peasant girl, who also threatened their role as advisors. Though Charles had accepted her initial message only a few weeks earlier, his habit of temporizing proved far harder to break. He not only hesitated, but stalled, taking nearly a month before giving in to her constant entreaties. At the end of the first week of June, the Dauphin finally agreed, but with one condition.

The Dauphin decided that Joan needed to clear the English possessions along the Loire River. She agreed, and must have departed like a blast from a cannon in her keenness to get underway. By June 10th she had returned to Orleans, and the next day reunited with the army outside Jargeau. Two days of furious fighting followed, with Joan leading from the front. The events included an incident where a stone crashed down on Joan's helmet sending her from a scaling ladder to the ground. But she bounded back up and cried for the soldiers to seize the town. Just as at the attacks at Orleans, her actions again inspired the French to renew their assault. Again, the English collapsed. The Earl of Suffolk, a leading officer among the English commanders, was captured.

From that point on, the French advanced like the wind knocking over a line of dominoes. Over the next five days, Joan passed between French controlled towns, where she was joyously welcomed as La Pucelle, and the last two English controlled towns. After a fierce frontal assault seized the bridge, one of the English possessions, Meung, opened the town to her when the garrison retreated into the castle's keep. The English troops at Beaugency fought, but were defeated, with the majority captured. Rather than ransom the nobles, the custom of the time, Joan allowed them to depart as long as they did not fight for the next ten days. The series of victories meant that the Loire River valley was now controlled by the French.

While the surrendered troops were marching out, the French received word that long-delayed English reinforcements were marching towards them. Joan welcomed this information and stated that a great victory would follow. In general, medieval face-to-face battles were bloody, indecisive affairs with results seldom causing any changes to the status quo. For this reason, open field battles were rare and far between. Fully aware of this, the French leaders had misgivings, but nonetheless followed Joan out to face the English. The armies met late on June 17th, exchanged heralds, and apparently agreed to give battle the next day before withdrawing for the night. Historians view what happened next as quite atypical – both sides made written narratives that agreed on the details.

The ensuing day, the armies lost track of each other in the mix of woods and fields around the village of Patay. The English had drawn up themselves in the standard formation that had always served them well. Positioned in a line to the front, longbowmen protected themselves by driving stakes into the ground forming a palisade wall before them with armored knights and men-at-arms to the rear. [78]

Not knowing the location of the French, the English decided to change the orientation of their formation. In the midst of that movement, a lone deer bounded before their ranks. The bowmen raised a hunting cry, broke ranks from their marching order, and became quite disorganized. The nearby and unseen French advance guard, hearing the cry, moved blindly into a full charge. Joan was not with them; she had stayed further back with the main body. In contrast to the past, now the French exhibited dauntless ardor and steely confidence.

The sudden attack destroyed the archers and the entire army fled. At least half of the 5,000 men force were killed or captured, including all their senior commanders from Talbot on down -- with one exception, Sir John Fastolf. [79] The French suffered nearly no casualties either in the assault or the thorough pursuit. This crushing defeat marked the end of England's ability to field an army capable of fighting on open ground for the foreseeable future. All that remained of English forces in France were garrisons – and a shattered reputation.

Joan celebrated the victory as she had each encounter at Orleans. Though ferocious during battle, afterwards she became the opposite. As she cradled a dying English soldier, she wept. She bitterly resented the cost of victory, especially for the dead who were unable to confess their sins before battle. She often shrank from the sight of blood after a battle, despite her role in

---

78 The English had deployed similar formations at their great victories over the French at Crecy (1346), Poitiers (1356), and Agincourt (1415), as well as numerous smaller affairs. Heavily outnumbered at each encounter, their archers caused massive casualties to the French, while disrupting their formations along with their ability to command and control.

79 Later, William Shakespeare used Fastolf's life and experiences as the model for Falstaff in four plays, Henry IV part 1, Henry IV part 2, Henry V, and The Merry Wives of Windsor. Though a popular buffoon in Shakespeare's works, the real Fastolf was a seasoned soldier. He was the only one of Talbot's officers who cautioned against fighting the French by reason of their string of successes and the resulting low morale of the English army. Clearly, had Fastolf's experience been fully appreciated and his advice heeded, the English may have avoided a disaster.

causing it to be shed. Though driven by her voices and belief in the justice of her cause, she far more preferred magnanimity and Christian charity. Those beliefs included her English opponents, as well as those in the Dauphin's court who constantly tried to undermine her influence.

But beyond the overwhelming satisfaction from the triumph at Patay, after decades of costly defeats, a more important event happened during this week of four victories. This incident eventually proved decisive for France's long-term future.

During her few weeks of warfare forming an army and fighting, Joan had met many men calling themselves warriors who wanted a place in this new force. Often following a brief meeting, Joan could decide if the claimant was full of fire and courage or just another summer soldier. The teenage girl had acquired renown within the French camp for what was described as "the seeing eye." She had the ability to look beyond the surface of a person and read their heart and capabilities, no matter what their experience or lineage. Such a moment occurred again before the taking of Beaugency.

Arthur de Richemont, the Constable of France -- titular chief general of France's armies -- had been exiled from the Dauphin's court a few years earlier due to the jealousy of his primary advisors. De Richemont now approached Joan's forces and volunteered to serve with his troops under her leadership. To repeat: the high lord and general-in-chief offered to serve under the peasant girl; Joan unquestionably performed miracles. The Dauphin himself had forbidden Joan's senior officers to speak with De Richemont, let alone to allow him to join them. Joan ignored this order, met the Constable, and welcomed him to their forces. Immediately after the victory at Patay, Joan took de Richemont to the Dauphin and reconciled them. In the short-term, this act seemed only of passing significance. However, long-term, it manifested itself as quite the opposite.

Following Joan's death and several more years of battlefield stalemate, King Charles VII again allowed de Richemont to lead his armies. He would continue to command them for the next 20 years, completing the ejection of the English armies from France. Even stranger, this nobleman, far from being a threat to the throne, mentored the indecisive and weakling king into becoming a warrior himself. It happened. What remains unknown is whether Joan recognized with her "seeing eye" that de Richemont would evolve into the one to complete her mission of restoring France. Selecting a successor capable of completing one's vision is an outstanding example of Joan's exceptional statesmanship.

The victory at Patay had opened the door to northern France. Joan – now accompanied by de Richemont -- immediately returned to the Dauphin and his court along the Loire River, well to the army's rear. For the next three days she earnestly implored Charles to advance straight to Reims.

With the English in total disarray, tactically it made sense to go to Paris, which was ripe for seizure. However, Joan's voices and plain common sense offered different strategic insight. Battle was not the way to win France, but uniting politics with the stamp of God would. As a number of her companions already knew, Joan believed that she was fighting against time. Her voices had informed her that she "only had a little more than one year" to complete her work. She did not know what may take place afterwards, but this internal timeline drove her, shared only with her closest companions. The Dauphin needed to go to Reims, be crowned, and consecrated by the church as Kings of France had done since the 8th century. Following this, they could tackle the English again – under an anointed King.

Yet, the Dauphin again dithered. He even brought Joan to tears by instructing her to rest while they stayed in place. Stewing in their jealousy, the Dauphin's advisors continued to argue for options that would block Joan's mission. Even the Archbishop of Reims, who had not even visited his cathedral for more than twenty years, resisted returning. Again, the Dauphin's very nature went against making decisions. Attesting to years of indolence, lack of imagination, and outright terror at having to actually wield power and exercise real responsibility, his feeble character casts a shadow on every conversation with Joan.

Over a week was squandered – allowing time for the English to begin regrouping at Paris. Perhaps the Dauphin made up his mind when Joan left the court for two days and slept in open fields in near despair. Eventually, he succumbed to her willpower and agreed to accompany the army towards Reims.

Finally, this French whirlwind regathered its strength and set out from Gien on June 29, swept all before it. English resistance no longer existed; those who remained had fled to Paris or remained locked in castle garrisons.

Accordingly, the Dauphin's army faced only England's French allies, primarily Burgundians, who controlled the richest cities in France along this 170-mile route.

The first city they reached was Auxerre. Joan pushed to storm the walls immediately and continue with speed to Reims. This time, Joan failed to convince the Dauphin. After a three-day delay, Auxerre agreed to provide supplies to the army – and (a rumored) two thousand gold crowns to the Dauphin's principal advisor, La Tremoillé. [80] Joan was unhappy both for the example it set, as well as the thought of leaving an enemy force in their rear.

The army continued northwards to the next major city, Troyes. Protected by an even stronger fortified wall, the Burgundian town refused to open their gates. They offered to do the same assistance as Auxerre. This time, the military leaders and Joan insisted on a council of war. Joan asked for two days, surprisingly with support from the Archbishop of Reims, and was granted the time. Intentionally, and in plain view of the city's walls, Joan immediately began preparations to assault. Clearly unnerved at the imminent bloodletting, the inhabitants of Troyes quickly offered to capitulate, rather than risk the fate of Beaugency. An addendum to this event, which must have given a wry smile to the Dauphin after the city's surrender, was the fact that the Treaty of Troyes had been signed here in 1420. With the signing of the treaty, his father had signed over the Dauphin's succession rights to his new brother-in-law, Henry V of England. The dominoes were falling in place.

The third major town along the route was Chalons sur Marne. With the example of Troyes behind them, Chalons opened its gates as soon as the French arrived. Chalons leaders even sent a formal note to Reims suggesting it do the same, and the Archbishop added a letter advising the cathedral city to prepare to welcome the Dauphin and himself. At the time, July 15th, the citizens and garrison of Reims had not made up their mind if they would welcome or fight this approaching cavalcade.

A side note here: Joan met two old family friends during the one night at Chalons – only a couple days journey from Domremy. A written account by one of them stated that Joan confided to them that her only real worry

---

80   Georges de La Tremoillé long had a reputation for adjusting his views based on contributions to his personal account.

now was treachery. This accurate premonition leads this modern observer to wonder whether Joan had exceptional foresight, wisdom beyond her teenage years, or another gift.

On July 16th the French Army, the Dauphin, and his court entered the open gates of Reims. The population had made their decision that day, and they turned out in force to welcome first the Archbishop on his visit "home" and several hours later, the Dauphin and the rest. From the vantage of today, it is impossible to know who the city was actually welcoming. Yet, one finds it hard to imagine the citizens cheering loudest for the long-absent Archbishop, an enemy army, or a Dauphin who three months ago was merely a pretender. In contrast, Joan was the living Miracle. A disquieting omen for the future, the crowds worked themselves into a frenzy hailing "La Pucelle" and even asked her blessings, while riding alongside the Dauphin. Royals choose to rule alone and do not accept competition, even from teenagers who have raised them to their throne.

Instructions had already been given that the next day, Sunday, would be the coronation. Absolute bedlam must have followed. The amount of effort required to construct and assemble such a royal spectacle – on virtually no notice for a city that had been the enemy only days before – was immense. Work went on throughout the night, but by morning, preparations for the splendid 13th century Gothic cathedral had completed. Attendees consisted of a significant percentage of the Peers of France, church dignitaries, other senior nobles, and as many knights and soldiers as could cram themselves under the lofty, vaulted arches by late morning. All the pageantry of a royal coronation was observed, including a distinctive element employed in crowning French kings for hundreds of years. The Archbishop anointed the new king with oil from a special vial that legend maintained had been brought by a snow-white pigeon to St Remi when he baptized Clovis in the late 5th century A.D. [81] Nearly a thousand years of history and tradition dictated that

---

81 Saint Remi became Bishop of Reims in the year 458 at age 21. In 496, he baptized King Clovis I, the first of the Teutonic Franks to move into Roman Gaul, along with 3000 of his warriors.

for anyone to be considered the true king, this oil sanctioned the difference between being ordained by God and being a mere pretender. [82]

All the preparation paid off; the ceremony and accompanying pageantry of this magnificent spectacle went off without a hitch. Not only were the participants swept up in the grandeur of the moment, but the entire city showed itself every bit as enthusiastic. Throughout the ceremony, only one detail differentiated this coronation from all others, before or since. Joan stood beside the Dauphin as he became King. None of the Peers, political or religious dignitaries, family, or knights joined her at his side; only the teenage peasant girl stood there with her battle standard, proudly, and with a radiant smile. [83]

Truly, this was a moment unique in all of history.

By force of will, Joan had completed a political act that would have been considered impossible just five months previously. Even more extraordinarily, at every step along the way, she had to overcome the resistance of those who should have initiated the necessary actions. She tenaciously held to her vision of what France needed, then persisted in achieving it despite seemingly insurmountable political, military, and cultural obstacles. She overcame the circumstances, including her gender and social status, and still made her visions a reality. Along the way and without any intention, she won over the hearts and souls of both the army and the general population. Furthermore, a remarkable fact, often overlooked, was that Joan, the battle leader at Orleans and along the Loire River garrison castles, was the statesperson on the march to Reims.

Joan had shifted from applying decisive military leadership to showing astute political shrewdness. This campaign had no casualties; no blood was spilled on the 2-week trek through enemy territory. But this time her opponents were French allies of the English. Joan understood the cultural and psychological differences between her foes and the proper way to deal with

---

82   This euphoria, of first the people of Reims and soon the majority of the people of France, underscored Joan's wisdom to insist that the coronation occur at Reims in the authentic, traditional manner.

83   Joan had a personal battle standard prepared before beginning the campaign at Orleans. It was a swallow-tailed pennant of white silk featuring a figure of the Lord flanked by angels on each side and the words, "Jhesus Maria" over a background of multiple, small gold French fleur-de-lys. These symbols clearly record the figures that inspired Joan in her mission to rescue France.

both. Would she have assaulted Auxerre if she had been given the okay? Or would her preparations – and potential bluff – have resulted, as they did at Troyes, with an abject capitulation from one group of Frenchmen to another? That will never be known. What can be said is that winning consecutive victories in what was effectively a civil war without shedding blood is a rare, if not unknown accomplishment. [84]

One would be hard pressed to find this portion of Joan's exploits recounted in a modern text on the history of statesmanship; yet it deserves to be there. During five weeks, she had led and completed a military campaign that opened up a French river system to her kingdom, destroyed a formerly invincible enemy, reconciled her ruler with her own eventual successor, conducted a bloodless march through disputed territory, and crowned a man as king who had failed to press his own legitimate claim. Perhaps, just as importantly, she united the population into realizing that they were first and foremost Frenchmen, bound to the soil and traditions of France. Joan possessed an intuitive audacity unknown in her era. She defied the rules and strictures of the age. What other peasant, a woman nonetheless, would dare to badger a future king? Who else would repeatedly travel – with an army much less a small band – well behind enemy lines? Yet Joan's successes were due to knowing when to adhere to norms, and more crucially, when to break from them boldly. Still, like the earlier events, these things happened, and Joan bore the sole responsibility for turning what seemed an impossible dream into France's new reality. One would need to search far and wide to discover a similar level of statesmanship.

In many ways, upon accomplishing the coronation, Joan should have accepted the King's suggestion and retired with full honors back to her home village. She had fulfilled the two primary objectives her voices had asked her to achieve, the relief of Orleans and the anointing of the Dauphin as the true King of France. Though the voices had declared that the English would be driven from France, they had not specifically revealed her involvement or a time frame involved. Her character and upcoming efforts remained unchanged despite this uncertainty. The selfless visionary insisted

---

84   The maxim that "the supreme art of war is to subdue the enemy without fighting" is attributed to the Chinese political and military theorist, Sun Tzu (5th century B.C.).

on attempting to achieve this last step of France's rebirth. However, Joan now fell afoul of King Charles VII's will and the policies he would undertake.

Consequently, Joan's influence began to wane immediately after the coronation. Under the new king, the traditional norms of the Middle Ages and feudal society, along with Charles' relationship with his long-established aristocratic advisors began to re-emerge. It was almost as if tradition had awakened from a dream. Joan had offended the political establishment by being both frank and correct. Without allies, there was a notable lack of effort to save her later. Her final goal – driving the English from France – occurred, but not under her leadership nor during the remainder of her short life. Her version of common sense now ran up against a wall that even she failed to surmount.

SECTION 3 - FAITH

CHAPTER 7

WASHINGTON, PRESERVING A REVOLUTION, APRIL 1775 – MARCH 1783: THE NEWBURGH ADDRESS

To the vast majority of Americans, George Washington's greatest achievement remains essentially unknown, both today and at the time it occurred. His fame and legacy largely center around his leadership and success in winning the War of Independence, as well as in setting the course and establishing key traditions as first president of the United States of America. After all, his example set a foundation that has held firm for more than 230 years, while continuing to inspire countries and people worldwide. Few, ever, have been able to match such accomplishments.

Nevertheless, his one decisive action on March 15, 1783, may even transcend these other accomplishments. It ensured that freedoms gained by the Revolution would be preserved, essentially paving the way for the future of democracy in the new Republic. Few military or political historians are even aware this event took place; some may know it as a mere footnote. Yet, this incident, in contrast to other historical examples of failed democracies, proved to be different. One man, George Washington, with democracy and the new nation's future governance perilously poised on a razor's edge, chose democracy over the opportunity to re-install an authoritarian government by military intervention.

In short, nearly all of the long-serving, professional officers of the American Army had decided that the only way to secure their entitlements was to march the army on the capital of Philadelphia and force Congress to grant them. In other words, their actions would be mutiny and set the stage for an American coup d'état with Congressional assistance. Such an action would have followed in the footsteps of earlier democratic governments in Athens, Rome, and other smaller European principalities. Each had been overthrown by armed coups. In all probability such a military takeover would have put an early end to American democracy and soundly nullified the words of our Founding Fathers in the Declaration of Independence.

The mutiny and the coup failed for a single reason: General Washington. When he learned of it, he immediately faced down nearly his entire officer corps, most of whom were friends and comrades that had served under his command for nearly eight years. To make matters even more difficult, Washington agreed with every one of their complaints and had been trying, unsuccessfully, for years to remedy them. Shortages of all types plagued the army – food, clothing and equipment, shelter, medical care, pay, and promised post-war benefits. He certainly understood their concerns and reasons for mutiny – and their willingness to sacrifice all that they had won. This man though had faith in the U.S. democratic system of government. He reasoned that despite all of its challenges, the new Republic still offered far better opportunities for its citizens than the alternatives of military governance or monarchy. Further, Washington had long been aware of whispered conversations to make him the king of an American monarchy.

Washington's action, now called the Newburgh Address, can only be understood by examining an extensive backstory running the full length of the war. This chapter provides context to the Address and insight into this incident. More importantly, it shows how Washington, ever-courageous and steadfastly faithful to the Republic, ended the revolt before it ever began, relegating the incident to a forgotten footnote rather than a memorable federal failure.

The backstory begins in Philadelphia at the 2nd Continental Congress in May 1775, less than a month after the first shots of the Revolution rang out at Lexington and Concord. This Congress, following in the footsteps of the 1st Continental Congress of 1774, had been organized the autumn before by 12 of Great Britain's 18 North American colonies. [85]

Like the 1st Congress, the goal of this 2nd assembly was to convince King George and the British Parliament to address the abused rights of its loyal subjects. The primary concern focused on taxation without representation. Most delegates were concerned citizens with fierce loyalty to their individual colony and distrust for outsiders. These colonists would have been insulted to be identified by reference other than their individual colony's name. All spoke English; few of them had met prior to 1774. Simply stated, the colonies were united more by common language than common interests.

However, incendiary events in Massachusetts caused the Congress to change its planned agenda. A minor military maneuver exploded into a raging revolution that would soon engulf the entire British Empire and much of Europe. The British Military Governor of Massachusetts, General Thomas Gage, made an effort to seize arms and powder from the local militia on April 19$^{th.}$ This operation met a completely different result than a similar, successful raid in 1774. Militia, along the route and pre-warned by the Sons of Liberty and riders Paul Revere and William Dawes, moved the munitions and mobilized to engage the British troops. Initially successful in the first exchanges of fire, the Redcoats arrived too late to find most of the munitions. During their return march to Boston, the British regulars were severely mauled by the militiamen, causing a disorganized retreat and significant losses. This news spread like wildfire throughout the Colonies just before the new Congress convened.

Accordingly, one delegate decided to attend the 2nd Congress not in normal business attire but rather in his battle-worn French and Indian War uniform, as a show of solidarity with the Massachusetts militiamen and colonists. As he was a Virginian, the uniformed man created a sensation from the moment he departed his plantation. People stood along the roadway to Philadelphia to doff their hats as he passed. Certainly, their gestures reflected respect for the Virginia gentleman, but perhaps the bystanders also realized

---

85 Georgia and the additional five colonies consisting of three in Canada (Quebec, Newfoundland and Arcadia – today's Maritime Provinces) and two in Florida (West and East Florida) had chosen not to participate. It is interesting to conjecture what could have happened if the other five colonies had been convinced to join in 1775.

the significance of the moment. They knew, likely as well as he did, that the colonies were heading down a one-way pathway for which there was no turning back. The impact in Philadelphia was every bit as pronounced, with the delegate's military attire suggesting that this assembly would be addressing much more than taxes. Of course, the uniformed delegate was George Washington, well-known throughout the colonies of 1775 for his exploits on the frontier, heroism in the earlier war, and success in farming. [86] Moreover, his physical stature, especially in uniform, impressed as striking. Weighing 200 pounds, immensely strong, and standing ramrod straight at six feet and two inches, he towered over the average man of the day. Adding to this statuesque impression was Washington's renown as an expert horseman who rode with grace and great stamina.

As the 2nd Continental Congress approached, King George and Parliament had not yet addressed the colonies' 1774 petition requesting relief or repeal of the Intolerable Acts. Though independence was not discussed openly, the delegates agreed that more forceful measures were needed to escalate their protests. Overwhelmingly, they voted to support the New England militia in its ongoing conflict by appointing a military commander. The only leader seriously discussed was Washington. However, he argued against the appointment, both in session and privately to many individual members. He believed he did not possess the ability nor experience necessary for success. By many accounts, Washington believed he would fail. He did not want to squander the colonies' opportunity through a bungled effort by a man who, by his own assessment, was more plantation farmer than professional soldier.

Congress believed differently and selected Washington. And despite his reservations and perceived inadequacy, he accepted. He had become convinced that he had the obligation to serve and lead. Using keywords that he later used in his Farewell Address as president, he believed – and lived – the concepts of duty, honor, and country. [87] As he wrote shortly after his selection, Washington also firmly believed "in the justice of our cause"

---

86 Benjamin Franklin was likely the only other household name in the colonies. However, he had lived in England for nearly 18 years, returning in May 1775 just in time for the start of this Congress.

87 Further in the future, in1803 these three words were incorporated as the motto of the United States Military Academy at West Point.

and would pursue his responsibility with all his ability and integrity. This point illustrated the strong faith that permeated his entire life. Examples included his conviction for Deism, his confidence in the upward progression of mankind per the teachings of the Enlightenment, and the opportunity presented to the colonies by standing up to King George. He strongly believed that the colonies were just in their cause and that faith in this cause would lead to triumph.

On this day, June 14, 1775, the American Army was born. It consisted initially of one member, General George Washington. His Congressional appointment allocated no troops, but it did allow him to assume command of the individual town militias in New England and employ them at his discretion. No resources were appropriated for the army – no salary for the militias, no uniforms, and nothing to purchase arms and ammunition, build shelters, or secure provisions. Faced with this situation, Washington set the tone for his needy army by stating that he would accept no payment for his service and requesting (not demanding) that he be reimbursed for personal expenses upon completion of his duties. Indeed, Washington and his army of militiamen were true citizen soldiers. He had been given the authority to lead, train and employ the army. But Congress, representing individual colonies – not yet a nation – lacked the funds and authority to levy taxes and support an army.

Eight days after acceptance of this commission, Washington departed Philadelphia to join "his" army – of complete strangers. Days before his departure, Congress held further deliberations and granted him the authority to enlist a small military staff. Further, Congress appointed four subordinate major generals, two of whom were already in Philadelphia. The other two commissions were to be given to militia leaders in the Boston area. Additionally, Congress gave Washington the authority to commission eight brigadier generals. The army that Washington hurried to join was not a federal army, but rather a loose colonial force composed of militias from various New England towns and villages with nominal control held by the respective colony. Accordingly, he realized that a key task ahead would be convincing these disparate groups to serve under a single commander and central leadership team.

For his journey north, Washington was accompanied by this new team, which included newly appointed Major Generals Charles Lee (former British Army officer and his second-in-command) and Philip Schuyler (landowner and leading New Yorker). Also, along for the ride were Adjutant General Horatio Gates (another ex-British officer and friend of Washington for twenty years); a military secretary, Pennsylvania politician Joseph Reed; and an aide, Thomas Mifflin (wealthy Pennsylvania merchant and orator). All but Schuyler were handpicked by Washington for their friendship and his admiration of their abilities. Congress selected Schuyler because of his role as an important figure in New York – seen as a key colony due to its population and status as the most practical route traveling to Canada. An additional factor was Schuyler's strong relationship with the Iroquois nation.

Of note, over the years ahead, an ironic result transpired: all members of this initial cadre but Schuyler turned against Washington during the war. Moreover, a number of times these individuals precipitated catastrophes that nearly caused the colonists to lose the war. Gates, especially, figured prominently in the Newburgh crisis of 1783. Fortunately, Washington proved to be at his best in times of crisis and capable of overcoming those who failed him.

Arriving outside Boston two weeks after the Battle of Bunker Hill (actually fought on Breed's Hill), Washington embarked on a tour of duty that would last more than eight years. His first task, as he saw it, was to convince the different militias and their relevant colonies that they must become a unified army and not representatives of individual New England town meetings. [88] The crux of this challenge meant organizing them, usually against their will. His first steps were to complete the chain of command by commissioning the other two major generals: Artemas Ward of Massachusetts and Israel Putnam of Connecticut. Ward brought disappointment because he thought he deserved the Army command, as his colony had led the revolt. Putnam brought experience as a veteran and hero of the French and Indian War. Washington also identified and commissioned the eight brigadier generals. He based the distribution on the size of the colonies and the militias they contributed to the cause. Immediately, arguments ensued over

---

88 Town militias could defend their area; town meetings were required to dispatch them beyond their local boundaries. Colonies could not issue that kind of order; only individual town meetings had that authority in New England.

who outranked whom. Conversely, these arguments could also be viewed as signs of tacit acceptance of the concept of a central leadership team. In any case, these first reactions proved no more than irritants, as progress towards achieving the goal of unity of command was underway.

With a rudimentary chain of command established, Washington and his staff commenced the hard work of sustaining an army. Feeding the troops ranked among his top priorities. This task included finding provisions for the men's families, who often accompanied their militiaman and performed camp work. He also sought to instill discipline and create esprit de corps by creating a means to identify ranks and designate units. He also reduced idle time by putting the troops to work and ensuring they were assigned simple, productive tasks to a defined standard. Soldiers built shelters of uniform design. Common hygiene practices were introduced and enforced in order to reduce the spread of contagious diseases. And commanders drilled their units in multiple militia-size formations, as village and town units had never soldiered together as combined groups.

These steps proved to be necessary, short-term measures to harden and professionalize the untested, largely untrained militiamen. Washington also recognized that basic long-term measures had to be implemented. Without pay, no fixed periods of enlistment could be maintained, which was essential to sustaining an army long enough to gain political victory. To enforce commanders' authority and orders, a disciplinary-justice system was sorely needed. Accordingly, he wrote and fired off a constant barrage of letters to Congress and colonial legislatures pleading for this authority, as well as for the necessary resources. All of these steps were critical for training, equipping, and sustaining an army, especially when the foe was the best-trained, best-equipped, and most successful professional fighting force in the world.

The organizational work to lay the foundation of the fledgling colonial army never ceased. Further, Washington had long ago learned that orders alone would never make things happen without leadership by example. To this end, he traveled on his horse from dawn to after dark daily, visiting units, supervising, helping, and getting acquainted with his hodgepodge army. He insisted that they must think and act like a national army, not a ragtag collection of individual militias. Additionally, he welcomed input from one and all, while ensuring his staff disseminated information both up and down the chain of command. He listened. With his senior officers, he hosted councils of war where each member was encouraged to assert his points. His willingness to accept input brought buy-in from all.

Nationalism was a new concept for the colonies and its army, and General Washington used every opportunity to promote it among his men.

Concurrent to all these endeavors was the fact that across from Boston harbor and at the opposite end of a narrow isthmus sat a large army supported by a number of formidable warships... Dire straits indeed. The British had the capability to strike at any moment. Washington held only a few mismatched cannons to support his army. Though nearly every soldier carried a musket, many varied in type and caliber. Standardized arms and ammunition did not exist. With that said, the biggest shortage of all was gunpowder for firing muskets and cannons. As happened at the third and final British charge at Breed's Hill, Washington's army might find itself again facing its attackers with only courage to arm its empty muskets, unless a means for replenishment was established.

In summary, Washington had been assigned a seemingly impossible mission – when weighing the pluses (few) against the minuses (many).

Yet, despite the odds, Washington proved to be a genius at leadership. He did, gradually, assemble adequate forces and resources necessary for success at Boston. At the same time, he was able to mask his army's initial weaknesses by a combination of stratagems that intimidated and pacified British forces. More than eight months later, he employed cannons and ammunition – captured from British forts in update New York and then hauled by oxen through winter snows – to drive the British away. The same qualities that carried him and his troops through the French and Indian War predominated again: resourcefulness and persistence. He never gave up, though he certainly thought about it. He even wrote to others outside of the army about his own inadequacies and concerns that "the game was pretty much up" later in the war when events looked just as dark. Yet, even in apparently hopeless times, he never showed a lack of confidence to those around him. Instead, he redoubled his efforts to inspire his soldiers to stay the course – because he always had a plan to work around whatever obstacles appeared in his path. These qualities sprung from the same source:

his faith. He genuinely believed in the justice of their cause and that they would eventually succeed if they persevered.

The years ahead produced many results, militarily and politically. During the vast majority of the war, the outcome appeared more often as a lost cause than a potential victory. Rather than attempt to describe in detail all of these events, the following chronological summary highlights the noteworthy losses, challenges, and the infrequent wins:

- 1775. Destruction of the two American forces sent to wrest control of Canada from the British

- 1776. Elimination of the remnants of those forces attempting to halt a subsequent British invasion down the New York water route of Lake Champlain, Lake George, and the Hudson River

- Near-destruction of Washington's Army in New York and New Jersey, plus the near-mutiny of General Lee, but followed by the startling victories at Trenton and Princeton

- 1777. Loss of Philadelphia, the American capital, and defeats at Brandywine, Paoli, and Germantown

- The Conway Cabal – the months-long attempt by a group of politicians and officers, including General Gates, Thomas Mifflin, and Inspector General Conway to replace Washington with Gates

- 1778. Stalemate with new French allies in coordinating any naval or military operations, while risking collapse of the new alliance

- Concerted assaults by Native Americans and British forces across the western frontier, stretching along the eastern side of the Appalachians from Georgia to New York

- 1779. Another lost campaigning season due to the lack of coordinated French involvement, amid British intimidation of French naval and ground forces

- 1779 - 1780. Loss of three southern colonies (Georgia, South Carolina, and North Carolina) due to a British expedition rampaging through the South

- 1780. A third lost campaigning season with the French

- Benedict Arnold – a most unexpected betrayal by Washington's protege, marked by Arnold's attempted handoff of the vital West Point fortress to the British

- Official threat by the British commander to throw away the semi-formalized "Rules of War" if the Americans hung the convicted spy, John Andre, who had served as Arnold's go-between. If initiated, the result could transform the ongoing Revolution into a vicious civil war.

- 1781. First substantial mutiny by complete units – Pennsylvania line troops, followed by New Jersey line troops a few weeks later – due to chronic shortages

- Ratification by all states of the Articles of Confederation, which confirmed a national government, but did not give Congress authority to independently raise revenue – hence, no Congressional ability to supply pay, uniforms, equipment, food, or proper medical attention to the army. The discontent caused by this failure planted the seeds for the future Newburgh uprising.

- Surrender at Yorktown of the main British forces in the South to the combined French navy, French army, and Washington's army, caused by surprising and surrounding Lord Cornwallis' army – effectively ending British efforts to win the war

- 1782. Focus by Washington to maintain government and military support amid British occupation of four cities and full naval control of the seas again – keeping the army together had never been harder

- Vote by Rhode Island against a resolution allowing Congress to raise funds by imposing duty on imports. This act confirmed no independent source of revenue for the national government or fulfillment of obligations to the army.

- 1782 – 1783. Attempt by a new cabal of Congressmen, financiers, and Washington's own officers to emplace a king or a similarly empowered strong, central government – in reaction to the Rhode Island vote

To review, it is now mid-February 1783. The army has been deployed in the field for nearly eight years under the following miserable conditions – unacceptable to any army of any nation in any era:

Pay. In general, most soldiers had received no pay for at least eighteen months. Those who participated in the Yorktown campaign gained two or three months' pay on the march south, courtesy of the French. Those who did not, obtained nothing. The previous large-scale payroll was delivered in the 1777 - 1778 campaigns when the army was based in the Philadelphia area. Officers received pay even less frequently than the enlisted men. On average, the long-term soldiers were owed between four to six **years** of backpay, according to Washington's own status report to Congress in 1783. Families or extended families who were dependent on their soldiers' pay needed to find other sources of income to sustain themselves. Additionally, when Congress paid the army, it was usually disbursed in devalued paper notes rather than hard currency. Consequently, few merchants accepted these notes' full value for purchases. Of course, throughout these many years, Congress repeatedly promised remittance but only rarely delivered on their payday promises. When they did, it was never enough to cover the many missing months and years. As previously noted, George Washington never took a cent in pay from the start of the war. He finally submitted his expenses – for the entire war – in late 1783.

Uniforms and footwear. Within Washington's main army, the national troops called the Continentals, these essential Army provisions improved after 1778 because the French allies provided annual resupplies. Still, at the surrender at Yorktown, the British observed obvious differences as they marched between files of French on one side and Americans on the other. The French outfitted their troops with gaudy white uniforms and presented an immaculate appearance. The Americans, their best outfitted troops standing proudly at attention, appeared as orderly ranks of ragamuffins. Continental soldiers who missed the annual occasions when uniforms were distributed, would await a year or more before the next lot arrived. Accordingly, they developed into experts with needle and thread, with regular patchwork making their tattered clothing appear more quilt-like than uniform-like. Footwear posed a more serious problem. As described in the Prelude, many soldiers marched to Trenton with blood-stained rags wrapped around their bare feet. The supply situation proved far worse in subsequent winters. For the majority of the militia-manned army, the troops' only uniforms were their own civilian clothes. Uniforms did not exist for them for the entirety of the war.

Food. Feeding the troops was a challenge that persisted throughout the war, especially during the winter months. Congress had two authorities to ensure the army was fed. Hired merchants accepted contracts to deliver foodstuffs. States received quota requisitions to supply both their militia units and their state regiments in the national army. However, Congress' ability to provide oversight and enforcement did not exist, as Congress did not have the authority under the Articles of Confederation to raise income by taxes or duties. Quality, quantity, and delivery of anything often proved elusive. Further, the army seldom had hard currency, which would have allowed it to feed itself. Local farmers expected payment in hard currency for their crops and livestock – which the nearby encampments of the British always used. The paper notes that Washington's army issued had limited or no value compared to British cash. As the army was quartered on their own lands, officially requisitioning or unofficially seizing provisions was not a viable option except during an emergency basis. Consequently, soldiers learned to be as resourceful as their commander in order to get by. In short, the men had to fend for themselves much of the time for their meals.

Shelter/winter quarters. As early as Breed's Hill in June 1775, the British were astounded at how capable the colonists were at erecting quick and effective earthworks for protection. That expertise translated to building expedient shelters whenever they settled between campaigns or during winter when movements usually stalled from November to April (in the North). Soldiers constructed their own huts without building supplies and by using their own axes and tools. They built shelters as the first pioneers had built log cabins by interlocking nicked logs and stuffing mud in the cracks. In contrast to the colonials' exposed, primitive winter quarters at Valley Forge or Morristown, the British wintered in comfortable, warm houses in the biggest cities of the colonies, such as Boston, New York, Philadelphia, and Charleston. On campaign, few tents existed for Washington's units. In general, when the army marched and slept, the men wrapped themselves in their blanket – if they had one. When they did not, they used their outer coat, rain or shine, hot or cold. The soldiers had always noted that Washington endured the same conditions as his men until food and shelter resources were available for all. Again, like the example he set of personally leading troops in combat when needed, his willingness to consistently share physical hardships with his men built camaraderie and also contributed to the mystique he earned as their revered commander.

Arms and Ammunition. The French definitely helped with muskets and bayonets beginning in the spring of 1778. Still, the average soldier, whether a short-term volunteer or Continental enlisted for the duration of the war, carried his own weapon and made his own musket balls. Gunpowder, though a severe shortage during the siege of Boston in 1775-1776, was adequately available for the remainder of the war, thanks to maritime resourcefulness. Hundreds of American merchant ships had been converted to privateers and commissioned by Congress, as well as individual states, to seize British ships and trade with Europe. Gunpowder was valued as the key item of their return cargos, whether seized or purchased in trade. Though far from the reliability of a factory assembly line, this process worked well enough to maintain the army's essential stocks of gunpowder and cannons.

Medical. At the outset of the Revolution, local militias usually brought along their village doctor, and units resisted any effort to create an organized medical structure, despite Washington's efforts to professionalize this necessity. His experiences from the earlier war, coupled with his appeals to Congress, eventually proved successful, allowing the organization and implementation of a formal, military medical system. Many more soldiers lost their lives to disease than battle, especially early in their enlistments. The colonies were overwhelmingly rural, and new enlistees became exposed to illnesses in the ranks that they had not encountered at their farm or village. Beginning in Boston and continuing in subsequent campaigns, Washington and his officers established, enforced, and gradually put into effect hygiene standards. And just as gradually, state-appointed officers grudgingly accepted the fact that their men lived longer if they accepted and enforced comprehensive medical standards and organizational structure. Though these standards became common practice among the Continental units, they continued throughout the war as a constant issue with the state-run militias. Finally, the army faced combat. Keep in mind, that if wounded in battle, antiseptics or anesthesia did not exist. Doctors conducted surgery with saws and probes, unsanitary and unrinsed between uses; infections were frequent. A swig of liquor followed by inserting a stick to a clenched mouth provided the only comforts for the patient during the primitive surgery that followed.

Benefits. Frankly, there were no material benefits to enlist as a soldier in the Continental Army. As the war progressed, states offered limited enlistment bounties, often in hard currency, to induce soldiers to volunteer their service. At the national level, the Continental Army (versus state militias) accepted volunteers for one-year, three-year, or full enlistments for the duration of the war, but had no funds for bounties. [89] The longer the term produced better unit cohesion and continuity, but the longer terms did not happen until several years into the Revolution. As noted earlier, the benefit of uniforms, equipment, and food at no charge did not turn out as publicized. In short, men volunteered for the cause, not the benefits.

But two failed promises, more than any of the ordeals described above, caused unrest among both the enlisted and officer ranks. The men grudgingly accepted all the other shortages and adversities, harsh as they may have been. But after Yorktown, when victory appeared almost certain, Congress began to waver on two of its most coveted guarantees. The first commitment concerned officers. Congress had committed to paying officers a pension of half pay under two conditions: if they served for the duration of the war and if they would return to duty if recalled following the war. Congress' second pledge pertained to all soldiers and promised grants of land in the Ohio Country – the new, undeveloped western territories conquered from the British and Native Americans. After years of financial deprivation, this assurance appeared to the suffering soldiers as the pot of gold at the end of the rainbow. Congress' land guarantee had given every soldier substantial incentive for enduring years of hardships – along with the moral prospect of winning liberty. [90]

Lastly, another group of soldiers existed: African Americans. They comprised a significant percentage of the Continentals. Many were free men.

---

89   In comparison to the Continentals, militia units, which were organized and maintained by states, provided a wide range of options ranging from weeks to extended periods of service. Part of that service might be with the national army for a few weeks, a campaign season, and occasionally longer – or served in defense of the state. Service for militia could be as a volunteer or conscripted by quotas set for towns or regions. Every state maintained their own requirements. Approximately 150,000 militia served with the Continental Army, while several hundred thousand more were retained on call in the states.

90   Congress passed legislation in 1776 for half pay pensions for the disabled; in 1778, it was extended to officers willing to serve for the duration of the war. The first Congressional act on land grants was passed on September 16, 1776; other Congressional acts and individual states enacted further measures later in the war. In lieu of pay, Congress had promised all soldiers land in the Northwest by 1779, plus their back pay, and half pay retirement pensions (the latter for officers only). This situation developed and progressed during the war as Congress proved increasingly incapable of fulfilling the basic benefits promised to enlisting Continentals.

As an addendum, Britain had done similar with land grants after the French and Indian War; the precedent existed already.

They fought for the words in the Declaration of Independence, "All Men are created Equal" and hoped that their contributions would make that a reality. Others, though, enlisted as slaves. [91] They fought for equality, but more importantly, for the commitment that a year of military service would secure their freedom. Both groups fought for a future that assured they would be treated as all other Americans.

Regardless of color, all of these soldiers stood as volunteers, true volunteers. Idealism had inspired them to join in the first place, furthered by their belief that freedom and independence were worth fighting for against the strongest empire in the world. They had endured years of grueling conditions to fulfill this common hope. They had accepted great risks to life and limb, while witnessing countless deaths and brutal injuries to friends and comrades. And now, with Congress wavering on the two most treasured benefits of pension and land, they realized that those years of endurance and sacrifice may be for naught. In victory, they would return home with hard-fought freedom, but facing a life of continuing hardships, financial ruin, and failure in their quest for the American Dream: private land ownership.

By 1782, soldiers were angry, nervous, and scared. But most of all, they felt betrayed. And it was these feelings of betrayal and broken promises that fueled the outbreak of mutinies, like the ones described earlier among Pennsylvania and New Jersey line troops. Congress had failed them, as had their individual states. Only one man had championed them. From beginning to end, he had shared their hardships. Soldiers recognized him as their commander. They always found him where the men needed him most – leading a march, consoling the wounded, conferring with subordinate officers, visiting a lone sentry, or huddling among troops at a campfire. They would follow him anywhere, and they aspired to follow his example always. Unlike every other senior officer, he had never, not once, taken leave from his duties. They knew he had requested, complained, and tried every way imaginable – with honor – to compel Congress and the states to deliver on

---

91   Slaves could be in the army for at least three different reasons. They could serve alongside their master. Another option was that they could volunteer to take the place of someone conscripted by their state for a militia position or allocated as a member for a Continental regiment – with their master's permission. Finally, others escaped from colonial owners who supported the British (called Tories) and volunteered to join the American army.

their obligations of supporting the army. Washington stood alone as the one man in America that they respected, trusted, and loved.

Most members of Congress realized all the above. Some of them had actually served with Washington in the army and sorely recognized these hardships, including two of his former aides, Alexander Hamilton and Thomas Mifflin. In an effort to resource the Revolution, several Congressmen and financiers had managed to secure international loans and grants despite no Congressional revenue. They had also established state banks that raised additional, though meager, funds. This financial wizardry of loans, grants, and state banks had maintained Congress and Washington's army, barely, for years. However, these men, like founding father Robert Morris, understood that in the long-term this was not sustainable. A system based on state reliance and unanimous agreement would prevent Congress from fulfilling its federal obligations and paying the national debts. The only other option was for Congress to be granted the authority to raise national revenue independent of state consent and support. [92] Following years of failure, in 1781 these men managed to convince Congress to pass a resolution giving Congress this authority – and security to forecast ahead. And during the nearly two years this resolution slowly wound its way through the state legislatures for approval, this group of politicians and financiers began communicating with disaffected officers under Washington's command. Horatio Gates, Washington's second in command, who resented Washington's successes while overlooking his own failures, stood at the center of this intrigue.

This background summarizes the situation that the country and its Continental Army found itself in during the long year of 1782. Peace negotiations dragged on with no end in sight. Further, Americans awaited confirmed recognition of the Colonies as a country. At the same time, the British continued to occupy New York City with a larger army than

---

92   The Articles of Confederation government was established in 1777 and confirmed in early 1781. It had three overriding limitations. No executive person or department existed; work was carried out by Congressional committees. Secondly, no resolutions passed by Congress could take effect until all 13 states ratified them. Not only did this make the procedure incredibly slow, but if one state rejected a law, it became invalid. Lastly, Congress did not have the authority to raise its own revenue. Instead, the states were responsible to supply Congress funds for national expenses – like the Continental Army. Unsurprisingly, the states refused to contribute to expenses beyond their boundaries.

Washington could maintain. The Continentals occupied camps north of the city with headquarters at Newburgh. Apparent victory could still be lost, and this British menace hung over Washington's under-resourced army like a dark storm cloud.

In May 1782, Washington received a letter from one of his colonels, Lewis Nicola. Whether Nicola operated entirely on his own initiative or that his individual effort served as a prelude to future events at Newburgh is unknown to history. In his letter, he formally outlined the army's complaints, explaining how Congress had repeatedly failed the army over the years and with no indication of improvements in the months ahead. Consequently, Nicola reasoned, only one path remained for the United States to become a strong and independent country: Washington must use the army "to lead in peace," take the title of "George I," and become king.

Washington immediately reacted. He categorically rejected Nicola's appeal. It marked the one and only letter Washington sent during the entire war for which he required his aides to confirm in writing that they had sealed the letter before dispatching.

Concurrent to these events, Congress' revenue-raising resolution continued its routing through state legislatures. The resolution would give itself authority to raise money via a customs duty (tax) on incoming goods from overseas. It could only be enacted if all 13 states agreed. Twelve states ratified the resolution, but in December 1782 Rhode Island rejected it. Shortly afterwards, Virginia changed its vote to reject it also. This rejection meant that without Congressional funds, the army would be disbanded after the upcoming peace treaty without prospects for backpay, pensions, nor land grants. Receipt of this depressing news caused consternation in the ranks and energized the malcontents.

Washington followed this rejection with another prompt action. He sent three of his senior officers to the capital at Philadelphia to insist that Congress meet its obligations. However, Congress confirmed to the delegation that it possessed neither the means to meet the obligations nor the power to demand the states deliver their promises on back pay and pensions, let alone land grants. It had overdrawn on all its own loans already and could not open new ones. Though Congressmen were appalled by the states' failure to honor these commitments, they were powerless to assist. Summarizing, the result conclusively demonstrated that the Articles of Confederation government was toothless. Congress had no authority over the states nor did an executive exist capable of overcoming states' refusal to meet their obligations.

Not all members of Congress chose inaction. Hamilton formed a group of several Congressmen to scheme against the parameters of the governing Articles of Confederation. Robert Morris added members to this group from the financial community who had helped underwrite earlier loans and grants. Morris, himself, served as Superintendent of Finance for the country in a role that preceded the future position of Secretary of the Treasury. Further, he had negotiated most of the foreign loans and was aware of whatever monetary options existed at the time. Additionally, prominent private citizens, who despaired the country's inability to gain self-sufficiency, met and supported this group. As mentioned, Gates and his staff had sounded out the army's officers during these past months and had confidence that the vast majority would not accept inaction if their benefits were revoked. The Philadelphia group, which included Hamilton and Morris, communicated their schemes back and forth with the army through Gates' staff and an unknown number of other officers who met and discussed clandestinely.

In mid-February 1783, Washington took delivery of a letter signed by Hamilton and alluding that he had support from members of the government and army officers. Knowing Washington as well as he did after serving directly under him for years, Hamilton phrased his words to appeal to Washington's sense of responsibility. He reasoned that if Washington temporized, he would be evading his duty. The request urged Washington to assert that the army would not disband until Congress and the states delivered on their promised benefits. Only Washington's influence and leadership could convince a majority of the government to do so. Or in Hamilton's words: "This Your Excellency's influence must effect." Additionally, Hamilton said: "It is of moment to the public tranquility that Your Excellency should preserve the confidence of the army without losing that of the people. This will enable you in case of extremity to guide the torrent, and bring order perhaps even good, out of confusion." The unspoken implication was that if Washington followed this recommendation, he could be asked to lead a change of government if Congress refused to grant restitution. Or if he refused to lead a changed government, he could retire after Congress' obligations to the army were satisfied. Politely phrased, Hamilton had extended Washington an invitation to lead a coup d'état – a sudden overthrow of an existing government by a small group holding positions of authority.

Washington took three immediate actions in response to this letter. First, he delayed responding to Hamilton for more than two weeks, allowing time to investigate the situation more fully. Secondly, he sent his own trusted men to assess the extent to which his officer corps was involved. Lastly, he corresponded with Joseph Jones, one Congressman whom Washington trusted. Jones' response warned him of "sinister practices" being used by conspirators to ruin his "reputation," and that they would proceed even against Washington's opposition. Reinforcing Washington's initial belief that the letter reflected a political plot, rather than a military mutiny, were questions raised by officers returning from Philadelphia. These questions implied that Washington was aware of plots in the capital.

Undoubtedly, Washington deliberated. He was determined to discover exactly what was occurring in the military ranks and to assess how widespread dissension had become. His answer to Hamilton on March 4th soundly refused the invitation to a coup. Washington insisted that he would continue to lead the army with peaceful petitions to Congress and that he was "under no *great* apprehension of its exceeding the bounds of reason and moderation."

However, on March 10th an unsigned letter circulated among the army camps at Newburgh. It called for an unofficial meeting of officers the next day to redress grievances unresolved by the officers who had been dispatched earlier to Philadelphia. Gate's aide, Major Armstrong, most likely wrote this letter with probable involvement by the staffs of Gates and Henry Knox, Washington's long-time chief of artillery. While intent on reading the unsigned letter, which had been openly posted throughout the camps, Washington also received a copy of an anonymous speech due to be given at the upcoming meeting. Only a commander holds the authority to convene a meeting of his officers; already this action violated regulations. Yet, ironically, the majority of the letter's content aligned with Washington's own feelings and frustrations. He was greatly moved. He also now fully understood how dangerous this movement had become. The words plainly demonstrated that this unrest existed as a military problem, as much as a political one. The letter conveyed a close approximation of the ground truth, and its call could inflame many. It recited their "toils" and "dangers," their sharing of "the cold hand of poverty," and "seen the insolence of wealth without a sigh." Does the country court their "return to private life with tears of gratitude and smiles of admiration" by granting them previously promised rewards? "Or is it rather a country that tramples upon your rights, disdains your cries, and insults your distresses?"

Up to this point, Washington agreed with the writer's words. However, they are followed by ones that caused him grave concern. The speech continued on by stating the army should "suspect the man who would advise to more moderation and longer forbearance." Finally, the letter concluded by earnestly demanding that the army remonstrate to Congress, with the demand that if Congress did not fulfill its obligations to the army, then the army would seize these assets and "retire to some unsettled country." Such an action implied that the country would be left undefended to the unlikely mercy of the British forces still stationed in America and of the Natives on the frontier. This harsh language combined with Hamilton's foreboding February letter and the involvement of many of his officers, convinced Washington of the severity of this threat. Clearly, Washington, the general and statesman, had some difficult and complicated decisions to make.

Washington grasped the fact that this dissension in the ranks and pending call to mutiny was as critical a challenge as any he had faced on the battlefield. Despite all the years of extraordinary adversities, he would never accept responsibility to act outside his core beliefs. He had resolved, and he would follow through with his commitment and employment of the army to secure the nation's independence as defined in the Declaration of Independence. Using the military to address grievances outside of this Declaration did not align with his beliefs.

The army, just like the rest of the population, needed faith that the government stood for them. Washington's challenge was to address the Army's legitimate concerns while adhering to his core beliefs. The solution might not be quick, might not feel quite fair, but it had to adhere to the principles outlined in the Declaration of Independence.

This moment – and his subsequent actions – separated Washington from many good, very good, leaders of the American War of Independence, some of whom were Founding Fathers of the United States. Without advice or assistance, the man who became known as the Father of our Country determined his next step. [93]

No surprise: Washington chose to face the issue head-on. Anger at their disregard of military discipline by calling an unauthorized meeting was not the answer. Attempting to placate them by agreeing with the letter and vowing to push Congress harder would solve nothing. Permitting them to drive the meeting forward per their plan would probably allow the sweep of events to get carried away, including over his own opposition. No, Washington opted to appeal to their idealism and the basis of their service. He also realized he had to do more than remind them of their pivotal role and example as officers. He would insist that they trust in "justice," remember their "common country" and "value your sacred honor." Still, he recognized that these efforts might not be enough. Whether planned or not, Washington would take one more measure.

Accordingly, Washington issued a command to cancel the anonymous meeting for March 11th but advised that there would be an official assembly on March 15th. [94] Further, he added that the assembly would be presided over by the senior officer who would then make a report to himself as commander-in-chief. This carefully worded message implied that he agreed with the meeting's agenda and that he would not be attending. As Gates acted as the leader of the military conspirators and served as the presiding senior officer, this proclamation reassured the ringleaders and gave them confidence that they would achieve their aims.

---

93 In early 1783, Washington's opportunity to ask advice or assistance was limited. The Congress that signed the Declaration of Independence in 1776 was missing many of its most notable members. John Adams, Benjamin Franklin, and John Jay were in Europe ensuring America's allies stayed engaged, while negotiating with Britain for the treaty ending the war. John Hancock, President of the 1776 Congress and first signer of the Declaration, served as governor of Massachusetts. Thomas Jefferson had been governor of Virginia, but held no office in early 1783 and had retired to his plantation. Hamilton and Morris were leaders in the group attempting to subvert the existing government. Of the most renowned Founding Fathers, only James Madison was serving in Congress at this time. Even so, given the era's speed of communication a thoughtful exchange of ideas was impractical between Philadelphia and Newburgh. Not for the last time in history, the burden of a key decision fell to the commander on the ground.

94 This chosen date was not a coincidence, but a deliberate choice. As noted previously, Washington was heavily steeped in Roman history. March 15th marked the anniversary of the Ides of March. On this date, Caesar's own friends and fellow patricians assassinated him for their belief that he threatened to end the Republic and become a tyrant.

The assembly was held in the town of Newburgh at an expansive hall with a high ceiling. It had received the nickname, "Temple of Virtue," after being built by the Army to host church services and dancing. It had also supposedly hosted earlier in the winter Washington's favorite play, *Cato*, an 18th century American favorite portraying resistance to Caesar seizing power in ancient Rome. [95] March 15th fell on a Saturday, meaning limited duties for soldiers. Officers crammed the hall from wall to wall as the midday meeting prepared to convene. Just as the gathering got underway, a side door opened and a clearly agitated General Washington strode onto the platform. A loud murmur of discontent greeted him, along with a dose of embarrassment and anger from those planning to conduct the meeting. No one had expected his attendance, let alone his seizure of the stage to address the crowd. This audience did not consist of willing listeners and earnest subordinates, the likes of which Washington had won over at the outset of the Revolution. On this occasion, the audience consisted of the disgruntled and disappointed, all of whom had lost their patience over lost entitlements.

Washington spoke briefly to the officers from a set of notes in his own large-size handwriting. [96] He reviewed their shared history together. He reminded them he had shared all their dangers and hardships and had never asked them to do anything he had not done himself. Nobody could doubt his efforts to gain justice for his men. Then, he asked them how this unknown writer was capable of achieving a better result than him? Did threatening Congress to gain their entitlements justify their sacrifices in the war and the loss of their comrades? Would leaving the country and moving with their families into the wilderness help themselves or the country they had defended for these many years? Was this person a friend – or an "insidious foe" who was "sowing the seeds of discord and separation?" He requested that they consider well what they decided. Further, he called on them to remember that Congress, as any democratic group, moved slowly and that their representatives in Philadelphia were fully aware of the army's sacrifices

95 Joseph Addison, an Englishman, wrote the play, *Cato*, in 1712. Cato, a stoic like Washington and a Senator in Rome during Caesar's career, championed the Roman republic and committed suicide rather than acknowledge Caesar's seizure of power during the Roman Civil War. The play symbolized two viewpoints: Caesar's success as a tyrant and Cato's noble failure and virtue.
96 Washington's complete Newburgh Address speech is listed at Appendix 7.

and Congress' commitments to it. His final words addressed their obligations: they owed it to themselves, the duties they had performed, the honor they had gained, and the country they had served to avoid overturning "the liberties of our country." He spoke for nearly five minutes before pausing.

Yet despite his powerful and personal appeal, Washington had failed to convince his officers. Few would meet his gaze, while most looked at the floor in silence. The atmosphere remained sullen.

After this uneasy pause, Washington reached into his pocket and pulled out another piece of paper. He declared that he had received a letter from Congress advising what its members were attempting to do to remedy the situation. He would read the letter aloud. Again, no reaction from his audience, as they had heard all this before.

Then the unexpected happened. Washington, their general, the man who always surmounted every crisis, who was famed for his calmness when chaos had engulfed them, fumbled about. He could not read the paper. All stared; their attention was now riveted on him. What was he doing? He reached back in his pocket, fumbled more, and then drew out something only his closest intimates had ever seen or even heard existed. It was a pair of glasses. He adjusted them uncomfortably on his face and looked at his officers.

Speaking now, not in his military command voice, but as one speaking to his friends, he explained, "Gentlemen, you will permit me to put on my spectacles, for I have not only grown gray but almost blind in the service of my country."

This small action, these few, unrehearsed words regarding his need for glasses, were delivered at exactly the right moment. During his speech the emotion had gradually built up within the hall. His appeal to their idealism and the practical results of "deserting our Country in the extremist hour" made sense to these faithful but frustrated veterans, as much as they resented it. Finally, his pause alerted everyone to focus their attention directly on him. And then the next words, presented in a tone for old friends, brought home to this battle-scarred group of grim soldiers the price they had all paid — the price of painful self-sacrifice for the purchase of freedom. The hall, full of hardened professionals, broke down in tears. Love, respect, and a willingness to continue to trust him flooded throughout the hall as he read the letter from Congress. The disgruntlement and disappointment, of course still lingered, but their willingness to be patient and resume their faith in their commander overwhelmed all other emotions.

Washington knew at this moment that he had turned the tide of mutiny and ended the possibility of a coup d'état. He already knew there was nothing more he needed to say. His action, like an earlier Ides of March, had served its purpose. Upon finishing the letter from Congress, he pocketed it, removed his glasses, and strode from the Temple returning to his headquarters alone, while his tearful men watched from the windows, now with stiffened resolve to side with their commander and remain committed to the cause of the Revolution.

This uncompromising – and unexpected – measure decisively ended the officer corps' conspiracy to overturn political control of the military. It stood – and stands – in contrast with many, many histories of antiquity. And the educated men of the 18ᵗʰ century were well versed from their education under the Enlightenment on these histories. Like Socrates, who accepted a cup of poison hemlock from his beloved city state of Athens for expressing his unbiased views, Washington, too, had the gift of knowing how and when to make the grand gesture.

He had determined that this issue had to be concluded without compromise. The direction of the country had been set by Thomas Paine's words, Congress' Declaration of Independence, and the actions of thousands of former colonists, now called Americans. The war was not yet won, but the dismantling of this potential mutiny would allow the United States to conclude its revolution and continue to move forward in unity. From a starting point that originated with an arbitrary, single-minded government, the opportunity now existed to begin and develop a "government of the people by the people for the people." [97] These United States must be established without military intervention. Washington had become fully convinced of the justice of this idea as far back as 1774, evidenced by his written correspondence. He had committed eight years of his life to realize this possibility. He valued the sacrifices that they had met and overcome; his faith was about to be rewarded with a country formed under the words,

---

97 Abraham Lincoln quote from his Gettysburg Address, November 19, 1863. Full Gettysburg Address at Appendix 11.

"All Men are created Equal." Time will heal all wounds. He believed. Ever faithful, he convinced others the wisdom of his faith, while appealing to their pride to live by it.

Unlikely as it may be, it is possible that another general or group of various commanders could have won independence on the Revolutionary War battlefield. It is also possible, yet unlikely, that another of America's brilliant Founding Fathers could have served admirably as the first president. However, it is far more difficult to imagine another person capable of facing down a hostile audience of his own mutinous comrades, with stakes as high as they were on that fateful day in Newburgh. And he succeeded not by force, but by a profound statement – and personal gesture – that brought them to tears. Washington stands alone in that regard as the only Father of our Country.

Thus ended the episode in which America came closest to facing a military overthrow of civilian rule. George Washington's belief in democracy and trust in civilian rule over the military has continued, undimmed and undaunted, during these many years since. Later leaders have accepted that rule – and tradition – as unnegotiable during other crises in our history.

This episode further reinforced Washington's reputation as a fair and faithful leader. Today, his actions at Newburgh are a forgotten footnote of the Revolutionary War, largely because the military's intervention was avoided. At the time, it represented, perhaps, his most admired deed by the few in the know – political leaders in Philadelphia and the military. Keeping in mind that the education of the day focused heavily on the philosophies of the ancient Romans and Greeks, Washington's countrymen and British alike compared him to Cincinnatus. By legend, Cincinnatus had been granted dictatorial powers twice by the Roman Senate during the Republican era to combat approaching enemies. He had already retired from civic life but was persuaded to return. Each time, he defeated the enemy and saved Rome. After each victory had been secured, Cincinnatus removed his badge of rank and returned to his farm and plow. The reward he sought was not wealth or power, but civic virtue. Both the legend and the life of George Washington demonstrated repeatedly that Washington was motivated by the same civic virtue and faith, rather than other ambitions. [98]

Rather than end this narrative of Washington's faith, three other short anecdotes are worth adding, as they convey important words and viewpoints of others of his era.

Washington died December 14, 1799, after a hard day's work in his fields during miserable weather. Arriving late for dinner in his home, he insisted on eating straight away as he had guests already waiting. His clothes were soaked, he developed pneumonia, and passed away a few days later at age 67.

Over the next two months, prominent citizens delivered at least 400 eulogies about him from newspapers and church pulpits across the land before a National Day of Mourning was held on February 22nd. His close friend, former general, and serving Congressman from Virginia, Richard Henry Lee, provided the most noted eulogy from Philadelphia. He spoke at length on Washington's career and gave examples of his values and successes by describing shared incidents and situations together. His final words sum up the man and have long been remembered as the finest description of George Washington:

> "First in war, first in peace, first in the hearts of his country-men, he was second to none in the humble scenes of private life. Pious, just, humane, temperate, and sincere; uniform, dignified, and commanding, his example was as edifying to all around him as were the effects of that example lasting."

In short, Washington inspired all to be better than they were.

Another eulogy was also delivered in Philadelphia by the Reverend Richard Allen, the Black pastor of the African Methodist Episcopal Church. In his remarks, Allen reminded his listeners that Washington had freed his

---

98 The Society of the Cincinnati formed in 1783. Led by many of Washington's senior officers (Knox, Hamilton, von Steuben, Lafayette, among others), it encouraged the ideals of Cincinnatus and the concept of democracy, while maintaining their American and French camaraderie. A few years later, as the French Revolution began with a wave of idealism, Washington's style of leadership motivated France's initial direction. Tragically, Washington's lieutenant, Lafayette, and others of like minds, failed to keep their hold on the reins of revolution. Ambitious men destroyed the idealism by blood and struggle for personal power. America had proved different.

slaves by his last will and testament and "was a sympathizing friend and tender father." Allen reasoned that since Washington cared so much for Black people, their duty required they follow the example of his Farewell Address of 1796 and be good citizens. Clearly, Washington's faith and actions served as examples to all Americans and cut across all aspects of American society.

To complete these tales of Washington – his character, statesmanship, and faith – a short account of a visit in mid-February 1778 summarizes the man and his most admirable attributes. He and the remnants of the Continental Army were quartered at Valley Forge following defeats at Brandywine, Germantown, and the loss of their capital, Philadelphia, to the British. As outlined earlier, the soldiers suffered in great need of food, clothing, shelter, and struggled to survive the harsh winter. From late December onward, supplies barely arrived as the severe winter closed in on their just-completed huts of green wood. By mid-February, the meager supplies dried up and for a full week they received no food at all. Cold, hungry, feeble, many ill, while encamped within striking distance of the British, this moment stood as one of the lowest points of the War for Independence. One evening after dark Washington's headquarters house heard a loud knocking. His aides opened the door and found a motley crew of armed, emaciated soldiers. They feared the worst and tried to close the door to protect themselves and Washington. The soldiers forced the door open and stepped inside. The aides started to draw weapons, when Washington joined them.

He asked the soldiers what they wanted.

One of the soldiers responded that they were a group of sergeants from all the regiments and had been elected as a committee to represent the army.

Washington stepped in front of his aides, stood tall, and asked what issues they were complaining about.

The sergeants were taken aback. They apologized and stated that they were not sent to complain, but rather to let their commander know that they understood the difficulties he was facing and attempting to resolve. They voiced their support for all his actions.

On such faith is built the ability to move mountains and overcome seemingly impossible obstacles, oftentimes incomprehensible to outsiders.

Truly, at Valley Forge and elsewhere across our young nation, drawing from the words of Paine's *Common Sense*, Washington served as the highest inspiration to his fellow citizens, notably by his character, statesmanship, and faith. May the United States of 2021 be so blessed. [99]

THE MARCH TO VALLEY FORGE, DECEMBER 19, 1777
BY WILLIAM B. T. TREGO
1883
OIL ON CANVAS
IMAGE COURTESY OF THE MUSEUM OF THE AMERICAN REVOLUTION

---

99 Washington's own sense of awe at what had been accomplished is summed up in a private letter dated February 3, 1783 to his most trusted general and successful independent commander, Nathanael Greene: "If historiographers should be hardy enough to fill the page of history with the advantages that have been gained with unequal numbers (on the part of America) in the course of this contest, and attempt to relate the distressing circumstances under which they have been obtained, it is more than probable that posterity will bestow on their labors the epithet and marks of fiction; for it will not be believed that such a force as Great Britain has employed for eight years in this country could be baffled, in their plan of subjugating it, by numbers infinitely less, composed of men oftentimes half starved, always in rags, without pay, and experiencing, at times, every species of distress which human nature is capable of undergoing."

CHAPTER 8
LINCOLN, REUNITING A COUNTRY, MARCH 1861 – APRIL 1865

Throughout much of 1864 the Civil War raged back and forth as each side struggled to gain ground in the divided nation's seemingly endless tug of war. The outcome remained unclear as to which side would win until autumn's successes forecasted that the North would finally prevail. It also appeared for most of the year that President Abraham Lincoln was unlikely to win the Republican Party's nomination for a second term, let alone win the presidential election on November 8th. A number of political rivals and foes launched efforts to prevent him from gaining the nomination and remaining in the White House, yet their efforts failed.

By Election Day the vast majority of voters proved to have a much different view. Lincoln was re-elected overwhelmingly with 55% of the popular vote and 212 of 233 possible Electoral College votes, carrying 22 of 25 states eligible to vote in the election. [100] The people of the Northern States and the soldiers of the Union Army, who were allowed to vote from the field for the first time, had spoken emphatically at the ballot box.

It is obvious today that they possessed a far clearer view of where the United States stood and vision of its future direction than Lincoln's

---

100   Two southern states largely occupied by the North, Louisiana and Tennessee, were allowed to participate in the popular vote, but their Electoral College votes were ineligible. The other nine Southern States did not vote. In fact, in 1864 Lincoln ran as a candidate of the National Union Party. A small segment of the Democratic Party had joined the Republicans in this bi-partisan endeavor because they believed in reunification first and foremost.

entrenched opponents in Washington, D.C. The president had won the backing of mainstream America by pushing 40 years of indecision and partisan politics aside and mobilizing the population to secure national unity. Along the way, he eliminated the cancer that had eaten away at America's soul since 1619 – when the first slaves arrived on American soil – with the Emancipation Proclamation.

Between the election and his second inauguration on March 4, 1865, Lincoln took two specific steps to show that the voters' faith in him was justified: one of action and one of deep thought. The action needed was obvious – continuing to support Generals U.S. Grant and William Sherman. Their aggressive prosecution of the war had resulted in a string of advances in the latter half of the year, brightening the prospects of reunification more than at any time since secession. The deep thought step was a bit more complicated.

Victory would provide opportunities but also challenges, especially with a Congress bitterly divided on key issues concerning the war. Whatever course of action Lincoln determined, he knew it would require persuading Congress and the people to support his strategy. As in 1861, he chose to announce the result of his reflections in the upcoming Inaugural Address. Accordingly, his message would inform both Congress and the public of his goals for the reunited nation. Unlike 1861, when he appealed to all Americans to unite and preserve the Union, in 1865 he described his vision of a future America. He kept his message short, simple, and humble. Slavery had caused the war, but in its outcome, slavery would be banished forever. Americans had fought a brutal war against each other, but soon peace would resume and Southerners would be welcomed back to the Union without retribution, except in extreme cases. In short, Lincoln envisioned a slave-free, re-unified nation that would move forward as one people.

Lincoln's Second Inaugural Address endures prominently on display for Americans today through its engraving on the Lincoln Memorial in Washington, D.C. It also made a deep impression on listeners at the time and has served to inspire other nation's leaders on how best to heal the wounds of war. For example, following World War II and borrowing from Lincoln's theme, Winston Churchill expressed his summary of how war should be conducted – to ensure it never happens again. His words personify how Lincoln directed the Civil War and envisioned its aftermath:

In War: Resolution

In Defeat: Defiance

In Victory: Magnanimity

In Peace: Good Will [101]

Lincoln's address sounded a clarion call to all Americans: North and South, Black and White. They bear repeating in full here.

Fellow-Countrymen:

At this second appearing to take the oath of the presidential office, there is less occasion for an extended address than there was at the first. Then a statement, somewhat in detail, of a course to be pursued, seemed fitting and proper. Now, at the expiration of four years, during which public declarations have been constantly called forth on every point and phase of the great contest which still absorbs the attention, and engrosses the energies of the nation, little that is new can be presented. The progress of our arms, upon which all else chiefly depends, is as well known to the public as to myself; and it is, I trust, reasonably satisfactory and encouraging to all. With high hope for the future, no prediction in regard to it is ventured.

On the occasion corresponding to this four years ago, all thoughts were anxiously directed to an impending civil war. All dreaded it – all sought to avert it. While the inaugurel (sic) address was being delivered from this place, devoted altogether to *saving* this Union without war, insurgent agents were in the city seeking to *destroy* it without war – seeking

---

101   Churchill wrote a six-volume history of the Second World War. With *Volume 1, The Second World War, The Gathering Storm,* this phrase became his motto ("Moral of the Work") for the entire series. However, he chose these words originally as an inscription for a memorial in France honoring the fallen of World War I.

to dissole (sic) the Union and divide effects, by negotiation. Both parties deprecated war; but one of them would *make* war rather than let the nation survive; and the other would *accept* war, rather than let it perish. And the war came.

One eighth of the whole population were colored slaves, not distributed generally over the Union, but localized in the Southern part of it. These slaves constituted a peculiar and powerful interest. All knew that this interest was, somehow, the cause of the war. To strengthen, perpetuate, and extend this interest was the object for which these insurgents would rend the Union, even by war; while the government claimed no right to do more than restrict the territorial enlargement of it. Neither party expected for the war, the magnitude, or the duration, for which it has already attained. Neither anticipated that the *cause* of the conflict might cease with, or even before, the conflict itself should cease. Each looked for an easier triumph, and a result less fundamental and astounding. Both read the same Bible, and pray to the same God; and each invokes His aid against the other. It may seem strange that any men should dare to ask a just God's assistance in wringing their bread from the sweat of other men's faces; but let us judge not that we be not judged. The prayers of both could not be answered; that of neither has been answered fully. The Almighty has his own purposes. "Woe unto the world because of offenses! For it must needs be that offenses come; but woe to that man by whom the offence cometh!" If we shall suppose that American Slavery is one of these offences which, in the providence of God, must needs come, but which, having continued through His appointed time, He now wills to remove, and that He gives to both North and South, this terrible war, as the woe due to those by whom the offence came, shall we discern therein any departure from those divine attributes which the believers in a Living God always ascribe to Him? Fondly do we hope —fervently do we pray —that this mighty scourge of war may speedily pass away. Yet, if God rules that it continue, until all the wealth piled by the bond-man's two hundred and fifty years of unrequited toil shall be sunk, and until every drop of blood drawn by the lash, shall be paid by another drawn by the sword, as was said three thousand years ago, so still it must be said, "the judgements of the Lord, are true and righteous altogether.

With malice toward none; with charity for all; with firmness in the right, as God gives us to see the right, let us strive on to finish the work we are in; to bind up the nation's wounds; to care for him who shall have borne the battle, and for his widow, and his orphan —to do all which may achieve and cherish a just and lasting peace, among ourselves, and with all nations.

Perusing these words today, the reader must understand the context in order to measure the true impact on his audience of anxious Americans across a fractured country. The stories from Lincoln's youth and early political years conveyed his strength of character. Likewise, the formation of a national Cabinet illustrated his emerging statesmanship. Accordingly, to understand Lincoln's faith, one needs to see the pathway that he and the nation had walked over the previous four years en route to re-election and the Second Inaugural Address. With that context in mind, it is clear that Lincoln's faith served as a beacon of hope for a better, reunified America.

Reviewing the previous four years, one must start with the war itself. Far more than the Second World War, the Vietnam War, or today's Middle East wars, the American Civil War directly impacted nearly every American. From a population of about 31,000,000 in 1860, an estimated 750,000 soldiers died; [102] tens, perhaps hundreds of thousands of civilians also died,

---

102   Soldier deaths. Most sources have long used Thomas Livermore's number (618,000) based on written records and published in 1900. But modern historians, including James McPherson, accept 750K as the number, primarily because all acknowledge that the Confederate records were incomplete and under-reported as well. J. David Hacker led the study.

either directly or indirectly from starvation, lack of medical care, or exposure. At least that many soldiers were wounded as well. As the era's main medical practice required amputation for arm or leg wounds, approximately half of the wounded remained crippled for the rest of their lives. [103] An example: the author's great grandfather was shot in 1864. He carried the bullet in his abdomen for the rest of his life and died of his war wound in 1899, according to his death certificate. He was not atypical. Many soldiers who survived the war would carry painful scars for life.

Further, hundreds of thousands of soldiers were also captured. For the first two years of the war, both sides exchanged prisoners of war. During the last two years, prisoners remained interned in prison camps, and more than 400,000 soldiers attempted to survive in dreadful conditions that persisted as terrible or worse. One camp, Andersonville, endures today as a metaphor for man's inhumanity to man. Thirty percent of soldiers imprisoned there died of disease or starvation, while the 32,000 survivors lingered as walking skeletons by war's end. [104] Finally, there existed the trauma of battle itself. Dozens of bloody battles were fought over the course of the Civil War; casualty rates at many were shocking. Consider, Antietam which lasted less than 14 hours, sustained more than 22,000 casualties – roughly 30% of all the soldiers on the battlefield that day, condensed in an area that can be walked across in an afternoon. Even now, it ranks as the bloodiest day in American military history, ever.

The Civil War commenced with the assault on the federal government's Fort Sumter on April 12, 1861 and its subsequent capture the next day. Yet, prior to that day, war was not a foregone conclusion. Political and military

---

103 During the Civil War, more than 5% of the nation's population was directly impacted by death or wounds. As the civilian numbers are unknown, the total percentage may approach 10%. In contrast, World War II impacted 0.4% of the nation.

In terms of Civil War wounds, technology had made devastatingly brutal strides since the eras of Washington and Joan of Arc. The expanding minie ball fired from long-range rifled muskets and rifled cannons with more explosive types of ordnance combined to cause mass casualties with horrific wounds, both physical and psychological. Now called the first modern war because of technological advances, any vestige of glory that may have ever existed on the battlefield had been stripped away.

104 Fittingly, Andersonville National Historic site is today home of the National Prisoner of War Museum.

leaders of the South made a conscious decision to launch this unprovoked attack, triggering the war.

Between Lincoln's election and inauguration, seven Southern States seceded by December. They seized unoccupied federal properties within their state boundaries. However, several forts garrisoned by Federal government soldiers had been left alone. Situated in the harbor of Charleston, South Carolina, Sumter was the only fort that affected commercial shipping. Consequently, the newly raised Southern Army demanded that it surrender a number of times between December and April.

The garrison commander, Major Anderson, refused. [105] In January prior to President Buchanan's departure from office, Confederate artillery fired upon a resupply ship, but deliberately missed. Rather than continue forward, the ship's captain accepted the warning and returned to the North. After Lincoln took office in March, one of his first challenges was to convince the diverse Cabinet to make a second attempt at resupplying the fort. As the resupply ships with naval escort assembled outside Charleston Harbor on April 11th, South Carolina's political and military leaders delivered an ultimatum to surrender or else the fort would be attacked. Anderson again rejected the ultimatum, and the newly designated Confederate Army initiated a bombardment that lasted 34 hours. The Southern leaders had chosen war. Anderson was forced to surrender. His fort had been reduced to rubble. His troops had expended nearly all of their ammunition. And his food stocks, without hope of resupply, could last for only another day or two.

Just as Lincoln had assured those who heard or read his 1861 Inauguration Address, he reacted promptly to the attack. His response called for 75,000 volunteers to "suppress insurrection and repel invasion." That appeal resulted in a flood of citizens volunteering to fight. It also swayed four more slave owning states to secede, though four others chose to remain in the Union.

These actions and responses led to war breaking out. The political and military machines on both sides moved into high gear. The emotional waves of patriotism swept many forward and any considerations of compromise

---

105 Demonstrating the divided loyalties of the war from the outset, Robert Anderson hailed from Kentucky, a slave holding state. He was very determined to hold this fort for the Union. Heightening this division on a more personal level, Anderson's prize pupil, while he was an instructor at West Point, was P.T. Beauregard – the commander of the Confederates at Charleston.

or negotiation had passed. Opposing sides stiffened. Feelings on both sides hardened, and they would only intensify as battles followed, one after the other ... and the war years mercilessly marched on.

The war started poorly for the North with reverses and set-backs in repeated efforts to push south into Virginia and down the Mississippi River. The Union troops fought well, but their enthusiasm was not matched by the competence of their generals. By comparison, the South was well-led by its field commanders. But despite battlefield successes, it could never quite convert those tactical wins into strategic victory and long-sought statehood. To achieve its aim, the South required one of two things to happen: recognition and support from the European powers or permanent expulsion of the Northern armies from the South's self-declared boundaries. One could compare the situation to a boxing match. Both sides expected a quick knockout, but instead had to settle for a long bout of hooks and jabs, essentially a battle of attrition over many grueling rounds.

Lincoln's actions were consistent throughout this first term and matched fully the intent he communicated in his First Inaugural Address. His sole goal was to restore the Union. That statement sounds clear now, but it was anything but clear from the moment he arrived in Washington, D.C.

Secretary of State nominee William Seward seemed determined to exert control over Lincoln, whom he still viewed as nothing more than a western bumpkin. Seward also planned to act as a type of prime minister from his perch as the ranking Republican. Further, Seward had no real issue allowing the South to secede. Instead, he had ideas to annex Canada (still a British colony), seize islands in the Caribbean, attack Mexico, and/or take over countries in South America as a way to compensate for losses of the Southern states – if they could not be compelled or enticed to return.

Lincoln had to utilize all his shrewdness to induce Seward to abandon these ideas, while maintaining the critical support the New Yorker commanded nationally. Despite these stark differences and initial expectations, Seward would become Lincoln's best public servant and strongest supporter over the years ahead. Along the way, he realized that Lincoln's ideas presented a better path to American success than any of his own.

The Europeans required persuading too. Cotton from the South fueled their factories, powered their Industrial Revolutions, and ensured their prosperities. Lincoln built a navy that enforced a blockade that kept southern cotton in the South and war materials out, while convincing the more powerful European empires that the justice of the North's cause was more valuable than any transient economic losses they suffered. Seward, with Lincoln's support, masterfully engineered and executed this diplomatic effort, allowing the North to concentrate its fight on a single war front.

Internally, Lincoln also faced the potential threat from a large and powerful military, commanded by an arrogant, disloyal, and ineffective general. George McClellan considered himself more important than the president and continually tried to convince Congressmen of this as well. Lincoln played the waiting game and allowed McClellan's own battlefield errors and hubris to give cause to remove him in late 1862. McClellan would return as a presidential campaign opponent in 1864, but his military removal enabled other commanders to succeed in the ensuing years. Taken together, Lincoln's deliberate actions and clear-eyed patience with Seward and McClellan were key in shaping the Union's strategic efforts to restore the country.

Concurrent with the war, the nation built and sustained rapid economic growth, despite the war losses. The president served not only as the war leader but also as the domestic leader, devoting the necessary time and attention to issues impacting Americans' day-to-day lives. Immigrants continued to pour in, contributing to 25% population growth over the next ten years. Westward settlement continued to expand without interruption. Ratified in 1862 by Congress, the Homestead Act encouraged this settlement and gave opportunity to pioneers looking for a fresh start on the frontier. A transcontinental railroad was authorized by Congress in 1862 and a year later began construction. Designed to connect the western territory of Nebraska (not a state until 1867) to the west coast in California, and thereby linking the U.S. from coast to coast by rail.

The war itself prompted other changes across the country. It sparked the rapid rise of American industrialization and technology, with new factories churning out high-demand war materials and new inventions that changed warfare. Examples include repeating rifles, metal ships, transporting troops by rail, and a number of new medical procedures and aids. [106] Also on the

---

106 The March 9, 1862 naval engagement between the ironclads, Monitor and Merrimack, made every wooden-hulled navy in the world obsolete in the course of 24 hours.

home front, Lincoln signed into law the first income tax to raise funds for the war. The tax only required payment by citizens well above the average laborer's wage. Other acts reserved land for universities in each state (Morrill Land-Grant Colleges Act) and provided the first federal protections for land that would later become Yosemite National Park. Additionally, statehood was established for West Virginia (1863) and Nevada (1864).

The war also sowed bitterness and conflict within the North. Secret societies of "Copperheads" opposed the war and sought to grant the South's independence, with retention of slavery. Riots flared up over these and other issues, including resistance to the military draft, especially among new immigrants. This turmoil caused crises that directly challenged the Union.

Lincoln reacted with a balance of firmness and tolerance. The Copperhead issue crested in mid-1863, then began to subside after its leader, Clement Vallandigham, was convicted by a military court martial for criticizing the war. Lincoln, eager to deny him a platform to continue agitating, exiled him to the Confederacy – as their problem. Later, battlefield successes gradually eased both opposition and violence, while gaining Lincoln more respect and admiration from the majority. All of these events and decisions combined to increase Lincoln's popularity and engender the public support essential to waging the seemingly endless war and restoring the Union.

Yet, Lincoln's primary focus was the conduct of the war where he faced a tremendous amount of difficulty urging hesitant commanders to engage the Southern forces, especially those commanded by General Lee. Lincoln compared several of his commanders to a horse, stating they had a case of the "slows." For much of the war, he had to walk a tightrope between exercising oversight in his role as commander-in-chief and allowing generals the freedom to demonstrate their own initiative and independent decision-making. He usually would accept their plans and always ensured they had appropriate resources to fulfill them.

After the appointment of General Grant as commanding general in early 1864, these difficulties eased away because Grant instinctively exercised initiative and doggedly followed through on his decisions until resolution, in stark contrast to his predecessors. Still, the war continued to drag on. Lincoln became a frequent visitor to the eastern armies. Part of his reason would be the formal requirements as commander-in-chief, but he also made a point to mix and mingle with the common soldiers and listen to their comments. He would do the same at hospitals. As many were centered around Washington, in his regular visits he gave attention to each and every patient, including Southerners.

Also, further demonstrating Lincoln's concern for rank-and-file soldiers was his official role over military justice cases. He was the final appellate authority for capital punishment cases, usually regarding desertion or cowardice under fire. The vast majority of the time he commuted these sentences by overruling the military tribunals, their commanders, and his Secretary of War ... to their repeated frustration. Lincoln believed in the common soldiers, was grateful for their service, and did his best to give them the benefit of the doubt.

Tied to that belief, words from his Gettysburg Address in November 1863, perfectly summarize how he recognized the deep devotion and costly sacrifices that the armies paid for the Union's cause (see Appendix 11). These types of actions endeared him to both the officer corps and the enlisted ranks. "Honest Abe", "Father Abraham", and "Uncle Abe" were all terms of endearment that Union soldiers used in describing their commander-in-chief, both around their campfires and in letters home.

Of course, the overarching issue, surpassing even the war itself, was slavery. As the primary cause of the war in the first place, the war between the states could not be resolved without slavery itself being resolved. No clear path for resolution existed. Even following secession, Congress remained bitterly divided on potential solutions. Lincoln himself realized that his goal of reuniting the country was doomed to failure unless he proved capable of convincing the vast majority of the public – and both main parties in Congress – to support his proposed solution. And it would require a new way of thinking.

An example was the challenge of addressing existing laws, like the Fugitive Slave Law. During the ten years between its passage as a section of the Compromise of 1850 until after his election as president, Lincoln publicly supported this federal law. It required that escaped slaves must be returned to their owners, if found. Anyone who prevented their return would be in violation of the law and face stiff penalties. Lincoln abided by the law despite the fact that, privately, he opposed slavery.

Once war had erupted, he expressed his new view succinctly in a letter to Horace Greeley, owner and editor of the *New York Tribune*, one of the few national newspapers of the time. His only aim was to preserve the entire country. He wrote, "If I could save the Union without freeing any slave I would do it, and if I could save it by freeing all the slaves I would do it; and if I could save it by freeing some and leaving others alone, I would also do that."

That is exactly how Lincoln proceeded, step by cautious step, informed by his continuous assessment of the war and the sentiments of the population. In hindsight, one can see that Lincoln used the powers Congress granted him to win the war and restore the Union to accomplish another goal – break the scourge of slavery. Eventually, his actions brought peace and reformed the country. However, at the outset of the war that result was not preordained.

Initially, he had supported a soft approach known as, "compensated emancipation." This provided that if the rebel states returned to the Union, slave owners would receive compensation from the federal government in return for their slaves' freedom. However, as the war ground on with increasing losses of American lives and treasure, Lincoln's attitude hardened and he soured on this softer approach.

The nation took its first small step towards emancipation in April 1862 with the passage of law whereby Congress freed the enslaved people within the District of Columbia. Two months later that measure was expanded to include all federal territories, largely the area between Kansas and California. In July, the president signed a Congressional act that all slaves who escaped to the lines of Northern forces were now considered free, essentially eliminating the old Fugitive Slave Law.

Yet sadly, by mid - 1862, the combined effect of these laws affected only about 10,000 slaves, less than a single percent of the nearly four million enslaved people in the United States. However, that summer Lincoln wrote the executive decree that would become known as the Emancipation Proclamation. The Cabinet reviewed it, recommended amendments, and approved it with the stipulation that the executive decree be enacted under Lincoln's Constitutional powers as commander-in-chief only after a significant battlefield victory. They believed a victory would lend gravitas and an emphasis; to do so absent this would be interpreted as a weak and halfhearted attempt by a desperate union grasping at straws.

Further, an announcement following a victory would help maintain Congressional support for this executive decree of emancipation and impress the watchful European powers. Accordingly, Lincoln held the proclamation. As a result of the inconclusive battle of Antietam, Lee's invading army was forced to retreat from the North. Five days after the battle, Lincoln declared victory and issued the Emancipation Proclamation on September 22nd. It decreed that, "all persons held as slaves within any State" or portion of a State in rebellion against the U.S., "shall be then, thenceforward, and forever free..." as of New Year's Day 1863. The announcement was a wartime measure only, excluding slaves from the four border states still in the Union, as well as slaves in occupied areas run by military governors. [107]

The Proclamation made the ramifications crystal clear for both sides. Even though no more than 25% of Southerners owned slaves and only 2-3% owned multiple slaves, the majority of the South convinced itself in 1861 that it had to fight. This majority fought to not only prevent invasion but to protect its way of life that featured a minority of their fellow Southerners owning slaves. In the North, beyond the ardent desire to restore the Union, the Proclamation added to the crusading belief held by many, although not all. Now, freedom for enslaved people would finally allow all Americans to achieve the ideal enshrined in the words of the Declaration of Independence – "that all men are created equal."

In due time, other consequences from the Proclamation began to unfold. In the parts of Louisiana controlled by the North, requisitioned plantations paid formerly enslaved people to work as laborers, demonstrating a potential economic alternative to enslaved labor. Due to the Proclamation and the never-ceasing demand for more Union soldiers, states were permitted to recruit and outfit the first Black soldiers, indeed entire regiments.

The 54th Massachusetts Regiment set the early standards for establishing the recruitment and training process. Its professionalism and courage in combat proved it was the equal to any unit on the battlefield. One of its

---

107   The Union border states still holding enslaved people were Missouri, Kentucky, Maryland, and Delaware. Federally occupied territories unaffected by the Proclamation were most of Tennessee, the future West Virginia, and the area around New Orleans.

early issues was the Black soldiers' refusal to accept lower wages. But the 54th's persistence paid off, and after a 16-month boycott, they received the same pay as White soldiers.

Politically, emancipation allowed Lincoln to introduce a test case. In late 1863, another presidential decree was released allowing seceded states to return to the Union via the ten percent rule. If 10% of registered voters pledged allegiance to the United States and signed a statement supporting emancipation, then that state could be readmitted. As the main population centers of Louisiana had fallen under Northern control, it was chosen as the initial test case.

Lastly, the Emancipation Proclamation ended once and for all, "repatriation" as an option for freed slaves. Discussed for over a generation at the highest circles of government, including within Lincoln's Cabinet, under this option freed enslaved people would be resettled overseas. The alternatives considered included Liberia in Africa, the Caribbean islands, or Central America. Freed Blacks vehemently objected to this option. Frederick Douglas – former slave, noted writer, speaker, and campaigner for slave liberation and women's suffrage – led a delegation to meet President Lincoln to ensure this option was terminated. The delegation eloquently convinced the president that repatriation would not be tolerated. Exactly like the Black soldiers of George Washington's army from over 80 years earlier, this delegation thought of themselves and those they represented as Americans first and nothing else. Although willing to allow any voluntary departures, they were here to stay – as free Americans.

The contentious question of formerly enslaved people's suffrage rights remained unanswered prior to Lincoln's 2nd Inaugural Address. As early as March 1864, Lincoln had cautiously queried the appointed governor of occupied Louisiana about allowing Black soldiers who had served, "gallantly in our ranks," the opportunity to vote under the 10% plan. Further, Congress approved in the Senate – although rejected in the House – an 1864 bill on voting rights in the Territory of Montana that would have begun to open the door for Black suffrage. Despite Congressmen holding ongoing discussions, this question stayed contentious and mired in Congress. The most commonly suggested option would allow male, property owners to vote, a common state (or colonial) requirement from the 1600s until about 1830.[108] In short, President Lincoln did not feel comfortable that the country was ready to take this step – yet.

Lincoln managed to lay the foundation to tackle this knotty question by implementing two other political measures in the short period between his 1864 re-election and second inaugural on March 4, 1865. A final pair of measures completed closure of the loopholes remaining from Lincoln's earlier wartime actions to resolve the war's primary cause – slavery.

Ensuring freedmen's voting rights and full equality still lay ahead, but ending slavery had to be finished in perpetuity. Above all, Lincoln insisted to his Cabinet and leading figures of the Republican party that the 13th Amendment must be ratified before the newly elected Congress could sit. The 13th Amendment abolished all slavery everywhere in the United States, filling the gaps in the Emancipation Proclamation and codifying this long-overdue step in the Constitution. As lawyer Lincoln knew well, a presidential executive decree could be changed by any successor; an amendment to the Constitution required support from both Houses of Congress and the States.

The Senate had already passed the proposed amendment in April 1864, but it had failed to pass the House in June by 13 votes. Voting generally followed party lines, but 35 representatives either abstained or were not in attendance. With the war showing signs of coming to an end and his re-election behind him, Lincoln resolved that the primary issue had to be settled. He knew that the advent of peacetime would bring many changes – and likely delays.

This risk was not acceptable to Lincoln; the necessity of full emancipation had to be finalized. Accordingly, during January 1865, he went to extraordinary lengths to convince members of the Democratic Party to change their votes and ensure passage with bi-partisan support. A number of Democrats met with the president one-on-one to discuss the need to pass the amendment. The result: 22 Democrats either changed their vote or

---

108 When the United States ratified the Constitution in 1789, most states stipulated that voters either had to own property, pay taxes, or both in order to have voting rights. Strangely enough, some states allowed Blacks and other states allowed Women (unmarried or widowed) to vote at this time. By the 1828 elections, the majority of states had removed the property and tax stipulations restricting males from voting (effectively creating universal White, male suffrage), but had also removed the openings that enabled Blacks and Women to exercise voting rights.

abstained, allowing the amendment to pass. The full story was an incredible and unexpected success, one that no one in the Cabinet or Congress believed was possible at the start of the new year. Yet, on January 31, it cleared the House with two votes to spare, thereby sending the Amendment to the States for ratification. [109]

Lincoln's statesmanship – and faith – had steered and resolved the country's longest lasting and thorniest contradiction to finally begin to eliminate slavery in the United States of America. [110]

Once the 13th Amendment had cleared Congress, Lincoln's final initiative was establishing the Freedman's Bureau in March 1865. This organization functioned with a wide range of roles and authority. It operated decentralized administrative bases throughout the former Confederacy to give support to formerly enslaved people. Part of the operation provided necessities of life – food, shelter, and essential work supplies. The Bureau also assisted families in attempting to track down and reunify with separated family members.

Few slaves had been taught to read, write, or had knowledge of anything beyond their plantations; another mandate in its charter was to provide opportunity through education and legal help. Lastly, the Bureau granted land to those formerly enslaved so they could establish themselves as farmers or tradesmen. Knowing in advance the difficulties the Bureau would face in permanently enforcing these actions, Lincoln ensured it did not function under a political department. Instead, the military controlled it, as a war department agency with one of U.S. Grant's leading officers, Major General O.O. Howard, as commanding officer.

Additionally, the Freedman's Bureau offered a further opportunity for women to contribute. This favorable development commenced in 1861 with the onset of the war. After armed conflict broke out, the government created

109 Sadly, Lincoln would not live to see the Amendment ratified by the States; that would not happen until December, 1865 – eight months after his assassination.
110 The 14th Amendment was ratified in 1868 and granted citizenship to all born in the U.S. The 15th Amendment, ratified in 1870, prevented the federal government or states from denying a citizen's right to vote based on race, color, or previous condition of servitude. Even with the Reconstruction trilogy, these amendments were just preliminary steps in achieving the full equality of rights as envisioned by Lincoln. Progress towards full rights was significantly thwarted in some parts of the country until a new Civil Rights movement began in the mid 20th century.

a military medical service called the United States Sanitation Commission. Although not considered for a senior management role in the Commission, Dorothea Dix was appointed as the first Superintendent of Army Nurses and given the authority to organize, recruit, and lead the Nursing section. The majority of nurses who served during the war were women, and they acquitted themselves professionally.

Based on these results, when the Freedman's Bureau formed in 1865, management opportunities opened for women. The majority of the Freedman's Bureau staff and its decentralized leaders were primarily female. The bureau performed its localized missions all across the South with assistance, if needed, from nearby military garrisons. This decision marked the first time that the federal government capitalized on its authority to grant executive power to an organization predominantly structured and directed by women.

Lincoln's accomplishments do not typically extend to recognition as an early pioneer of women's rights. Yet, because he believed in meritocracy, he ensured those who performed well received increased responsibilities, regardless of gender. The formation of the Sanitation Commission and later the Freedman's Bureau provided initial opportunities for women to contribute in leadership roles at the national level, a first for the United States.

Lincoln took one final step, on his own initiative and without Congressional approval. It was April 11, 1865 – two days after the surrender of Lee's Army at Appomattox effectively ended the war. Before an excited crowd celebrating the surrender and the upcoming cessation of hostilities, Lincoln delivered a speech from a balcony at the White House. [111] The exuberant listeners – and journalists – were taken aback by Lincoln's sober tone and his words.

For him, the end of the war was just the beginning of the process to make America whole again. This speech marked his first formal effort to initiate a national program that would join the remaining one eighth of Americans, formerly enslaved people, into the political system of the country. Freedom, military service, and education were first steps; voting rights would continue their progression to full citizenship.

---

111 Appendix 8 records the complete speech of April 11, 1865.

His speech addressed limited enfranchisement in Louisiana. He proposed to take advantage of the rudimentary self-government in place there through the 10% rule and extend voting rights as the legislature had requested – giving the right to vote to Black people. It could serve as a test case for Louisiana's former slaves – and the rest of the South.

Tragically, due to his assassination three days later, Lincoln could not complete this final step toward making all Americans full citizens. The chaos surrounding his murder combined with the complications associated with the onset of peace, prevented the measure from being implemented in an impartial manner with bi-partisan support.

The president's proposal publicly broke a national taboo that had been unresolved since 1776 – discussion of voting rights for Black Americans. However, it remained for Lincoln's successors to follow up. Although they managed to institute laws and legal protections to confirm all enslaved people were free, unfortunately America's political leaders were unable to gain widespread acceptance of former slaves as full Americans. In contrast to what Washington's leadership and example had accomplished with religious toleration, after Lincoln's assassination this incredible challenge fell to men far less able – it continues to haunt the United States to this very day.

No president since George Washington had faced such a combined burden of political pressure, civil strife, and the need for nationwide post-war recovery. Compounding these burdens was a series of personal heartaches, which by themselves would have broken any other man.

His wife, Mary, was disheartened when the family moved into the dilapidated White House, seeing it as unfit for a president and the nation. She quickly and substantially overspent the established budget to refurbish the home to what she saw as a fitting condition. Funding the work required special action by Congress, which likely necessitated some arm twisting from the president himself. Mary's actions clearly created the appearance of frivolous, unessential spending in the midst of a costly war. In an era when the White House and First Lady's staffs were not very robust, homelife produced a number of unwelcome distractions from Lincoln's primary focus.

Also on the troubled home front, Lincoln's third-born son, Willie, died at age 11 in February 1862, likely of typhoid fever. Willie was the Lincolns' second child to die young. After his death, Mary suffered severe depression for weeks and even after finally recovering, still had periodic and unpredictable fits throughout the rest of the war. Mental health had no medical treatment in this era, except for the allowance of time and rest. The White House stood as the least likely place in the country where such could happen.

Lastly, Lincoln's eldest son, Robert, reached adulthood during the war and pressed his parents intensely to allow him to enlist. Mary forbade it for years, stating the family had already sacrificed enough. After Robert graduated from Harvard, Lincoln obliged his son by obtaining him an appointment on General Grant's staff in January 1865, just before the war's end. Yet, even this relatively safe position still incurred the wrath of Mary.

There was no oasis in Lincoln's presidency where he could relax and recharge himself, especially after Willie's death. He took no holidays or extended respites during his presidency; the closest periods he had to a break in responsibilities occurred during his visits to the armies and hospitals. The strain on him is starkly evident when comparing any photo of the president from 1861 or earlier to those of 1864 -1865 (note photos of Lincoln in 1860 and 1865).

Still, Lincoln did maintain one pressure-release valve: his sense of humor. He employed the act of telling stories both as a means for personal relief, and also as a way to illustrate solutions to conflicts without demonizing his critics. Laughter and his stories allowed an outlet that he needed from the pressures and strain brought on by not only the war, but also the majority of his own political party as well.

Let us return to March 4, 1865, and the Inaugural Address. Lincoln stood on the podium before the Capitol building surrounded by a large crowd containing members of Congress, the government, soldiers, and supporters.[112] Though the war had not yet ended, it would endure for barely five more weeks. The hint of the victory to come was something that all were aware of. The country had survived four very long years.

---

112 The crowd was estimated to be more than 10,000 people.

ABRAHAM LINCOLN, JUNE 3, 1860 – PRESIDENTIAL
CAMPAIGN PHOTO – ALEXANDER HESLER

ABRAHAM LINCOLN, APRIL 10, 1865 – SHOWING THE STRESS OF THE
OFFICE FIVE DAYS PRIOR TO HIS ASSASSINATION – A GARDNER PHOTO.

The primary cause of the Civil War had been remedied by the 13th
Amendment. But, the dead numbered hundreds of thousands with many
more Americans crippled or broken in body, mind, or in assets. The trauma
of a divided, warring nation had been felt by nearly all of its citizens. No one

could blame the majority of Congress and plenty of other Americans who expected revenge and wanted to punish the South. The inaugural crowd and the war-torn nation eagerly, anxiously awaited hearing President Lincoln's plans for the victorious United States.

However, Lincoln's address focused only on reconciliation. He spoke for no more than five minutes. His first words briefly summarized where the country stood four years ago and the events that had passed since then. All present knew this history; he saw no need to embellish it or glorify it. He recalled to the crowd how the government had attempted to prevent a civil war and placate the other party; an effort that failed. His next words surprised many, even most present.

He discussed the institution of slavery and how it had existed for 250 years in America, rather than blaming only the South. Lincoln believed that a price must be paid by the country for "wringing their bread from the sweat of other men's faces." He reminded his listeners that both sides prayed to the same God and asked Him for help. Yet, that power would Himself judge what the full price was that must be paid for "blood drawn with the lash." Both the South and the North were guilty; both had a debt to pay. As all present knew, the North also profited from the South's economy built on slavery. Society's civil conflict and the war would persevere until divine justice had been served. The crowd had not expected to hear such a sentiment, especially the self-righteous audience members who only blamed the South, which included several of the leaders of Lincoln's party in Congress.

That lead-in made Lincoln's last words all the more powerful. "With malice toward none; with charity for all," he insisted that the time had come for "the nation," not just the North, to heal itself, all of it. Americans were obligated to repair the wounds – people, property, lifestyle – and to care for those who had borne the heaviest load – soldiers, widows, and families (North and South). He asked his fellow citizens to make "a just and lasting peace" for all their fellow countrymen and with all nations. [113]

Lincoln reminded and expected them to remember that they existed as one people who could and should move forward as one. He did not speak of punishment, revenge, or reparations. There can be no doubt that his recent

---

113 In his epic documentary, *The Civil War*, filmmaker Ken Burns called the war, "a family tragedy." As with most challenges in the war, Lincoln grasped this fundamental truth before anyone.

actions – prosecuting the war, 13th Amendment, 10% rule, Freedman's Bureau – demonstrated Lincoln's faith that America could be restored and fully free. He specified a path that could give Americans the opportunity to reunite as one people – if they could put their anger behind them. However, just as soldiers in blue and gray had done on countless battlefields, a mere 37 days later Lincoln gave his "last full measure" in the balcony at Ford's Theatre. [114]

Distressingly, his loss only underscored what others, later, would fail to fulfill. A brief moment in time existed at the end of the war where the right person at the right place may, perhaps, have completed the task of making America a better and more equal United States. Lincoln's murder ended the opportunity, which had been within grasp.

Lincoln's faith in justice coupled with his belief in the American people, all of them, carried the country through the Civil War. The huge displays of grief after his death and the reverence future generations have paid to his memory clearly shows how tragic his loss was for fellow Americans – even those unborn at the time. It also gave Americans cause to consider the tragedies that might have been avoided, had they possessed something Lincoln had in abundance: common sense.

---

114 A phrase from the Gettysburg Address (Appendix 11) in a passage where Lincoln describes the "honored dead" who gave their lives in the war.

CHAPTER 9
JOAN, STAYING THE COURSE, JULY 1429 – MAY 1431

George Washington and Abraham Lincoln had faith in the justice of their causes. One believed that his country should be free and united. The other's beliefs were nearly the same, but importantly believed his country had to be united first before it could remain free. Both proved capable of leading the majority of their countrymen to achieve these goals. Joan of Arc had a far more difficult road to travel to realize her faith in her vision of a united country. She hoped to lead the unification struggle herself. The opportunity presented itself after the crowning of the Dauphin. Although her dream eventually came true, it happened long after she paid the ultimate price – her life

As covered in chapter 3, Joan's quest began with hearing voices. To her, their call – and demands – were crystal clear. The Dauphin must be crowned King of France, and the English had to be driven out so that the French would be governed by their newly crowned king, Charles VII. As happened during her own lifetime, one may argue the nature and source of the voices: factual or a ruse, divinely inspired, genius, or madness. It really does not matter. What mattered is that Joan believed the voices came from God. She had total faith in them, acted accordingly, and achieved miracles that no one would have believed possible weeks before they occurred. Her faith and passion formed an aura around her. She not only convinced the vast majority of the people of France, but swept them to action in support of her quest. This wave of support marked the beginning of the end of English dominance of France and confirmed the ascension of the Dauphin as the legitimate king of the French.

Chapters 3 and 6 of this book described the details of those actions. Like Washington and Lincoln, Joan successfully achieved her aims. Unlike them, she was not long celebrated by the beneficiaries of her efforts. The people that she most helped, particularly the new king, abandoned her. Her later efforts proceeded without the support of the King and his entourage and led to her capture by the King's enemies. In contrast to the universally accepted custom of the time, her liege lord, Charles, made no effort to ransom her. Absolutely nothing was attempted on her behalf, despite there being multiple opportunities to do so. Consequently, another bidder, the English, bought her from her captors. They had two goals. First, they sought to utterly discredit her legitimacy – and King Charles VII – by having the church declare her a heretic. Secondly, they intended to destroy her by fire, forcefully exterminating the only previously successful enemy leader and thereby sending a clear warning to others.

On May 30, 1431 after a sham trial, Joan was declared a relapsed heretic by the Church and this nineteen-year-old girl was burned at the stake. The English were ecstatic. They had killed their primary enemy and discredited her. Now, governance could resume to the status quo ante with the re-establishment of their candidate, Henry VI, as ruler of France. Yes, they expected a few odds and ends would need to be cleaned up due to Joan's successes in 1429. But with her gone, they envisioned few difficulties. Or so, the English thought.

Events proved that the English were wrong – very, very wrong. Despite Charles VII's inaction and lack of character, despite the Church having reversed its decision that Joan's voices were legitimate, and despite the many, previously unsuccessful leaders of the French loyalist forces, Joan's vision proved correct. She had convinced the French people that France existed as one nation, and their own monarch should rule them. The soldiers and their chiefs had learned self-confidence and proved to themselves that they could defeat the English. Further, more than a few leaders, political and religious, were ashamed that Joan had not been supported and endeavored to continue her quest. It took a number of years for change to occur. But by 1453, the French had driven their enemies out of France except a small area around the town of Calais. [115] Even more importantly for France's future, by 1456 at the Trial of Rehabilitation, the Church under the Pope's guidance had declared that their 1431 verdict was mistaken. Joan was innocent, she was now a martyr of the Church, and all questions on King Charles VII legitimacy ended. She eventually did win, but at the cost of a terrible, painful execution.

How could this have become her end? This is really an extension on the earlier question, how did she manage to achieve power in the first place and gain the triumphs she did attain? Her leadership, character, and vision spurred her to accomplish two declared goals, the relief of Orleans and the crowning of the Dauphin. Along the way, she destroyed the English field army and the confidence it had built by 90 years of continuous victories. Yet, those same three traits proved to be exactly what caused her downfall.

Historical patterns, which swirled about Europe before Joan's birth and during her life, also require mentioning. A recap of key events helps make sense of the era. These included a series of disasters in Europe, which disrupted the economic, religious, and political stability of the continent. They created a culture where innovation came to be seen as the greatest peril in society.

Following several centuries of rapid economic and population growth, three years of failed harvests and cattle epidemics caused the Great Famine of 1315 - 1317. Populations fell 10 -15% as extreme levels of crime, disease, mass death, and even cannibalism took hold across much of Europe. Likely triggered by a volcanic eruption, whatever the actual cause, millions of Europeans died. A generation later, the Black Death followed. Not just

---

115 By the treaty ending the 100 Years War, the port of Calais remained English. Its purpose was to provide an exclusive trading post for the now French, Duke of Burgundy, and his most important customers via his textile trade. The settlement served as a reward for his allegiance.

a one-off event between 1347 - 1353, the bubonic plague struck again in the 1360s, 1370s, 1380s, and 1400. Up to 60% of Europe's population perished. [116].

Politically, there arose many challenges to the thousand years of Catholic dominance of society. The Church itself had divided allegiance between two series of different Popes from 1378 to 1417. After a series of legitimate popes resided at Avignon, France (1309 – 1376), Pope Gregory XI returned the papacy to Rome. Following his death in 1378, rival groups of cardinals supported claimants who resided at Rome and Avignon. It took nine years of negotiations and two Church Councils to conclusively re-unify the papacy in 1417. Another threat to religious unity were the Hussite Crusades (see chapter 3) that followed Jan Hus' burning in 1415 and continued until 1434. The ecclesiastical leadership viewed the Hussites and their 'heresy' in the same way as terrorism is perceived today.

Additionally, the Byzantine Empire was gradually losing territories in southeast Europe to the Ottoman Turks. By 1431, only the capital city of Constantinople (today's Istanbul) survived; the last government linked to the Roman empire would soon totally vanish. Although the Eastern Orthodox Christians of the Byzantines were distinct from the Catholics of the West, they both ineffectually resisted the ongoing progress of the Muslim Turks into the Balkans.

Finally, as described above, the 100 Years War had ravished France. The 30-year madness of Charles VI, the question of whether he actually was the dauphin's father, and the estrangement from his mother – a supporter of Burgundy and the English – all ensured that France stood as anything but a bastion of stability. This undercurrent of turmoil permeated every step of the way that Joan traveled from the Savior of France to becoming pronounced as a burned heretic less than two years later.

---

116 Although Europe's exact population was unknown in 1347; a widely accepted estimate was about 80 million people. Sixty percent of that amount, just under 50 million people, would die over the next six years from the plague. Both the population and percentage of deaths from western Asia, primarily the Muslim empires, and East Asia, were undocumented but probably similar. In comparison, globally the Second World War saw a similar number killed. But the worldwide population then was over 2.5 billion, a 3% mortality rate, not 60% (one twentieth of the plague's death rate). With Covid-19, from a worldwide population of 7.9 billion, about 3 million have died, a fraction of less than 1% (fewer than 4 per 10,000 people).

The seeds of Joan's fall were planted at the height of her success. The day after the coronation, Joan and the army were set to depart to subjugate Paris, the main Anglo-Burgundian stronghold in France. Planned as a four- or five-day march, Joan anticipated arriving before the latest group of English reinforcements. However, the now King Charles VII forbade them to depart. Philip, the Duke of Burgundy, England's main French ally and likely the richest noble in Europe, had cast an enticing lure to Charles. Though invited to the crowning, Philip ignored it, even though granted a safe pass along with a personal request direct from Joan to unite. He had not gained his position by sitting back and watching events. He knew that Charles, as well as his principal advisors, had a weakness – gold. He responded to the invitation with a letter and his own offer. Whether offered as a "gift" to the new King (and his advisors) or as an out and out bribe, nobody could determine then, or now.

The results though, settled the question clearly. Charles withheld his army from advancing for four days. Then after the delay, he unexpectedly accompanied the army and prevented it from marching directly to Paris. Instead, they meandered towards the Loire region (heading south rather than southwest towards Paris). The army bypassed Burgundian towns that were prepared to capitulate without accepting their surrender. On August 5th, nineteen days after his crowning, King Charles VII concluded a new 15-day truce with Burgundy. Philip had promised to relinquish Paris to Charles at the end of this truce. Yet, everyone in France knew that no love existed between these two men. [117] The probability that Philip would turn over his largest and most powerful holding to the new king without a struggle was as unlikely as the English voluntarily leaving France after 90 years of aggression and possession.

Joan and all of the senior figures from the siege of Orleans, Battle of Patay, and the campaign to Rheims realized exactly what these decisions meant. With the nobles' support, she raged against the new king's decrees.

---

117 Ten years earlier as dauphin, Charles had stood idly by – within touching distance – while assassins murdered and mutilated Philip's father, John the Fearless. Despite witnessing the act during what was supposed to be a diplomatic meeting on a neutral bridge, Charles did nothing then – or afterwards. Though unproven, history credits Charles with pre-existing knowledge of, if not directing, the murder.

He attempted to conciliate her and them. With Joan, he told her that her mission was complete, and that he would handle affairs from here. She could retire to a life back at her beloved village with the reward of lifetime tax relief. However, she would have none of it; her voices had said she had a limited time to clear the English out of France. Too much time had already been lost, and she was determined to complete her mission. Joan had no confidence that Charles would achieve liberation. She all-too-frankly asserted that a truce was a farce, simply a ploy by the King's enemies to gain time, and to give them an opportunity to build up defenses again. She pleaded with him to let her and the army free to enable her to win the rest of his kingdom!

Among the nobles, especially the ones with families tied directly to the throne, their support of Joan began to wane. Perhaps, Burgundian gold had gone to some of them as well. More likely, accepting that they had a real king now, they did not want to be on the wrong side of him and their own futures. They would have known, as military leaders, that one always follows up success by pressing the initiative. They had it and recognized if they hesitated, they could well lose it. The English and their allies remained as a very formidable foe and more than capable of recovering given time. Consequently, they hesitated and wavered in their support of Joan. This moment set in motion the process that resulted in the isolation of Joan from the new leadership of France.

Charles rejected their pleas. The truce would stand. When it ended, Philip did not turn over Paris, and no discussion ever publicly explained why. Another armistice, initiated on August 29th, gave Philip permission to send more troops to Paris, though both sides understood that the French army intended to attack shortly. None of this makes sense today; it surely did not then either.

One certainty resulted: the ardor of the French and their belief in their King markedly diminished. What was he up to? He continued to hold Joan and the army on leash until September 8th. Nearly two months had been lost, enemy reinforcements had entered Paris, and had been allowed to staunchly prepare Paris' defenses for the upcoming assault.

Accordingly, instead of storming a weakened and disheartened Paris in July, the French army faced their old foe that had been given the time to recover and regain their poise. As professional soldiers, the English and

Burgundians had prepared for exactly what they expected to hit them. Their experiences at Orleans and the fortifications along the Loire had taught them tactical lessons. Paris stood as a far larger fortress than Orleans. With additional time to enhance its walls, strengthen obstacles, and a newly reinforced garrison, it was also far stronger – and ready. Despite all that, when the French launched their assault, it was ferocious.

The English and Burgundian defense was similarly fierce with a barrage of arrows, stones, and burning oil greeting the attackers. Still, the French surged across a dry moat, through the water moat, and gained the ground beneath the city walls. While attempting to raise ladders to scale the ramparts, as at Les Tourelles Joan was wounded, again an arrow, which sank deep into her thigh. Her standard bearer was killed trying to protect her. The French dragged her away and pulled their forces back. Joan urged them to regroup and charge again. This time, they refused and she could not remount to lead them forward over their protests as she had done several times earlier.

The next morning, the French military leaders were discussing when and where to strike next when two emissaries from the King arrived. They ordered that the wounded Joan be taken to the King immediately. The French army remained motivated for the fight, having already built a bridge across the Seine to attack Paris from the south. Yet, their King, the leader they had raised to the throne and to whom they had pledged their allegiance had, unbeknownst to them, destroyed the bridge secretly overnight. The assault on Paris ended.

During the next two weeks, Charles took the army away from Paris and retired to the Loire River town of Gien 90 miles away. He then disbanded the army. His main general, Duke d'Alençon, who had risen to prominence with these victories and was also Joan's closest friend and confidante, was sent home. The King kept Joan with his court, but her status was more akin to that of a prisoner than that of a trusted field commander or inspirational leader. [118] Whatever his motives may have been, they undermined the cause that so many had already sacrificed their lives and committed their honor toward attaining. However one weighs the balance sheet of these recent

---

118 Though predating Niccolò Machiavelli's treatise on governance, *The Prince*, by more than a century, Charles seemingly concurred with his famous admonition: "Keep your friends close, keep your enemies closer."

events, one must realize that French politics of this era were undecipherable to the outsider.

Rather than acknowledge the setback at Paris was due to delays, insufficient forces, lack of financial and logistical support, or his own calculating politics, Charles and his advisors openly claimed that God had abandoned Joan. Her voices could no longer be believed. Accordingly, the king no longer had an obligation to support her militarily. By enabling the army to fail before Paris, he had accomplished one goal. He had raised doubt to counter the adoration of the army and the people of France for this living symbol whom he perhaps feared as a rival – despite all proof to the contrary. The king's moves to counteract the people's fervor also came close to breaking Joan's spirit and faith. She gathered her armor and captured trophies, and left them before the shrine of Our Lady at the cathedral of St Denis as the army began to retire. Even Machiavelli's *The Prince* did not recount an act as cold hearted as Charles' actions. If he intended to insulate his throne against his most faithful supporter, he clearly succeeded. Yet he paid a cost; his callous actions spurned the chance to earn the love and affection of his subjects.

Sixth century Christianity codified a list of seven deadly sins that had origins dating back to Aristotle: Pride, Greed, Lust, Envy, Gluttony, Wrath, and Sloth. All of these sins except gluttony figured prominently as possible motivations for Charles with any attempt to logically explain what occurred between his accession to the throne in July and the dismantling of the still successful French national army barely two months later.

It bears remembering that Charles had long demonstrated his mastery of survival and cunning at

Medieval politics. The threat of Joan returning to the field could provide opportunities for extracting payment from the Anglo-Burgundians, while her very presence at court could intimidate the English and their allies. With Joan at court, a potential weapon remained sheathed. Her mission mattered not to Charles nor her anxiety to complete it within a year.

This unrelenting young dynamo had been reduced to inactivity. She had no responsibilities nor any activities that furthered her mission. Finally, after a couple of months at the end of autumn, he released her. Joan joined a small force sent to seize two towns along the Loire River before winter ended the campaign season. Not by coincidence, these towns previously belonged to Charles' minister, La Tremoillé – and their loss to the Burgundians cut into his fief income. Despite the small number of troops involved and a lack of supplies and funds, one town, Saint Pierre-le-Moutier was recaptured. However, the French forces failed to take La Charité before winter closed in and rendered a siege impractical, and they broke it off. If nothing else, these small actions kept Bedford and Philip off balance; they knew Charles remained gullible and greedy, but also quite clever. What was he up to?

Under orders, Joan returned to court and remained another four months. Charles then enacted a third truce with Burgundy that endured from December to March. A cunning and quite self-interested leader himself, Philip may well have wanted this latest truce, so that he could marry for the third time (January 10th). Whether necessary for connubial activities or not, a truce protected him against any winter surprises. [119] With the French "army" disbanded since September and the leaders sent away, all that now persevered were small bands of knights without connections to the royal family or major dukedoms. They were kept well away from Court during the winter and were consequently unable to influence royal advisors. These adherents to France remained as armed groups because they believed in Joan and her mission. Joan, now alone, tried to rouse the King and the court to complete the reunification of France. At best, she met with only apathy.

However, in late March, Charles again permitted her to depart the court. She joined a small contingent of men-at-arms without any of the senior nobles from the preceding year. They planned to clear the towns east and north of Paris from English/ Burgundian control. Success would give them the opportunity to strike Paris again from a position of strength, while holding the towns and countryside in their rear secure unlike the year before. This force did conduct victorious attacks on Melun and Lagny. However, the band's small size – they were more a troop than an army – limited what was possible. Small groups could not continue to attack walled towns without cannons, scaling equipment, nor carry the day against foes that outnumbered them, even with La Pucelle at their head. It appears that Joan had again been set up to fail. Charles had not re-formed the army, granted her no funds, gave

---

119 Philip accumulated 24 mistresses at various times and fathered at least 16 illegitimate children. His sexual proclivities appear to have had an unsurprisingly large effect on his decision making.

her no supplies, and chose not to personally command these soldiers thereby denying a degree of legitimacy to their cause. Despite what must have been obvious to her and any veteran soldier, these zealous followers of Joan – and France – never ceased to make the best of the situation. They continued to gain additional triumphs against towns and robber bands – while carrying Joan's standard for France.

Word reached Joan's troop that new English reinforcements had landed and were marching to join Philip's Burgundians outside the town of Compiegne, north of Paris. Other small groups of French, more independent bands without a central commander, gathered under Joan to deny consolidation of enemy forces and protect Compiegne. In due course on May 23, 1430 during a preliminary skirmish outside the town, the Burgundians counterattacked Joan's band. The band attempted to retreat back to the town. However, the garrison commander closed the drawbridge before the last of the rearguard, led by Joan, could gain access. Cut-off and fighting furiously outside the walls, she was eventually knocked off her horse and captured by soldiers of the Duke of Luxembourg, a vassal of the Duke of Burgundy.

There were several other suspicious occurrences around this time. The Archbishop of Rheims, who had crowned Charles as king, had been with Joan the day prior to the drawbridge incident. Immediately after her capture, he sent a strange note to the court implying that justice had been done. It was almost as if he had expected her capture.

Joan's original plan for the day's raid had been thwarted by a minor French commander who blocked her from using a bridge that would have permitted an attack from the rear. Instead, it forced her to undertake a riskier frontal assault. Perhaps, Joan's luck had run out, exactly as her voices had predicted. But treachery must also be considered. The Archbishop had proved to be no friend of hers – neither the previous year when he vehemently argued against the crowning, nor after her capture.

Two minor commanders refused to assist La Pucelle of France? That would not have happened the year before, and was nearly inconceivable even now. One must wonder how much direct or indirect influence Charles had exercised for events to unfold like this. The entire campaign had apparently been set up to fail by his lack of support, while he maintained a safe distance away. Nonetheless, the common French soldiers added an odd postscript.

Her leadership – and capture – inspired the defenders of Compiegne to resist valiantly and successfully held out against the besieging Burgundians and English. Compiegne persisted as a French citadel – and remembered Joan.

Nearly seven more months passed by. Luxembourg held Joan in genteel captivity, as befitted her position at Charles' court, as did Burgundy when she was transferred to him later. However, by the end of the year, she was sold to the English, arriving in late December, 1430. During that period, Charles made no effort to liberate her. The standard process for captured nobility at the time required that their liege lord ransom them from the captors. Charles never sent anyone to Luxembourg or Burgundy to negotiate, nor did he make an offer for Joan's release. No efforts followed to rescue her. Rather, the king rejected military leaders' requests to attempt to free her.

An alternative, when a liege lord failed to provide a ransom, was for opposing forces to exchange prisoners. It bears remembering that the previous year Joan had collected a significant group of senior English lords that she turned over to Charles to aid him in raising funds, rather than ransoming them herself. Lastly, once the English had taken her and began the process to hold an ecclesiastical trial in France, the Church's Primate in the country, the Archbishop of Rheims, might have exercised his influence on Joan's behalf. He never said a word. He had the authority to order the court to cease and threaten any that participated in a trial by excommunication, the most powerful weapon a Prince of the Church had at his disposal. Any combination of these options may have freed Joan. However, only silence ensued from Charles and Rheims. Their lack of action confirmed these people were not her friends – nor felt any obligation to save her.

Joan had every reason to doubt King Charles VII by this point in time. She was not naive. The common sense she utilized to achieve miracles the previous year, as well as her daily interactions with noble and peasant alike demonstrated that even with her young age, she recognized frauds and hypocrites. Yet, her faith in France and her liege lord never wavered. No words of anger or self-pity were ever recorded or even hinted during the long period of her captivity. If she did question why, she kept it to herself. Instead, she always exhibited a brave and defiant attitude in defense of Charles and his kingdom. She persisted with absolute confidence in the justice of this cause. She continued to state, repeatedly, that she expected that Charles would save her, while maintaining her attire as a knight of France rather than as a woman. She refused all entreaties by her captors to deny her King. A number of sources recorded that she used her puckish humor to bait her keepers with two consistent barbs – the English would be driven out of France, and the Burgundians would support Charles. At least one incident resulted in an enraged English nobleman assaulting the manacled and defenseless teenager with a knife.

Joan did have her limits. After learning that Philip had sold her to the English, she jumped from the parapet of her castle prison to the bottom of a dry moat 70 feet below. Amazingly, she lived and suffered no serious injuries beyond a possible concussion. The failed escape, as she described the leap, had not weakened her resolve. She resumed obstinate behavior towards her captors when she regained consciousness. Nothing had changed her faith nor her character. Despite the fact that Charles had clearly abandoned her, and her arch enemies resolved to put her on trial for her life, she refused to lose belief in the divine justice of France's cause. Everything she had done had been sanctioned by God, and Charles was the true and sanctified ruler of France. [120] Yet, her determination to escape and belief that God would take care of her surpassed all other concerns. Joan had reserves of resolution and faith that did restore her when hope appeared lost.

While held by Luxembourg and Burgundy, Joan had been treated as a noble. No dank and dark dungeon held her, rather she kept her own rooms and was allowed the freedom to wander parts of the castle grounds. That changed immediately when the English took custody at their citadel city of Rouen in Normandy, northwestern France. The English isolated her in a miserable stone cell and chained her to a bed with an iron manacle around the ankle. Furthermore, English guards sat *inside* her cell watching her 24 hours a day without any chance for privacy.

The Duke of Bedford, serving as regent for the child king Henry VI, had determined a process he believed would return England to its dominant role of France. Gaining custody of Joan marked the start of his plan. He

---

120   Curiously, when describing the leap, Joan freely admitted that the desperate attempt at escape went directly against the instructions of her voices. Psychologically, her action was baffling – she acted against her voices, contrary to common sense, and risked suicide (a mortal sin according to church teachings).

arranged to have a church inquisition trial which would examine whether Joan had committed heresy. Bishop Pierre Cauchon, a longtime supporter of England's claim to the French throne, accepted an appointment as chief inquisitor/ judge along with a Dominican Prior, Jean Lemaistre. Additionally, the English recruited a jury that included another 64 scholars holding doctors or bachelors of degrees in theology, law, and medicine from the University of Paris. The jury also included Bedford's uncle – an English cardinal, five other French and English bishops, three abbots, and a host of church and legal clerks, plus administrators who were assembled to try the lone defendant. Each member of the jury except clerks and administrators had the right to interrogate Joan. All members of her inquisition trial came from English held lands. Bedford ensured that each understood the verdict he expected that they would provide. This immense group of the learned and religious had been convened to prove that Joan's achievements had not been consecrated by God, thereby making Charles' rule illegitimate and unsanctified. Odds were egregiously stacked against the nineteen-year-old.

To properly understand an inquisition trial, some cultural history of the Middle Ages is necessary. In the 1400s, the dominant Christian church in Western Europe was the Catholic Church. [121] Pockets of Muslims remained in Iberia (Spain and Portugal), and there was a mix of the Muslims and orthodox Christians intermingled in southeast Europe. Nonetheless, the vast majority of Europeans looked to the Pope in Rome as their spiritual leader. In the Middle Ages, popes had far more temporal authority and ability to influence civil rulers and their decisions than they have had since the Reformation. Beginning in 1184, the Church authorized inquisitions to root out heresy – teachings against church doctrine. Every diocese had an appointed inquisitor. Torture was permitted and based on the decision of the local inquisitor. If determined to be guilty, the church had the prerogative to remove a convict's rights as a member of the church and turn the party over to secular authorities for capital punishment. In the 1400s, that normally meant being burnt at the stake. Joan would have been very aware of this process, as well as that the judge/ inquisitor had the authority to be

---

121 Underscoring this universality, "catholic" with lower case letters means "universal." Indeed, even Protestants who pray the Nicene Creed acknowledge belief in, "one holy, catholic, and apostolic church."

as subjective as they chose. The unlikelihood of receiving justice from an investigation and trial conducted by one's enemy would have been disquieting to anyone – even La Pucelle.

Joan's trial failed to meet basic, established legal rules of her time and unsurprisingly proved to be a sham. The structure of the trial itself evidenced this fact. In 1429, the Archbishop of Rheims had led a formal examination of Joan by church officials at Poitiers, cleared her of any violations of church teachings, and pronounced her mission as inspired by God. [122] As the top religious official in France, the Archbishop's court served as the highest church court in the land. Bishop Cauchon did not even have jurisdiction for the Rouen region; his Beauvais diocese was located in another part of France. A lower authority (i.e., Bishop Cauchon) did not have the authority to overrule the Archbishop's higher court.

Augmenting this abuse of structural legal requirements, neither Joan's testimony from the earlier trial nor the evidence and rulings of the archbishop were allowed. An additional church rule mandated that a delegate of the Pope must preside over inquisition trials, that is to serve as the Chief Inquisitor himself. The Chief Inquisitor of France refused to attend; Lemaistre was only an assistant. Joan received no legal counsel of her own choosing as required; instead, the court advised her to choose among her prosecutors. She had no chance to review or prepare her defense in advance, as she only received the charges after the trial began. Nor was she permitted to call witnesses on her behalf. Lastly, church doctrine allowed trials for accused heretics to appeal directly to either the Pope or the general Church Council (then meeting at Basel, Switzerland) for their judgement. Bishop Cauchon's court repeatedly ignored her requests to do so.

Bedford and Cauchon continued this travesty. In confinement for a church trial, Joan had the right – and expectation – to be held at an ecclesiastical nunnery and guarded by women. Instead, the English confined her throughout the trial in the secular cell and under conditions described earlier, without an opportunity to speak to anyone in her own language. Lemaistre, as a monastic prior below Cauchon's rank of bishop, permitted himself to be bullied rather than insisting on treatment as a co-chief judge

---

122 In fact, in his judgement the archbishop referenced at least one female Biblical warrior, Deborah.

per normal procedure. Though dismayed at the entire process, he refused to assert himself in his assigned role. The trial was initially open to the public, but Joan's unexpectedly robust solo defense of one against more than sixty learned men resulted in vigorous public support for her by the citizens of Rouen who attended. This was one reason the judges closed the trial to the public, thwarting the potential for domestic unrest. A second reason to restrict attendance also existed as other investigations into Joan proceeded concurrently with the trial. The Duke of Bedford's own wife led a delegation of doctors to again confirm that Joan was a virgin, proving the devil could not have had intercourse with her. Per Church dogma, her voices could not therefore be evil. Another delegation had traveled to Domremy to check Joan's character. Again, this new report declared her character to be untainted. The court did not want this information to be disseminated; both results stayed outside of public knowledge.

To compound the failure to follow the legal process and operational fairness, the English and Church leaders also used psychological means to break her. In addition to the constant presence of the guards in her cell, an obvious peephole opened directly on her bed. Watchers periodically spied on her at random intervals. Not one, but two priests, posed as other prisoners from Lorraine and endeavored to trick her into admitting transgressions. One of them actually convinced her to confess to him – while being observed through the peephole. During the trial once her spirited defense became evident, Cauchon and several of his closest cronies took her to the Inquisition torture chamber. They threatened her with all the Inquisition's instruments and introduced her to the brutal tormentors who would employ them. At least one attempted to rape her. Following this incident, the English jail commander replaced all the guards. They could not risk having it revealed that – as expected – she had been forced into confessing.

The most critical maltreatment was the deliberately wearing down of Joan's ability to resist. Her captors kept her manacled, under constant watch by enemy guards, fed only a non-nourishing starvation-level diet, and exhausted by being awakened at all hours of the night by the guards. [123] One

---

123 Terrible as this treatment was, one might observe that these same means are portrayed in George Orwell's classic work on 20th century politics, *1984*. Indeed, these very procedures have been widely used in the past century by many totalitarian regimes.

meal, a "gift" from the bishop of a carp (a delicacy of the time), was apparently poisoned and made Joan terribly ill for four days, bringing her close to death. Likely, it was a miscalculation carried too far, as the English and court wanted the trial to complete. Yet, it illustrated another example of the efforts to crush her spirit. As the trial advanced, Joan's weight and appearance noticeably changed from robust to haggard. No one, no matter their strength of character, can survive indefinitely without sufficient sleep and a reasonable diet. Joan's imprisonment by the English lasted over five months. Every effort was made to break her will while presenting the facade of fairness. Meanwhile, she continued to waste away physically. Bedford's goal was the elimination of Joan; the methods were irrelevant to him.

Still, Joan responded with the spunk that she had exhibited in the campaign to liberate France from the English. At one point, a deputation of senior English and French leaders, including her former captor the Duke of Luxembourg, visited her cell. Luxembourg sought to convince her to promise to give up fighting. If so, he offered to buy her back and release her. She laughed. She said matter-of- factly she knew that the English only wanted her dead in order to reclaim France again. She was quoted as adding, "But, even if there were a hundred thousand Godons, [124] more than they are now, they should not have the kingdom." The senior Englishman present, the Earl of Warwick, had to hold back another English lord from stabbing her to death on the spot.

Joan "lived" under these conditions from late December until the end, May 30th. Beginning on February 21st, she endured over twenty sessions where she needed to be mentally sharp enough to rebut the charges, as well as just survive her debilitating imprisonment. It is amazing that despite the conditions she endured, until almost the very end, Joan stoutly maintained faith in the justice of her cause. Additionally, she frequently assured the court that Charles would have her rescued.

Joan set the tone for the trial at the beginning of the first session. Asked to make an oath on the Bible promising to answer all questions, she refused. She emphatically stated that some questions might concern topics that she had previously sworn not to disclose. The infuriated inquisitors sent her

---

124 French term of reproach for English soldiers due to their propensity for cursing, "God Damn."

away. At the next session, Joan did suggest and agreed on a modified oath. The judges remained angry, but accepted the compromise she offered. A similar routine played out across all the early sessions. To many questions, she merely answered "Passez outre" (Pass). Her response meant either it did not apply because of the oath she had sworn, or it applied to the political mission she had embarked on for France – which did not apply for a religious trial.

The judges did not appreciate being reminded by the unschooled youth that they had strayed outside the boundaries of her oath. The earlier sessions demonstrated that she was proud, decisive, and convinced of the righteousness of her cause and actions needed to unite France under the duly crowned king.

The transcript of the trial covered more than 150 pages. It remains beyond the scope of this discussion to go into every detail of the day-to-day interrogations. However, a few of these exchanges will serve to illustrate to startling effect who had the superior mind and heart: the illiterate, teenage peasant girl or the learned theologians, lawyers and churchmen.

Bishop Cauchon warned her she must answer their tribunal. Joan's answer in turn warned the bishop, "You say that you are my judge; I do not know if you are or not; but be very careful not to judge me wrongly, for you would be putting yourself in grave danger. I am warning you of it now, so that if our Lord punishes you for it, I shall have done my duty in telling you." [125] Later, well into the trial, it had become clear that the trial transcript had been altered by removing portions of her responses. She told Cauchon, "Oh, you write the things which are against me, but not the things which are in my favor." Lastly, there is a famous quotation often used to describe this battle of a female David against the hierarchy of the Church. Asked whether she was in a state of God's grace, Joan again wisely demurred, "If I am not, may God put me there; if I am, may God so keep me." Even against the weight of church and state, Joan maintained phenomenal grace under pressure.

As the sessions progressed, Joan began to show signs of exhaustion from the ordeal. Her frustration increased as the same questions were repeatedly asked in different sessions, sometimes verbatim and other times reworded.

---

125 Joan meant that persecuting her unfairly could cost him his eternal soul and cause him to be sent to Hell.

But it remained obvious that their goal was attempting to dupe her into giving different answers. The strain of striving to stay consistent and avoid the inquisitors' verbal and theological trick questions added mental fatigue to the physical duress of poor diet and lack of sleep. As she had from the very beginning, she begged to be allowed to attend Mass and Communion, two cornerstones of her lifelong daily rituals. Her requests, which became desperate pleas, continued to be refused. Again, with the Church conducting her trial, one would imagine that spiritual aid would be a priority for both sides. Instead, spiritual deprivation simply provided another tool that her captors wielded to obtain their desired goals. Eventually, in mid-April, she fell deathly ill a second time.

Gradually, Joan started to answer questions that she had refused earlier. Her expectation of rescue by the King and his soldiers faded and she realized the trial would conclude without legal counsel, defense witnesses, evidence from Poitiers, nor intervention by the Pope. Perhaps, she gave answers exactly as she remembered them. But as these later answers differed significantly from her earlier refusals concerning the same topics, both before and after imprisonment, another probability exists. Likely, she gave answers that she figured the judges would accept to stop further questions. Her new answers described her voices in great detail as physical beings, rather than the bodies of light identified earlier. It could well have been an attempt to describe a picture in her memory that her limited vocabulary and education had no words, but that the jury could accept based on 15th century cultural concepts. Further, these answers stopped the repetitive questions from being asked. She did the same when explaining the sign that the Dauphin had requested, which had long stayed a secret. The tale she now told became long and elaborate, like a religious painting of this era. The transcripts record that while relating this, she had to backtrack several times, as if she was making it up on the spot. However, the inquisitors accepted her new explanations, and no further questions followed in later sessions.

The court time and again bombarded Joan with demands to switch to female attire. Partway through the trial, despite the earlier rape attempt, she agreed. Cauchon and Lemaistre had consented that if she would wear a full dress, they would allow her to attend Mass. She consented to wear it to Mass and then would change back to protect herself from her guards on return.

However, nothing ever came of their request except more pressure later; she stayed in her male attire. Likely, it was just another ploy played on her.

After five weeks of trial and interrogation, the court finally read all 70 charges to Joan, entitled the Acts of Accusation. The readings took two days, March 27th and 28th – more than three months since her arrival at Rouen and five weeks since the trial began. The prosecutors advised her that she had the opportunity to review and change her responses. She refused. She did declare that she obeyed the church, followed its routines as a good Christian, but the last words she would follow were God's instructions. Her reply was not submission to the Church – or Cauchon.

In response a week later, Cauchon and his key advisors chose to reduce the charges to just twelve. Evidently, they doubted that the 70 charges would win over all the jury. They submitted the revised Acts of Accusation to all the other assessors and requested their comments. Two more weeks passed by, extending Joan's grim confinement to mid-April before the charges were finalized. The reduced charges focused on three areas: who spoke to her through the "voices" (some "sorcery" charges were dropped), dressing as a man (a "perversion to God" and "rebellion" against the Church), and her unwillingness to accept the primacy of the churchmen's authority (rather than direct from "God's" voices). Cauchon's challenge was to prove that Joan's voices were illusions; her attire, a trick; and her mission, a perversion of nature. [126]

In the meantime, she remained in her cell, manacled, with no activity or diversion, and grew weaker. During this period, she contracted her second serious illness. She lingered close to death for at least another two weeks and even asked for Last Rites including Confession. Still, she repeated her answer twice, once during this illness after the revised charges were delivered to her in her cell by Cauchon and those key advisors. Prior to her second response, she had met the full assembly of judges and jury on May 2nd. The court had a member preach a sermon to her requesting she accept their authority, and she responded by asking for time to reflect. The second answer occurred later, during the May 8th trip to the torture chamber. The effort to intimidate her backfired; it roused her to again reject their charges. Her defiance and

---

126 See Appendix 9 for chart outlining a summarized version of the 12 Acts of Accusation and Joan's responses.

faith sustained her each time, stating even if she was tortured and coerced to confess, she would later deny their charges even if they compelled her to "face the fire."

More time passed. The clerics held discussions where they decided not to torture her. By May 23rd. Bishop Cauchon, Lemaistre, and the assessors all agreed on their judgement. Their decision had been sent back to the University of Paris' senior academics and received their endorsement as well. They determined to declare her guilty as a "heretic, sorceress, schismatic, and apostate." That verdict would allow the Church to turn her over to the English, as she would no longer be a member of the Catholic faith. However, this verdict would not address the legitimacy of King Charles VII, one of Bedford's two goals demanded of Cauchon from the start. Joan must be made to admit to the charges. Accordingly, on this day, they read the 12 charges to her again in order to intimidate her. She again refused to change her responses, even if she was to "stand in the fire" (stronger words than her earlier ones of willingness to "face the fire").

These charges did not please the Duke of Bedford and the English. They had paid 10,000 pieces of gold for her (a fortune) and paid the costs of the trial, yet after more than five months appeared to have achieved only one of their essential aims. Fully aware of the situation, Cauchon and his fellow assessors realized that their personal well-being would be directly affected if they did not fulfill Bedford's expectation. The parties schemed to complete both of Bedford's aims – finding Joan guilty and undermining Charles' legitimacy. The churchmen resolved to repeat this hearing the next day in public at the city square before the stake having wood piled around it ready for use. The vast majority of participating Church and University jurors from the trial attended, as did armed soldiers, the English leadership in France from Bedford on down, and every citizen of Rouen who could cram into the space available. Joan had neither friends nor support when her English guards marched the exhausted and emaciated girl into the overwhelming pandemonium of this seething mass.

A spokesperson for the court delivered an oration to Joan about Charles being a heretic and schismatic. She interrupted and, even now, defended Charles. She again requested to have her case sent to the Pope. They refused. Bishop Cauchon then read her sentence. The Court declared her excommunicated, a heretic, and to be turned over to the secular authorities for their justice at once. Obviously, that meant the fire.

The spent girl finally broke down. At this moment of supreme isolation and weakness, as the ongoing clamor assaulted her senses, Joan's spirit and strength deserted her. She affirmed that she would submit to the authority of the Church. She no longer supported nor believed in her voices. And she repeated both affirmations several times.

The crowd erupted into near chaos. A clerk, conveniently located adjacent to Joan, pulled out a document and insisted that she sign. The facts of what actually occurred next remain confused due to contradictory accounts. What was certain: Joan did make a mark; several reports stated she drew a circle, and others that she depicted a cross. But she did not write her name. Joan had been taught to sign her name and had also used a code with a circle or cross while with the French army. Consequently, it made it impossible then, let alone today, to understand if Joan genuinely intended a valid confession – or was hedging or merely sought a respite.

All around her the crowd argued about burning or release. The English shouted their disapproval to the Church authorities, who themselves shouted back. Later, witnesses stated that the document she signed consisted of only a few lines; the one submitted as part of the record of the trial was substantially longer. Whatever the case, since she had recanted to save her life, Cauchon proclaimed a new sentence: lifetime imprisonment on bread and water under control of the Church.

Suspiciously, the bishop already had this second judgement prepared in advance. Cauchon's cronies in the square had advised Joan that if she recanted, they would release her to a church prison staffed by French Women, rather than English soldiers. Joan had saved her life. Yet, as she soon realized, she had also admitted that her mission was not sanctified by God and that Charles could therefore be declared illegitimate as King. She had paid a price by forswearing that her voices had not come from God.

Instead, partly on her own and partly dragged by the guards, the dazed Joan trudged back to her cell – also shocking and dismaying the English dignitaries in the crowd. They had been expecting to be able to burn her upon sentencing and reacted with fury towards Cauchon. Curiously, the only reports of Bedford, who had sat quietly throughout this spectacle, record that he did not say or do anything except continue to watch. He knew, possibly others did too, that this setback did not mark the end of the contest of wills.

Returned to the cell, Joan resumed her place as if she had never left. Again, the soldiers manacled her to the bed, and three of the five guards stayed in her cell. Outside the tumult continued, but she had to face the consequences of her just completed actions – and her conscience. She had washed away years of belief in a couple of minutes. Had she spoken rightly? wrongly? cowardly? Or had she betrayed her beloved voices? Later in the day, a group of church officials led by Lemaistre re-entered her cell. They praised her for submitting to the Church and its mercy. Then, they told her that she must show her acceptance by abandoning her men's clothing and wearing the woman's dress they brought. Further, she must shave her head to remove her boyish cut. She agreed and did so.

Questions remain on what took place next. Four more days elapsed. Cauchon did not follow through on the promises he had made to Joan at the square. However, sometime during this lull the English informed Cauchon that Joan had resumed wearing men's clothing. At least three times, low-level church officials had been sent to confirm, but armed and angry English soldiers chased them away with violent threats. Finally, Cauchon himself led a group unhampered to her cell on May 28th. According to the transcript made at the time, Joan stated that she had changed back to men's clothing of her own free will. Her reasons were that the Church had refused to permit her to attend Mass as promised, had not removed her manacles, nor transferred her to a women's prison. She also revealed that she had heard her voices again, and they had declared that she had betrayed God. She would not forsake her voices again. Joan demanded to recant the confession she had signed under duress. Charles was the true king, and she had undertaken all her endeavors because God wanted Charles as King of the French.

The uncertainty over what happened is largely due to accounts by different church officials presented at Joan's 1456 Rehabilitation Trial. Joan claimed that when she responded to a call of nature, the soldiers stole her female clothing. In its place, they returned her male clothing. She donned it, lest she expose herself to the Englishmen. Though Joan never admitted the next incident, it is probable that the English assaulted and raped her at least once. Lastly, during Cauchon's May 28th visit he and fellow church officials saw that Joan had clearly suffered a severe beating. [127]

Authorities of the Church, led by Cauchon, and the English, led by Bedford, had already attempted nearly every imaginable coercion to extract the desired testimony from Joan. In doing so, they made a travesty of the trial and any pretense of caring for their prisoner's welfare. They had never sought a fair trial in search of justice as their aim. Joan's recantation at the stake had served their purpose in challenging King Charles' legitimacy. Yet, La Pucelle still lived. The Maid of France remained the sole enemy who had threatened English dominance over the past 90 years. Destroying her reputation as La Pucelle, the Maid, followed by her extermination would allow the return of all as it had been previously, they believed. [128] Bedford had already pursued every other means to achieve his desired end. One final act remained to add an exclamation point to her "guilt" and punish her impertinence.

Cauchon and his cohorts acted promptly and immediately provided her with the means to sign the renunciation, despite voicing that she would lose her soul as a relapsed heretic. She signed her retraction. From Cauchon's narrow canonical viewpoint, his work had completed. As a relapsed heretic, an apostate, Joan was no longer a member of the church – or entitled to its protections. The Church could wash their hands of her and transfer Joan to the secular authorities and their leader, the Duke of Bedford.

Bedford was now finally satisfied. Having 'proven' Joan to be a false prophetess, had also rendered Charles VII's rule illegitimate. The crowning of Henry VI, the legitimate heir, as King of France could now take place. Having stripped the French military of its inspirational heart and soul, Bedford could now eradicate it. England would again be ascendant – as he had planned.

The English wasted no time. The stake in the Rouen city square was still in place with the faggots piled around. It took a day to revise the documents.

---

127 The witness statements at the 1456 trial that nullified Joan's conviction included several officials who accompanied Cauchon during this visit to her cell, as well as other visits that took place over the next two days – Joan's final two days.

128 The belief at the time was that a virgin could not be influenced by the devil. To declare Joan a heretic and a sorceress, they had to show the devil's involvement. Violating her perversely confirmed their predetermined judgements.

They set the time for her execution at 8am the next morning, May 30th. Bedford brought out all his troops, redoubled the watch on the walls to ensure there would be no attempt to spirit Joan away, and garrisoned the square to ensure that all could enjoy a proper burning.

Joan had no famous last words. If the battered, bruised, and starving girl uttered anything, her words were suppressed. Yet, as she exited her cell and marched back to the square, Joan displayed no signs of her earlier exhaustion or fear. She strode purposely to the stake, though requiring assistance by Dominican priests due to her injuries. En route, an English soldier handed her a wooden cross; she grasped it and thanked him. Two members of the ecclesiastical tribunal broke ranks with their peers and brought forth a large metal cross. Joan asked them to raise it in front of her in order that she could lock her eyes on it once the fires were lit.

Again, a church official addressed her with a formal pronouncement about relapsing as a heretic. Given the opportunity to pray, she did – and asked forgiveness for those of the Church who had done harm to her. As was the case six days earlier, soldiers, English gentry leaders, Church dignitaries, and as much of the population of Rouen that could squeeze inside had packed the square. Yells, threats, and cries – some for and others against her – resonated throughout the square once she was released to the executioner. Accounts stated that he asked her to forgive him for what he was about to do. She acceded to the request, and he set about his work. He had her tied to the stake, and then ignited the stacked pile of tar-soaked wood pile. Silence reigned until Joan's first screams rang out. Yet, witnesses record that she soon stopped screaming, locked her eyes on the cross, and called upon Jesus. She died quickly. Joan was all of 19 years old.

Bedford made certain that the execution was completed with no half-measures. The executioner was instructed to stop the fire once she was clearly dead. He had to prove that she was neither devil nor male by stripping the body to display her anatomy to the crowd. Following that, he had to restart the fire, reduce her corpse to a pile of ashes, and throw them into the nearby Seine River, to preclude future efforts to claim she was anything other than a heretic. Transcripts document that the executioner claimed he could not burn her heart. He feared that he had burnt a saint and asked for absolution to the Dominican priests after the square cleared.

No doubt that after these events transpired, Bedford and his senior leaders – with or without Bishop Cauchon and his cronies – would have gathered to celebrate their victory. Likely, they raised a toast and expressed a fervent expectation that English arms would soon regain all that they had lost since April, 1429. After all, the French were a cowed and unworthy foe – without Joan as their leader. Cauchon, who now expected promotion to Archbishop of Rouen, would also have been satisfied that the Court had met his expectations.

Yet, history records that Bedford, Cauchon, and other senior English and allied French leaders heard whispers and even harbored doubts about what they had done. Joan's character along with her unwaveringly pious and surprisingly competent performance at the trial caused uncomfortable contemplation. The trial lasted far longer than expected and resulted in convictions on only 12 modified and dubious counts – out of 70 charges. Far too often, the rustic girl from Lorraine had impressed them with her sincerity – and outfoxed them on complicated religious doctrine. If Joan's voices came from God, then they had just burned a saint, and their souls would be damned, just as Joan had implied during the trial. Cauchon and the others would have remembered that more than a few jurors had walked out of the trial and refused to participate. They had not agreed on either the court's actions nor Cauchon's instructions to find her guilty, despite threats to their own personal safety and prospects.

Unfortunately, history did not record in detail what these key members of the prosecuting group thought in the years ahead. Bedford did have Henry VI crowned King of France in December 1431, but in Paris, not Rheims. The French retained control of Rheims. Henry's legitimacy became even more questioned because he had not been crowned at the traditional site with the prescribed ritual for inaugurating a new reign. Bedford himself proved unable to regain England's previous holdings and stature, either militarily or administratively.

On a personal level, Bedford's beloved French wife died of the plague the next year. [129] The French, no longer cowed or feeling unworthy, refused to give up their gains. English reinforcements and financial strength were

---

129 Anne was sister of Philip, Duke of Burgundy, and an integral link in the Anglo-Burgundian alliance.

not enough in the upcoming years to enable them to recover from the losses of 1429. Their attempt at re-conquest became a war of attrition. Four years later, Bedford died at the relatively young age of 46. Days later, England's primary ally, Philip, switched allegiance to Charles, and the English aim of dominion of France had finished. Continuously driven back over the next 22 years, they proved unable to prevent a steady progression of French victories in reclaiming their provinces. By 1453, the English held only the port of Calais. Their weak king, Henry VI, never rose to the military challenges France raised.

As for Cauchon, he never received his expected reward of becoming Archbishop of Rouen. Ironically, he never returned to his diocese of Beauvais. Joan's forces had retaken the area and maintained control even after her capture. Cauchon ended up exchanging that diocese for one in England's now smaller holdings in France. Further ambitions, either as Primate of France or as a cardinal, never materialized. That sums up Joan's lasting effect on England and its allies.

What did come to pass were prophecies Joan made during her time with King Charles VII and again during her trial. As she foretold several times, the French did drive the English out of Paris within six years. The only error she made was in timing. It took barely four years before Bedford died and Burgundy allied with Charles. By April 1436, a little less than five years, Paris opened its gates to the Bastard of Orleans and Constable de Richemont. Joan's main prophecy, the one she hoped to accomplish in the year she foretold she would be active, did come true also – the elimination of the English political and military presence in France. It just took until 1453 without her leadership.

The French experienced less turmoil; they simply waited. Charles VII, never keen to be a warrior, nonetheless ended up leading his army in the field years later under de Richemont's tutoring. Along the way, Charles developed his skill at survival into what may be called expertise. France gained territories and allies at the negotiation table, erased its previously destitute situation by raising funds, became self-sufficient, and – whenever the English were preoccupied elsewhere – seized one English town/region after another. Charles used most of the next 30 years of the reign into which

Joan had elevated him to completely fulfill her voices' prophecies. Despite his manifest weaknesses, Charles became the King that reclaimed France.

One might wonder if Charles ever had an uneasy conscience for what he had done. The young teenage girl who believed in him had elevated him to the throne against his own judgement, and in doing so convinced the population of France that he had God's divine mandate. Yet, she was the same person he willfully allowed to be burnt at the stake.

George Bernard Shaw wrote a play, *Saint Joan*, in 1923 that considered whether that may have been the case. In the epilogue, Charles has a dream after Joan's 1456 re-trial that reversed the 1431 verdict. Joan's ghost as well as the main characters involved between 1429 – 1431 join him. Joan, cheerful at the start, converses with all. The others informed her that she had become a church martyr and likely would be canonized as a saint. Joan asked if she can return to life now, as saints performed miracles. Right? One by one the other ghosts depart, as does Charles. The last to depart is the simple English soldier from Rouen who gave her the wooden cross. This act of mercy entitles him to a day off from Hell on the anniversary of Joan's death, but he must return to Hell as the day ends. None but the soldier proved willing to support a Saint such as her. Politics, power, and ambition continued to be more important than the plain faith and courage of a teenage country lass who reminded them that she was a better noble than any of the famed and powerful high-born lords.

Faith. Regardless of how one tries to interpret her voices and regardless of where one believes the voices originated is immaterial. What mattered was Joan's sincere belief in the legitimacy of Charles as the rightful King of France and that the English did not belong in her land. Despite every physical, cultural, and spiritual obstacle put in her path she not only endured, but won. Her whirlwind of actions and successes in 1429 laid the groundwork for all that followed. Militarily, it remains perfectly feasible that if given support, Joan may have driven the English out of Paris in the days immediately after the coronation.

Had that happened, Joan may very well have persisted with that onslaught against France's foes for the remainder of the year that she claimed her voices would support her. As the Duke of Burgundy later showed, his allegiance to the English was not unbreakable. The events of the next 24 years may very well have happened within a few months. Politically, Charles chose a different way. He still won. He still secured all that Joan stated he would. Could he have done so without her faith in him and the inspiration she provided not only to him, but to all of France?

There is no indication that Charles had either the strength of character or the willingness to inspire anyone to even dream what Joan did. Of course, nobody can ever know that answer. Yet, this 17- year-old girl, a true heroine in every sense of the word, did initiate the path that began to win a king-dom – by herself – while inspiring others to persist after her capture. And as a 19-year-old, Joan chose to dedicate her life to France accepting that it would end in a fiery death. Even more important to her, she remained true to her vision inspired by God, despite the threats – and actions – of worldly prelates that she was risking her life and her immortal soul. She maintained her faith in her ordained King – and the French nation.

Has anyone in history ever achieved so much with so little yet paid such a great cost?

Great as Washington, Lincoln, and other figures throughout the annals of history are, none followed a more unlikely or comparable path. Joan is unique. Joan's strength of character, her vision, and her faith gave her the ability to work miracles. Today's world, as a general rule, lacks such faith. Where faith exists, all too often it remains intolerant, far more like Bishop Cauchon, the Duke of Bedford, and even Joan's revered Dauphin. Perhaps one day, the world will be prepared to embrace the faith of Saint Joan, the character of George Washington, the statesmanship of Abraham Lincoln, and the common sense and vision that all three so aptly demonstrated. [130]

---

130   Mark Twain wrote an historical novel on Joan of Arc, *Personal Recollections of Joan of Arc.* Published in 1896, it is based on the actual transcripts of her trial. In contrast to any of his other books, he provided a long discussion on his impressions of this remarkable young woman. See Appendix 10 for his observations.

SECTION 4 - FORWARD TOGETHER

CHAPTER 10:
COMMON SENSE IN THE YEAR 2021 - AN ESSAY

Common Sense. Though an everyday expression with a simple meaning, it is much easier said than done. Common sense remains both evasive and difficult in its application, as evidenced in our own history. America has had many well-meaning, very intelligent, and committed political leaders throughout its 245-year democracy. They have convinced citizens to support them with their votes, won elections, and endeavored to carry through with their cherished campaign goals and programs. Few, though, have truly stood out by making good on their promises.

Washington and Lincoln are remembered and honored because they resolved existential challenges while keeping their pledges, initiated exceptionally effective programs by building consensus, and accomplished many of their goals within their terms of office. They proved capable of translating their ideas and beliefs into practical solutions and achieving results – for the benefit of the country. A more difficult challenge than evaluating American presidents, Joan of Arc introduces challenges of understanding a foreign culture in the Middle Ages. Yet, she also proved capable of adhering to her values while resolving an existential crisis under completely different parameters. However, in some ways, her example is more applicable to today's challenges because she came to prominence outside traditional, recognized pathways to nationwide influence and represents an example that greatness is possible to any person from any background willing and capable enough.

Those times and actions have become history, now little remembered. In 2021, a new president has taken leadership of the Executive Branch, and consequently the nation. Like all of his 44 predecessors except Washington himself, he faces challenges inherited from his predecessor. Recent presidents and congresses have allowed themselves to be paralyzed by the number and complexity of the obstacles facing them and have passed the difficult ones along. President Biden has the opportunity to learn from their failures and follow the lead that Washington, Lincoln, Joan – and others – have shown. To resolve them, the president must first focus on the primary issue and either set aside the secondary ones until later or employ them in pursuit of his main goal. Lincoln knew his primary goal – that to which all other priorities had to bend – was national unity. Similarly, Biden's most pressing challenge is to find bi-partisan solutions that both sides of Congress and mainstream America support. He must mobilize every resource of his office and use his character, vision for the nation, statesmanship, and faith in America to build consensus solutions that endure.

President Joe Biden began his presidency by delivering an inspiring Inauguration Address. [131]Neither long nor abstract, his inaugural themes and priorities zeroed in on many of the major issues that lie ahead for America. He spoke to the entire country. He appealed to Americans' memories of our shared past. And he pointed out the pride that Americans have long cherished as the guiding light of modern democracy. The president reminded his fellow citizens to be aware of the difficulty maintaining democracy even on the grounds where many of these traditions were formed and the memorials to the nation's greatest achievements now stand. He listed a series of traits that Americans view as distinctly our own and that define our greatness. Then, President Biden provided a dose of current-day reality by outlining some of the major challenges that the country and his presidency now face.

His introduction complete, the president clearly stated that the solution is before us – unity. To reinforce his point, he referenced Abraham Lincoln and the Emancipation Proclamation. And he emphasized that this solution is "the most elusive of all things in a democracy." President Biden asserted he is totally committed to this cause, and he urged all Americans to join him.

---

131 Appendix 12 contains the entire text of President Biden's spoken Inaugural Address.

He envisioned what unity can accomplish, while providing examples from American history. Paraphrasing, he meant that if we unite, we will succeed. He does not have an issue with those who disagree with him. In fact, he described the right to disagree peacefully as "perhaps our nation's greatest strength" ... as long as disagreement does "not lead to disunion." Pursuing this thought, he said disagreement should be accompanied by "tolerance and humility" along with the willingness "to stand in the other person's shoes." The president displayed both courtesy and graciousness in not referring to recent events – or people – that have cast a dark shadow over this concept.

Even with unity, the challenges ahead are many. President Biden stressed the necessity of working together to overcome the pandemic, difficult as that may be. In order to overcome the pandemic, he declared that America must "engage with the world" and lead by example to demonstrate the moral authority we have long been noted for. And the president made no secret of acknowledging numerous other significant challenges that would require equally decisive and concurrent actions. He summarized his challenge in these six words: "Are we going to step up?"

As with Lincoln's Second Inaugural Address, Biden reiterated that he and the country will be judged how they resolve these crises. He wants the future to judge his administration's legacy by remembering that "they gave their best, they did their duty, they healed a broken land." The president encouraged his fellow countrymen to have "hope, not fear." And with unity and a resolved purpose, America can again be a "beacon to the world."

The president manifested a fair amount of common sense. He said the right things. The question that remains unanswered is whether these words will be converted into effective deeds and results – or slip away as forgotten platitudes of an inoffensive speech. As in 1776, "these are the times that try men's souls." Will President Biden reveal himself to be a summer soldier or a sunshine patriot? Can he prove to be one who deserves "the love and thanks of man and woman?" Can he exhibit the character, statesmanship, and faith crucial to resolve the primary issue that he claims is threatening to overwhelm the United States – lack of unity? Nearly as important and directly impacting on unity are three major secondary ones he himself highlights: the pandemic, economic issues, and foreign affairs.

This chapter will look at this primary present-day challenge and the three major secondary ones by considering how they may have been addressed by the leaders profiled in this book. Specifically, what might Lincoln, Joan of Arc, and Washington have done if they had faced today's political polarization, the covid pandemic, and economic development / foreign affairs' crises, respectively. A host of other secondary challenges are important, even critical, but none are likely to be fully resolved until this foremost set of problems has been successfully settled or is on track for resolution. [132] We have seen how the trio has employed common sense to focus on their primary concerns. Concentrating on their top priorities, they achieved success while allowing the secondary concerns to be addressed later when time and the situation permitted. The military calls this focus, "the mission;" and it is ... Accordingly, this chapter will consider how to address today's primary challenge first, and then briefly consider the three main secondary issues that the president pointed out.

With that statement, another should be added. The author is not recommending specific solutions; this essay seeks to be apolitical. However, the essential elements to achieve solutions, as President Biden requests, require bi-partisan input and support from Congress. *And* he requires input from as wide a range of experts in the appropriate fields representing as large a cross-section of the country as the president can convince to participate. He can use the May 13-15, 1908 Conference of Governors (also called the Conference on the Conservation of Natural Resources) as an example of a successful American model to gather input and begin to garner national support. [133]

---

132 Appendix 13 outlines many of these secondary challenges, as well as points to potential solutions – following common sense using lessons from the past and the opportunities of today.

133 President Teddy Roosevelt hosted this White House conference with the goal of developing a plan to responsibly use and conserve the nation's natural resources. He invited and assembled all the state governors, many members of Congress from all parties, the entire Supreme Court, business and philanthropic leaders, senior civil servants from most branches of the government, and experts in both conservation and resource management: water, forests, land, and minerals. Hundreds of distinguished leaders collaborated on and issued a document shortly afterwards. It became the framework for national conservation and resource use policies and endured for decades. Appendix 14 outlines Roosevelt's description of the person who endeavors to achieve compared to the person who criticizes.

Unity. Upon winning the election, President Lincoln also faced a fractured country. Indeed, in 1860 the land was on the verge of imminent disintegration due to lack of unity. In stark contrast to President Biden however, Lincoln had the support of the outgoing, albeit feckless, president. Yet, he also inherited the loss of a quarter of the states, which had seceded from the country before Inauguration Day, and others were threatening to do the same. Comparing the two situations, one can see the challenges were similar, if not more drastic for Lincoln's America.

Both presidents focused on unity in their Inauguration Addresses. However, Lincoln made a strong effort, even before assuming office, to unite all political parties and factions, despite a lack of even knowing many of the senior, national politicians. He intuitively knew that unity meant everybody. He worked with his vice-president, another with whom he had never previously worked, and developed a plan to have a representative Cabinet comprising all points of view – Democrats and Republicans, abolitionists and slave owners, representatives from every area of the country breaking from decades-long precedents, as well as including those directly opposed to him. His intent was to govern with bi-partisan support that incorporated diverse viewpoints to ensure lasting solutions. His Cabinet had a voice in executive decisions while Lincoln maintained links to all parts of Congress and thereby the entire nation.

President Biden has nominated a Cabinet that is certainly diverse based on race and gender. While ethnicity is one facet of inclusiveness, he made no recognized effort to reach out to either the other party or his main rivals to give all outlooks a direct voice in executive deliberations.

That oversight appears even more marked by the fact that the president has lived and worked in Washington D.C. for much of the past 47 years. Unlike Lincoln, he knows an extensive range of reputable, competent political and business leaders nationwide. Even with convincing wins in the popular vote (7 million) and electoral college (306 versus 232), upon closer examination Biden's victory margin was perilously thin. A change of 125,000 votes in four key states (Arizona, Georgia, Pennsylvania, and Michigan – Republican states in 2016) could have swung the 2020 electoral victory to Trump. If President Biden hopes his agenda will endure past the next election or two, he needs to convince Republican voters and even skeptical members of his own party that their views will be considered. Giving all viewpoints an opportunity to have a direct role in resolving challenges is common sense – and the best way to proceed, as Lincoln did by the range of membership in his Cabinet. If so, unity gains more stakeholders.

Lincoln also made strong efforts to establish bonds with mainstream America. Prior to his inauguration, he made a "whistle-stop" train tour of many key population centers across the country. He met local dignitaries, shook hands until his hand swelled, and made short, personal speeches in many public places, both during brief pauses along the route and the overnight stops. He even took advantage of his noted lack of good looks by growing a beard – as urged by a young enthusiast. He turned his new beard into a public relations masterpiece when he met her on his tour. He encouraged folks to talk, speak their mind to him, and regaled them with stories that applied to their own experiences. The result of these efforts was to gain a reputation, with people *and* the press, as approachable, willing to listen and follow up, nor behaving differently than any other citizen – despite being president-elect.

Granted, President Biden's travels have been curtailed by the raging Coronavirus. However, unlike professional sports organizations and his immediate predecessor who successfully worked around the virus, he has not attempted to take his message direct to day-to-day citizens by joining them on their home ground. He could take advantage of travel to counter his own glaring disadvantages – his age and reputation as a long-time political insider to connect with all Americans – with the requisite effort. [134]

Bearing in mind that recent events and the election show that a notable percentage of the country does not trust him or his party, especially in the 'Rust-belt', the South, and rural areas, the president has a short window of opportunity to convince his fellow citizens that he stands for the vast majority of them. A honeymoon period continues, but will pass away without

---

134 By comparison, Washington took command of the Continental Army at age 43 in 1775 and was 57 upon assuming the Presidency in 1789. Lincoln began his presidency at age 52 in 1861. Joan left home as a teenager – and died as one. FDR (Franklin Delano Roosevelt) was 50 and died in office at 63. Elected in the middle of the Great Depression in 1932, he took office the same month that Hitler seized power in Germany and faced two of the major challenges of the 20th century. Biden, elected at 78, has to contend with not only the challenges engulfing the country, but with Father Time as well.

a determined endeavor to win over his compatriots both emotionally and intellectually against a perception of a half century of central government neglect.

Lastly, during and after the recent failed impeachment trials of his predecessor, President Biden has been largely silent. An opportunity exists to not only woo the former president's political supporters in the capital, but also to reassure mainstream America with healing words of civility and graciousness. For a short period, the president can project himself to stand above this fray as the protector of the Constitutional process, which has been adhered to by Congress.

With the election settled, now is the time to move forward together. Otherwise, time will march on. And his honeymoon will end with the primary challenge facing him unresolved by Biden's party holding its slim majority. Without a determined effort to reach out to the Republicans and the American people, much of the country will remain divided by long-running mistrust. Unity may remain elusive.

It is vital that President Biden follows up to his inaugural plea and dedicates his presidency to making bi-partisan, consensus decision making his overriding priority. The challenge of unifying enough of the country to make cross-party progress provides more opportunity, real opportunities unseen in a generation. He could emulate Lincoln, who took advantage of the crisis he faced, to establish a multi-party coalition at the advent of the Civil War. If President Biden can demonstrate to the nation that he understands and is committed to bi-partisan solutions, then he can begin to convince others to feel the same.

He currently speaks of crises, not one, but many. Few of these crises have received serious, comprehensive action to resolve in decades. If the president can gain unity, he can build momentum after beginning to address these deep challenges. That progress can allow him to utilize the full prestige of the executive office and the legislative branch together to tackle more of these wide-ranging series of issues, problems, and questions.

While President Lincoln used the Civil War as an opportunity to end slavery, he also used the secession crisis to support Congressional legislation, rather than governing primarily through executive decrees. That cooperation enabled the country to surge forward with prosperity and growth. These

"secondary" initiatives included the transcontinental railroad, higher education, industrialization, and new inventions. Lincoln exhibited vision – and
convinced others to participate and initiate action under his stewardship – to
take advantage of these opportunities, while his primary focus was firmly
fixed on reuniting the United States.

Another president, John F. Kennedy, issued a call to: "Ask not what your
country can do for you, ask what you can do for your country." That message still resonates with some today, both to achieve unity and resolve the
many challenges awaiting action. [135] President Biden has similar opportunities as Kennedy – and Lincoln – plus the benefit of knowing what has been
accomplished in earlier times of strife and change. It remains up to him to
seize the moment for his primary objective, draw on our past experience, and
mobilize all of America's vast resources as the most powerful representative
government in human history.

Accordingly, President Biden can issue his own clarion call to America.
He can champion the need to assemble America's best and brightest – and
other nations that share democratic goals – to address many of these secondary crises. [136] The United States has done it before.

Among the country's most successful solutions were the Manhattan
Project – a technical and political problem solved with significant contributions by allied and refugee scientists, and the Marshall Plan – the economic/
social rebuilding of a broken post-war Europe. [137] The former occurred during
the midst of the Second World War, FDR's and the nation's primary focus.

---

135 Inaugural Address, January 21, 1961.

136 The term "the Best and the Brightest" originated in the 1700s as satire. It reappeared again
during the Vietnam War to describe the disastrous results of decisions made by bureaucrats thousands of miles away. Supposedly intellectuals, they had no direct responsibility for the execution
and results of their ivory-tower pronouncements. However, when utilized in a cooperative framework, as per the examples outlined, great successes can result.

137 The Manhattan Project. Following the confirmation of nuclear fission by German scientists
in 1938, the United States responded by initiating the Manhattan Project in late 1939. In less than
6 years, with multinational support, the first atomic bomb was developed, tested, and used, which
forced the end of the Second World War – saving millions of lives and costs.
The Marshall Plan. See Chapter 4, note 36 for cost. The Marshall Plan was executed between
1948 – 1952 in Western Europe, turning much of a continent ravaged by war, death, hunger,
pestilence, poverty, and moribund economies back into stable and prosperous societies that have
been at peace with one another ever since.
Appendix 13 outlines more details on these two programs, including costs and results.

The latter began just after the war completed. Although the U.S. was well on the way to recovery and prosperity, the nations of Europe were stuck in economic and social doldrums. After the 1946 elections, the Democratic party's minority in Congress faced a Republican majority that had been elected on a platform focused on domestic issues, not overseas commitments. Yet, President Truman worked to gain bi-partisan support and Congress approved the Marshall Plan.

Lincoln too led a major outreach asking Americans to help. He assembled America's best railroad men to support the logistics of the Civil War armies, inventors to develop new weapons and medicines, and politicians to participate as officers in the war. He made every effort to gather widespread support for his battle to reunite the country.

The effort to develop a vaccine for Covid only had national assistance to stimulate decentralized research and provide purchase guarantees for successful results, rather than a coordinated program. Imagine what can be possible if a combined team of volunteers, "enlisted" by the president with Congressional support, was coordinated nationally incorporating the country's best researchers, business leaders, civil servants and military for a targeted goal.

The Manhattan Project developed and succeeded in this manner. Scientific endeavors can be undertaken to address a multitude of huge secondary challenges that can contribute to the primary goal – achieving unity. Success in research and implementation brings the country together – and builds prosperity. In other words, a national scientific effort of similar scale as the Manhattan Project would contribute to unity, without distracting from that main focus. One can visualize the leaders of this project asking the Federal Government, as Churchill did in 1941: "Give us the tools, and we will finish the job." [138]

As with the Marshall Plan, social and economic progress followed an earlier domestic initiative, the U.S. Civilian Conservation Corps (CCC)

---

138   The last sentence from a radio broadcast to Britain, the Commonwealth, and the United States on February 9, 1941.

during the Great Depression of the 1930s. [139] In both programs, teams of decentralized leaders were assembled, trained, given clear goals and authority, and instructed to resolve major problems – in a short timeframe with a limited budget.

As President Biden alluded to in his Inaugural Address and actioned with his call for a third stimulus bill, the work and job situation in the country appears to paint a dismal picture. But as many Americans already know, the not-so-flattering work picture has been building for over a generation comprising a large section of the population, especially in the central region of the country. A half century of economic changes has turned parts of the land from secure, productive, career vocations to insecure, service-oriented, transient jobs. Part of that change is simply the natural evolution of work patterns. However, part of it has resulted by a lack of government support for industries that have moved elsewhere or to entice new ones to replace those lost.

Using the stimulus as a short-term temporary measure will not fix the damage from the pandemic – long-term. It is also not the same as a comprehensive economic development bi-partisan bill that seeks to encourage and build *lifetime* occupations along with the educational resources that will support that concept. Focusing particularly on the most depressed parts of the country would enable this problem to turn into a long-term opportunity for a solution. Coincidentally, those regions most affected are the ones that are least supportive of the president and his party. Again, this secondary effort supports the overall mission – building unity.

Comparing these challenges to Lincoln's, one remembers the incredible bi-partisan national efforts to resolve domestic concerns during his administration – in the midst of a civil war. Beyond rail these included: using the Homestead Act to settle the West, building more extensive roads, and encouraging the boom in factories that provided work and opportunities for both those born in America and the surging numbers of new immigrants. Like Lincoln's projects, the Conference of Governors, the Manhattan Project,

139   The CCC commenced in 1933 to provide unemployed, single men the opportunity to volunteer to perform public work projects. Results included construction of much of the infrastructure for national parks, state and national forests, and dams (supplying electricity for many rural areas), as well as reforestation, erosion control, and conservation programs.

the Marshall Plan, and the CCC, new programs provide the potential to build both unity and prosperity – particularly in parts of the country crying out for help. Studying Lincoln, one has no doubt that he would never hesitate to assemble such teams, listen to them, confront these "secondary" problems, and turn them into opportunities – to improve and unite America.

One can pick and choose from among the secondary crises the nation faces. Still, without unity, without controlling the pandemic, without providing career opportunities for our fellow countrymen, none can be completely resolved. Yet, a united America that serves the majority of the population rather than pandering to vocal minorities – while nonetheless listening to them – could certainly surmount obstacles that have been long deemed as unconquerable. Indirectly, many of the secondary issues may well be partially or fully resolved in the process of working through the primary challenge. The lessons from Lincoln's – and Washington's – presidencies give clear examples of results from that focus.

Many of today's specific problems and questions were unimaginable in Lincoln's time. However, the challenges facing him had a single, simple solution – unity achieved through rigorous application of common sense. With unity, he won a civil war, ended 250 years of bondage for a significant percentage of Americans, and unleashed an era of prosperity and growth for the vast majority of the country. Lincoln achieved unity by connecting politically with Congress and emotionally with the American people. His success was confirmed at the ballot box in November 1864.

President Biden asked in his Inaugural Address: "are we going to step up?" The answer could well be 'yes,' but only if he follows his own call to unity by seeking and gaining bi-partisan support in Congress with legislation. Relying on executive orders is not the same as reaching out to all Americans to bring us together again.

Pandemic. As with the covid pandemic, Joan of Arc also faced an enemy that was ravaging her land – 90 years of incessant warfare waged by the invading and victorious English. The French leaders responsible for defeating the enemy had done nothing in decades to advance the nation's cause. In fact, they generally ignored the war unless it upset their comfortable lifestyles. In contrast, the population suffered miserably in every measurable criterion – for generations.

Crops, a year's worth of food, and family shelter could disappear in an instant at the hands of English – or lawless – raiders, plundering and burning homes and villages. Friends and family members could vanish suddenly. Those not slain might flee seeking a better life by running off to someplace imagined may be safer. Endless warfare caused economic insecurity and life itself to be precarious. The unceasing and unexpected attacks affected cities and the tradesmen that had made urban areas hives of bustle and prosperity. Wherever one looked – whether peasants or the nobility – the world appeared unstable with social, religious, economic, and political uncertainty in every direction. Armed enemies sometimes seemed to be the only certainty. Whenever actions were taken to restore stability, efforts were uncoordinated and inconsequential due to the war or lack of decisive leadership. In short, unending war impacted everyone in France – a land bereft of character, statesmanship, and faith.

Joan, though, did not accept the status quo. Despite arriving long after the onslaught began and having absolutely no status nor reasons to be considered as a leader, she took charge. She convinced a variety of incumbent leaders to support her – gaining multi-partisan consensus. Ironically, for decades these same leaders had been waging civil war against each other. Joan induced a change of their focus from selfish, personal objectives to a national goal.

The 17-year-old organized the means to attack seemingly invincible foes – by convincing rich and poor, educated and ignorant that she had the answers to victory. Frenchmen and women who had never sacrificed nor joined a movement, now became ardent believers and supporters. Joan was fearless; not only did she lead by example, but she drove at the enemy's strengths rather than avoiding them. And she overwhelmed them to the surprise and shock of her own supporters and reluctant allies. Joan's solution by enacting this total change from selfish and personal objectives to a national goal meant unity. Success followed.

President Biden has a comparable challenge to destroy his invisible enemy: Covid-19. The difference is that he begins with lesser challenges than faced by the teenage, peasant girl. He knows what is required to ensure that

Covid loses – coordinating a policy urging social distancing, masks, constant cleaning, massive testing, comprehensive contact tracing, and controlled quarantine with suspected cases and confirmed cases separated from the population. And the policy cannot be effective unless the president persuades, not orders, local and national bodies to implement and enforce.

Success has already happened in a number of countries under varying circumstances, which are applying different procedures to resolve the pandemic, including Taiwan, New Zealand, Singapore, and Australia. These locations already have gained control of the pandemic, carry on day-to-day activities similar to pre-Covid, and have rebounded economically. The one point these countries all have in common is persuading their citizens to unite and follow agreed procedures. In other words, they pursue Joan's solution – unity.

Joan waged total war in an era that had never known such an event. Despite her lack of education and experience, she knew that this war could only be won by utilizing every resource she could muster; no half measures were accepted. That meant total war.

President Biden has the resources and the authority to combat and defeat the foe, the virus, by inspiring Americans to wage our own version of total war. It cannot happen overnight, even with the technological advances of various vaccines. But combining the existing and growing scientific solutions, the knowledge of what has worked elsewhere, and common-sense leadership, he can quickly deploy the means to destroy Covid.

What is required is leadership by example, just as Joan, Washington, and Lincoln exhibited. The president needs to utilize every means he has including media, aggressively crisscrossing the land as is done in an election campaign, and cajoling every other national and local leader he can arm-twist – to gain public support and cooperation. Such an effort will provide the opportunity to end this menace sooner, rather than risk future waves of mutated covid-19 variants that will certainly return. Importantly, success will build America's primary need – unity, just as victory did in 15th century France (see 1957 photo of Elvis Presley assisting the government by encouraging teenagers to vaccinate for polio).

Perhaps nearly as important, a national effort, led by the president that includes assisting others in the international community, can raise American self-esteem and global standing. Many in the rest of the world, battered by similar problems that face the United States, would welcome U.S. leadership and example again. Such results can initiate the realization of other dreams. Joan's military victory enabled the coronation of her beloved Dauphin. Victory against covid can allow President Biden to focus on his and America's other dreams – and essential needs.

Economic Development and Foreign Affairs. George Washington assumed office in 1789. The country, which he had been elected to lead, was literally broke. The United States not only had debts dating back to the start of the American War of Independence, but had no means to pay them off. Manufacturing barely existed. High end and technical products were available only through imports. In exchange, the country relied totally on its agrarian industry – with a substantial amount of the labor provided by that "peculiar institution," slavery. The Army numbered in the hundreds; the Navy had been disbanded despite foreign aggressors on the high seas and all frontiers. Up until the revolution, the new nation had depended almost entirely on its mother country, Great Britain, as principal supplier and market for its goods. Accordingly, no clear paths for economic prosperity or security led anywhere for the new nation – except to try the uncharted paths of opportunity.

Though not eager to accept the role as first president, Washington never hesitated to tackle the intimidating list of challenges awaiting him. He identified and asked the wisest and most competent individuals in the country to join the government as Cabinet members. He relied upon them to research, directly advise, and execute well-discussed decisions from a wide range of views. He worked closely, in both public and private sessions, direct with members of Congress to ensure both branches pursued the same goals. And he actively canvassed leading experts around the country on various business or economic topics. He accepted anyone, regardless of their background, as long as they produced results.

The first president's economic achievements included establishing a financial system, paying off all debts while maintaining a balanced budget, implementing fair taxes to raise revenue, and encouraging investments in new fields. If these challenges sound familiar, it is because these are similar to the country's financial needs today.

One specific 18th century project was exploring how to link the east coast to the Ohio River valley to provide timely market access for settlers on the frontier. Later, this idea developed into the Erie Canal. Washington himself rode the projected route during his presidency and looked at it with the eye of a surveyor, just as he had done with a potential Potomac River – Ohio River canal.

Washington met and encouraged Oliver Evans who developed America's first automated mills and subsequently, the country's first steam engine. Evans registered the third patent ever issued by the U.S. patent office – another initiative Washington supported. As Washington traveled about America during Congressional recesses, he always included stops to survey important economic developments – factories making new types of manufactured goods, ports opening to new overseas markets, and the local infrastructure sustaining them. As with his estate at Mt. Vernon, his goal was to make America as self-sufficient as possible.

Yet, few of these initiatives were altogether new ideas. Many of these concepts harkened back to the 1760s and Washington's early years as a successful farmer, innovator, and developer of subsidiary industries for his plantations. Not only did he base his ideas on his own observations, but he welcomed input from his constant stream of visitors, official and unofficial, as he would later as president. Simply put, he ensured common sense was applied to the challenges confronting the United States by his capable and diverse team of leading citizens. His leadership and solutions provided the foundation that America's economic successes have been built on ever since.

The point of these vignettes from Washington's presidency is to illustrate his certainty that his personal involvement with entrepreneurs would spur them – and the country – to greater achievements. One can say the same about Lincoln's personal involvement to ensure rapid passage of the 13th Amendment, or Joan's interviews with volunteers – her seeing eye. Meeting and encouraging people face-to-face from a position of authority inspires people to excel. It also adds to the effect that such personal involvement can help resolve other issues, such as the pandemic.

Washington's lessons are directly applicable for mainstream America's concerns today. This group, particularly the great swath between the coasts stretching across the Midwest and the South, largely supported former President Trump. Well within current memory, part of this area served as the economic hub – and heartland – of the wealthiest country in the world. It no longer is and has sat as an empty shell for far too long. Again, that presents an opportunity for President Biden. Gathering input and setting conditions to encourage economic growth in the most depressed areas of the country, as Washington did, allow positive change to return. Self-sufficiency, gainful employment, and investing in our fellow citizens provides hope, builds passion, and nurtures innovation among people to share in America's successes. If the president can follow those examples and work hand-in-hand with Congress to ensure these efforts last longer than a single election cycle, he will share another trait with Washington – common sense.

Jobs, jobs, and more jobs that can provide a lifetime career once existed and are still remembered across much of the former manufacturing heartland. The economic upheaval caused by Covid 19 presents an ideal opportunity to address this challenge head-on. The president can call a national assembly, similar to Roosevelt's Conference of Governors, gather input, and submit a draft plan to the American people. A logical next step would be to establish an organization like the Marshall Plan with clear objectives, a reasonable budget sufficient to reach targets, and a rigid timeline for implementation. Finally, these economic – and social – challenges provide an opportunity to involve a wide cross-section of Americans in this task force and provide solutions – experts and business leaders, along with young people, volunteers, immigrants, and any other groups that need a voice. The result of a comprehensive jobs program can bring businesses back, encourage local ones to grow, builds prosperity, and contributes to President Biden's declared intent – unity.

The federal government has ignored this demise for over a generation; emotions are bitter against the insiders of Washington, D.C. who have forgotten these people. The president can furnish hope again to this significant portion of the country by remembering historical examples and enlisting the nation's top experts to develop imaginative, cross-party legislative solutions that endure. If so, the response of support and acclaim – and unity – that follows may very well surprise those in the corridors of power. That is, if such a policy and follow-up effort is rigorously applied and maintained with broad-based support. In his Inaugural Address, President Biden stated how he would like to be remembered, this example; showcasing the best of the American way in action, would be an accomplishment worth remembering.

With foreign affairs, the earlier chapters on Washington noted how he steered a neutral path around powerful empires, revolutionary forces, and pirate kingdoms. He believed that open and fair commerce with like-minded partners could navigate these challenges, as well as begin to build American prosperity and economic opportunities. Today's world is not substantially different. However, America's position is totally different. The country has evolved from a small-scale regional actor to a global superpower. American leadership – and example – is essential to ensure open and fair commerce – and world peace. Non-engagement with the world means a vacuum that others intend to fill.

Eighteenth century empires, like Britain and France, captured American sailors to man their fleets and incited attacks on the American frontier. Compare this with Russia attempting to subvert U.S. elections and China's theft of corporate and national security secrets. American security services are also certain that they have poisoned people in other lands, shot down airliners, have fomented revolutions or threatened neighbors, and buy influence through financial or military means. Pirates from the Barbary coast may be compared to today's rogue states that threaten other U.S. interests – North Korea's missiles and Iran's nuclear program. The challenge today persists: how should the world influence one-party states that attempt to subvert free countries in ways that fall short of war, even as they restrict their own citizens' rights? This remains every bit as big a challenge now as then.

President Biden has untold diplomatic, economic, military, and intelligence resources to protect the country and the allies that President Washington never had. The State Department maintains sizable staff in every capital in the world; they have global expertise and experiences – thus, influence. The country has the planet's largest and most diverse economy. All of the world's leading democracies have close political and economic ties to the U.S., including military alliances. Also, America leads the world in nearly every realm of industry and technological innovation, as well as cultural norms and entertainment. Consequently, the vast majority of countries seek closer ties with our nation.

The United States also has unprecedented soft power. Ambitious citizens from every nation in the world, including our main rivals, aspire to continue their learning inside our shores. Many endeavor to stay afterwards. Nowhere else provides an equivalent range of work opportunities, lifestyle, and freedoms.

Finally, another potential avenue exists for the United States to conduct foreign policy based on both international law and America's best idealistic aspirations. That avenue is the United Nations (UN). Sadly, it struggles as an underused organization riven by politics, inefficiencies, and failures. However, it still represents an ideal above and beyond any sovereign nation's government – and has succeeded at some moments of crisis in the past. Furthermore, the UN Charter encompasses the highest ideals of mankind. All nations, including those mentioned above, have signed and committed to following its covenants. Despite the UN's history and current state of flaws, it still presents an opportunity – a possible tool – for use in combination with all of America's other assets, to ensure global peace and prosperity.

Washington's Farewell Address remains just as relevant today, particularly when he states "that honesty is always the best policy," treat others as we wish to be treated, and to have no permanent affections or animosities towards any nation. Such wisdom and the resources listed above present President Biden the opportunity to enact changes and improvements – for a safer, more prosperous America – and planet.

Nowhere are these tools more applicable today than in relations with China (see Appendix 13 for more detail). China requires special attention – careful handling, time, and patience. Washington himself would likely have also recognized it as a unique case. But to again borrow a phrase from Winston Churchill, China "is a riddle, wrapped in a mystery, inside an enigma; but perhaps there is a key." [140] That key is China's "self-interest."

---

140 Churchill's description of another communist dictatorship – the Soviet Union – in a radio broadcast from October 1939. The Soviet Union had signed a non-aggression pact several weeks earlier with their mortal enemy, Nazi Germany, and then cooperated with it in carving up Poland rather than join the western Allies in opposing Hitler.

China has signed the UN Charter. China's signature obligates it to adhere to specific commitments for international laws and recognize universal freedoms and rights, internally and abroad. [141] America's resources and China's treaty commitments can provide an opportunity to assure China that America becomes more of a partner than a rival. President Biden can marshal this knowledge, experience, and these institutions to follow Washington's advice and combine it with the potential of the UN. A working agreement between the two superpowers under UN auspices would further not just China's self-interest, but allow cooperation on other matters that build global prosperity, progress, and perhaps the UN's prestige. Such was the intent when the UN Charter was ratified in 1945 by the 50 original signatories – the U.S. and China among them.

Accordingly, this is the challenge where President Biden himself has to "step up," to use his own words. The task demands imagination and the willingness to apply innovative thinking – outside the "box" – yet beyond the concepts that George Washington outlined. Advancing U.S. interests solely by exercising economic and military power may lead Chairman Xi Jinping, a one-party autocrat for life, to believe he is threatened. If so, he could choose the path of the mid-20th century dictators who launched the Second World War when they believed their lands were at a pinnacle of power and their opponents unable or unwilling to respond.

The president can extend an olive branch – an ancient symbol offering peace or reconciliation from conflict – through internal resources as well as through the UN. In the background, the president would also need to persuade the world's main democracies, many of them long-time allies or trade partners, to back his initiatives, peacefully. Finally, he must ensure that Congress supports his actions – from both sides of the House aisle. The U.S. acting on its own has not worked well, recently or historically. It has failed to make effective use of its many advantages. Summarizing: wooing China to return to being a partner and treaty-abiding global citizen in the

---

141 An extract from the UN Charter's Preamble and Article 1: Preserve international peace and security; guarantee fundamental human rights irrespective of race, sex, language, or religion; ensure equal rights for all people and all nations; maintain justice and respect for international law and treaties; develop social progress with better standards of life and freedoms; exhibit tolerance and being good neighbors; provide economic advancement for all. This charter supersedes all other treaties.

international community is common sense. To do so will require the highest standards of character, statesmanship, and faith from the president and signify that he can "step up" for both his office and the nation.

In summary, President Biden's presidency provides opportunities unparalleled for a generation ***because*** of the extensive national and worldwide crises. He has the authority and responsibility to reunite the country again. Now is the time to issue that summons for volunteers and service. Now is the time to assemble America's finest in teams, as we have done with the Manhattan Project, the Marshall Plan, and other events in our past. Now is the time to calmly and methodically attack these intractable problems by focusing on the primary challenge first, with the president leading by example, teams steered by the nation's top leaders, and aided by our enthusiastic youth.

Some may consider these goals and programs beyond the country's capability in the current, divisive times. Yet, remember what the leaders profiled in the book did and consider what those who emulate them might achieve today. As always, we have the wisdom of revered leaders and examples of their successes to guide us. What better gift than national unity could a 78-year-old lifetime public servant bestow on the country that he has given his life to serve and pledged by oath to "preserve, protect, and defend?" Thomas Paine would declare such a legacy to be common sense.

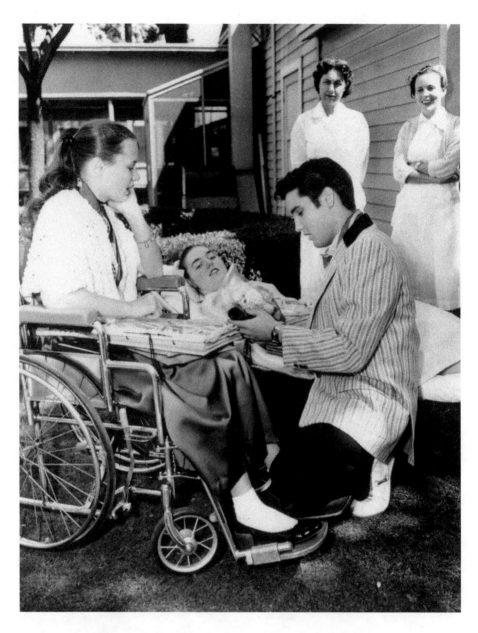

ELVIS PRESLEY. THIS MAY 1957 PHOTO SHOWS HIM VISITING POLIO
VICTIMS, BETH CURRIER, 14, AND ELAINE BROCKWAY, 18, TO ENCOURAGE
TEENS TO VACCINATE IN SUPPORT OF PRESIDENT EISENHOWER AND
THE NATIONAL EFFORT LED BY THE MARCH OF DIMES.

APPENDICES

1. BACKGROUND TO THE PAMPHLET
COMMON SENSE, 1763 - 1776

The American colonists' revolt against Great Britain built up over a pe-riod of twelve years, beginning in 1763 after the end of the French and Indian War. The British government insisted that the colonists pay their share of the costs of the war debt. The colonists were willing, but expected to be able to tax themselves, as they had in the past. They also expected that the debt would be adjusted for the fact that most of the war was fought on colonial lands. Their cry was "No taxation without Representation!" This disagreement, never resolved over the years, was the root cause of the American Revolution. Armed revolt broke out in April 1775 when British forces attempted to seize militia arms, ammunition, and several colonial leaders. Battles ensued at Lexington and Concord, followed two months later at Bunker Hill (Breed's Hill). Results were mixed, but despite severe deficits in arms, training, manpower, and leadership, the colonists had stood up successfully against the British troops.

The colonists' political leaders gathered for a second meeting, called the 2nd Continental Congress, at Philadelphia in May 1775. [142] Incensed by the brutality of the British in ignoring their "rights" as fellow Englishmen and inspired by their initial battle results – they needed someone to command their volunteer militias. They voted, nearly unanimously, to select one of their own to gather arms, organize the men, and provide the leadership they knew was needed for success. The man was George Washington. Starting

---

142   The First Continental Congress lasted seven weeks during September - October 1774, con-sisting of all 13 colonies except Georgia. Its purpose was to discuss a combined plan of action in response to the British Parliament's punitive Intolerable Acts/ Coercive Acts against the city of Boston following the Boston Tea Party. This Congress agreed to meet again in May 1775 after sending King George III a petition requesting relief.

with almost nothing, his job was to build an army capable of defeating what was then the mightiest military organization in the world.

Yet, there was no agreement in 1775 how best to define "success." Was it to convince King George III to recognize their rights? Was it to create some form of self-government under English stewardship? Or was it independence?

Thomas Paine, more than any other individual, provided answers to these questions when he published *Common Sense* on January 10, 1776. It was not long, less than 100 pages. Yet, Paine's concise pamphlet appeared at the right time and place to give all colonists, not yet Americans, pause for thought and cause for hope. It focused on Britain's failure to recognize colonial rights and their history of local, representative government. It also illuminated opportunities that lay ahead. Weaving these threads together, Paine created a fabric of unmistakably simple language – convincing readers there was no reasonable option other than to declare independence.

Paine's pamphlet swept across the Colonies. Initial copies were exhausted quickly, followed by many reprintings in subsequent weeks and months. It appealed so broadly to the colonists that in most towns and cities it was read aloud in public squares. Debates and arguments arose, but more than any other action or event at the time, *Common Sense* served to unify a majority of the colonists with common purpose and direction. And it can be said its publication compelled the Congress, still meeting in Philadelphia, to draft a Declaration of Independence. Even those who disagreed with the declaration, did agree that it was common sense.

2. RUDYARD KIPLING'S POEM - *IF*

If you can keep your head when all about you
Are losing theirs, and blaming it on you;
If you can trust yourself when all men doubt you,
But make allowance for their doubting, too;
If you can wait and not be tired by waiting,
Or being lied about, don't deal in lies,
Or being hated, don't give way to hating,
And yet don't look too good not talk too wise...
If you can dream – and not make dreams your master
If you can think – and not make thoughts your aim,
If you can meet with Triumph and Disaster,
And treat those two imposters just the same;
If you can bear to hear the truth you've spoken
Twisted by knaves to make a trap for fools,
Or watch the things you give your life to, broken,
And stoop and build'em up with worn-out tools;
If you can make one heap of all your winnings,
And risk it on one turn of pitch-and-toss,
And lose, and start again at your beginnings,
And never breathe a word about your loss;
If you can force your heart and nerve and sinew
To serve your turn long after they are gone,
And so, hold on when there is nothing in you
Except the will which says to them: "Hold on!"
If you can talk with crowds and keep your virtue,
or walk with kings - nor lose the common touch,
If neither foes nor loving friends can hurt you,
If all men count with you, but none too much;
If you can fill the unforgiving minute
With sixty seconds' worth of distance run,
Yours is the Earth and everything that's in it,
And – which is more – you'll be a Man, my Son!

3. WASHINGTON'S FAREWELL LETTER TO HIS OFFICERS IN THE FRENCH AND INDIAN WAR, 1759

(his response to a "humble address" from 27 of his officers thanking him and asking him to stay on)

To Captain Robert Stewart and Gentlemen Officers of the Virginia Regiment.

MY DEAR GENTLEMEN,

If I had words that could express the deep sense I entertain of your most obliging & affectionate address to me, I should endeavour to shew you that *gratitude* is not the smallest engredient of a character you have been pleased to celebrate; rather, give me leave to add, as the effect of your partiality & politeness, than of my deserving.

That I have for some years (under uncommon difficulties, which few were thoroughly acquainted with) been able to conduct myself so much to your satisfaction, affords the greatest pleasure I am capable of feeling; as I almost despared of attaining that end – so hard a matter is it to please, when one is acting under disagreeable restraints! But your having, nevertheless, so fully, so affectionately & so publicly declared your approbation of my conduct during my command of the Virginia Troops, I must esteem an honor that will constitute the greatest happiness of my life, and afford in my latest hours the most pleasing reflections. – I had nothing to boast, but a steady honesty – this I made the invariable rule of my actions; and I find my reward in it.

I am bound, Gentlemen, in honor, by inclination & by every affectionate tye to promote the reputation & interest of a Corps I was once a member of; though the Fates have disjoined me from it now, I beseech you to command, with equal confidence & a greater degree of freedom than ever, my best services. Your Address is in the hands of the Governor, and will be presented by him to the Council. I hope (but cannot ascertain it) that matters may be settled agreeable to your wishes. On me, depend for my best endeavours to accomplish this end.

I should dwell longer on this subject, and be more particular in my answer, did your address lye before me. Permit me then to conclude with the following acknowledgements: first, that I always thought it, as it really was, the greatest honor of my life to command Gentlemen, who made me happy in their company & easy by conduct secondly, that had every thing contributed as fully as your obliging endeavours did to render me satisfied, I never should have been otherwise, or have had cause to know the pangs I have felt at parting with a Regiment, that has shared my toils, and experienced every hardship & danger, which I have encountered. But this brings on reflections that fill me with grief & I must strive to forget them; in thanking you, Gentlemen, with uncommon sincerity & true affection for the honor you have done me – for if I have acquired any reputation, it is from you I derive it. I thank you also for the love and regard you have all shewn me. It is in this I am rewarded. It is herein I glory. And lastly I must thank you for your kind wishes. To assure you, that I feel every generous return of mutual regard – that I wish you every honor as a collective Body & every felicity in your private Character, is, Gentlemen, I hope unnecessary – Shew me how I can demonstrate it, and you never shall find me otherwise than

Your Most obedient,
New Kent County) most obliged and
10th January 1759) most affectionate
//s// G_e Washington.

Manuscript is in the collection of the Rosenbach Library, Philadelphia
Spelling and grammar note: The original 18th century spelling and style is re-
tained (same for Appendices 5 and 7). While not the same as today (21th Century),
the meaning nevertheless still resounds clearly as it exhibits the two-way exchange
of respect and friendship following arduous duty and time spent together.

4. JOAN OF ARC'S LETTER (DICTATED) TO KING HENRY VI AND JOHN OF LANCASTER, THE DUKE OF BEDFORD, MARCH 22, 1429

Jesus Maria. King of England, and you, Duke of Bedford, calling yourself Regent of France; William de la Pole, Earl of Suffolk; John Lord Talbot, and you, Thomas Lord Scales, calling yourself lieutenants of the said Bedford – do right to the King of Heaven. Render to the Maid (Pucelle) who has been sent by God the King of Heaven the keys of all the good towns you have taken and violated in France. She is sent hither by God, to restore the blood royal. She is very ready to make peace if you will do her right by giving up France and paying for what you have held. And you archers, companions of war, noble and otherwise, who are before the good city of Orleans, begone into your own land in God's name, or await news from the Maid who will shortly go to see you to your very great detriment. King of England, if you do not so, I am chief of war, and wherever I shall find your people in France, I will drive them out, willing or not willing; and if they do not obey I will slay them all. But if they obey, I will take to them to mercy. I am come hither by God, the King of Heaven, body for body, to put you out of France, in spite of those who would work treason and mischief against the kingdom. Think not you shall ever hold the kingdom from the King of Heaven, the Son of the blessed Mary; King Charles, the true heir, shall hold it, for God wills it so, and has revealed it to him by the Maid; in which he will enter Paris after a good campaign. If you believe not the news sent by God through the Maid, wherever we shall meet you we will strike boldly and make such a noise as has not been in France these thousand years. Be sure that God can send more strength to the Maid than you can bring to any assault against her and her good men-at-arms; and then we shall see who has the better right, the King of Heaven, or you. Duke of Bedford, the Maid prays you not to bring about your own destruction. If you do her right, you may yet go in her company where the French shall do the finest deed that has been done in Christendom (go on a Crusade), and if you refuse, remember the great detriment which will overtake you.

Written on this Tuesday of Holy Week

//s// La Pucelle

Joan was taught to write "La Pucelle" and that is how she signed her name on all documents she dictated.

There are a number of similar versions of this letter as it is translated from medieval French. For comparison, this note is nearly 200 years older than Shakespeare's handwritten manuscripts.

Translated by the author from the French; cross checked with other English translations.

5. WASHINGTON'S FAREWELL ADDRESS, SEPTEMBER 1796

Friends and Citizens:

The period for a new election of a citizen to administer the executive government of the United States being not far distant, and the time actually arrived when your thoughts must be employed in designating the person who is to be clothed with that important trust, it appears to me proper, especially as it may conduce to a more distinct expression of the public voice, that I should now apprise you of the resolution I have formed, to decline being considered among the number of those out of whom a choice is to be made.

I beg you, at the same time, to do me the justice to be assured that this resolution has not been taken without a strict regard to all the considerations appertaining to the relation which binds a dutiful citizen to his country; and that in withdrawing the tender of service, which silence in my situation might imply, I am influenced by no diminution of zeal for your future interest, no deficiency of grateful respect for your past kindness, but am supported by a full conviction that the step is compatible with both.

The acceptance of, and continuance hitherto in, the office to which your suffrages have twice called me have been a uniform sacrifice of inclination to the opinion of duty and to a deference for what appeared to be your desire. I constantly hoped that it would have been much earlier in my power, consistently with motives which I was not at liberty to disregard, to return to that retirement from which I had been reluctantly drawn. The strength of my inclination to do this, previous to the last election, had even led to the preparation of an address to declare it to you; but mature reflection on the then perplexed and critical posture of our affairs with foreign nations, and the unanimous advice of persons entitled to my confidence, impelled me to abandon the idea.

I rejoice that the state of your concerns, external as well as internal, no longer renders the pursuit of inclination incompatible with the sentiment of duty or propriety, and am persuaded , whatever partiality may be retained for my services, that, in the present circumstances of our country, you will not disapprove my determination to retire.

The impressions with which I first undertook the arduous trust were explained on the proper occasion. In the discharge of this trust, I will only say that I have, with good intentions, contributed towards the organization and administration of the government the best exertions of which a very fallible judgement was capable. Not unconscious in the outset of the inferiority of my qualifications, experience in my own eyes, perhaps still more in the eyes of others, has strengthened the motives to diffidence of myself; and every day the increasing weight of years admonishes me more and more that the shade of retirement is as necessary to me as it will be welcome. Satisfied that if any circumstances have given peculiar value to my services, they were temporary. I have the consolation to believe that, while choice and prudence invite me to quit the political scene, patriotism does not forbid it.

In looking forward to the moment which is intended to terminate the career of my public life, my feelings do not permit me to suspend the deep acknowledgement of that debt of gratitude which I owe to my beloved country for the many honors it has conferred upon me; still more for the steadfast confidence with which it has supported me; and for the opportunities I have thence enjoyed of manifesting my inviolable attachment, by services faithful and persevering, though in usefulness unequal to my zeal. If benefits have resulted to our country from these services, let it always be remembered to your praise, and as an instructive example in our annals, that under circumstances in which the passions, agitated in every direction, were liable to mislead, amidst appearances sometimes dubious, vicissitudes of fortune often discouraging, in situations in which not unfrequently want of success has countenanced the spirit of criticism, the constancy of your support was the essential prop of the efforts, and a guarantee of the plans by which they were effected. Profoundly penetrated with this idea, I shall carry it with me to my grave, as a strong incitement to unceasing vows that heaven may continue to you the choicest tokens of its beneficence; that your union and brotherly affection may be perpetual; that the free Constitution, which is the work of your hands, may be sacredly maintained; that its administration in every department may be stamped with wisdom and virtue; that, in fine, the happiness of the people of these States, under the auspices of liberty, may be made complete by so careful a preservation and so prudent a use of this blessing as will acquire to them the glory of recommending it to the applause, the affection, and adoption of every nation which is yet a stranger to it.

Here, perhaps, I ought to stop. But a solicitude for your welfare, which cannot end but with my life, and the apprehension of danger, natural to that solicitude, urge me, on an occasion like the present, to offer to your solemn contemplation, and to recommend to your frequent review, some sentiments which are the result of much reflection, of no inconsiderable observation, and which appear to me all-important to the permanency of your felicity as a people. These will be offered to you with the more freedom, as you can only see in them the disinterested warnings of a parting friend, who can possibly have no personal motive to bias his counsel. Nor can I forget, as an encouragement to it, your indulgent reception of my sentiments on a former and not dissimilar occasion.

Interwoven as is the love of liberty with every ligament of your hearts, no recommendation of mine is necessary to fortify or confirm the attachment.

The unity of government which constitutes you one people is also now dear to you. It is justly so, for it is a main pillar in the edifice of your real independence, the support of your tranquility at home, your peace abroad; of your safety; of your prosperity; of that very liberty which you so highly prize. But as it is easy to foresee that, from different causes and from different quarters, much pains will be taken, many artifices employed to weaken in your minds the conviction of this truth; as this is the point in your political fortress against which the batteries of internal and external enemies will be most constantly and actively (though often covertly and insidiously) directed, it is of infinite moment that you should properly estimate the immense value of your national union to your collective and individual happiness; that you should cherish a cordial, habitual, and immovable attachment to it; accustoming yourselves to think and speak of it as of the palladium of your political safety and prosperity; watching for its preservation with jealous anxiety; discountenancing whatever may suggest even a suspicion that it can in any event be abandoned; and indignantly frowning upon the first dawning of every attempt to alienate any portion of our country from the rest, or to enfeeble the sacred ties which now link together the various parts.

For this you have every inducement of sympathy and interest. Citizens, by birth or choice, of a common country, that country has a right to concentrate your affections. The name of American, which belongs to you in your national capacity, must always exalt the just pride of patriotism more than any appellation derived from local discriminations. With slight shades of difference, you have the same religion, manners, habits, and political principles. You have in a common cause fought and triumphed together; the independence and liberty you possess are the work of joint counsels, and joint efforts of common dangers, sufferings, and successes.

But these considerations, however powerfully they address themselves to your sensibility, are greatly outweighed by those which apply more immediately to your interest. Here every portion of our country finds the most commanding motives for carefully guarding and preserving the union of the whole.

The North, in an unrestrained intercourse with the South, protected by the equal laws of a common government, finds in the productions of the latter great additional resources of maritime and commercial enterprise and precious materials of manufacturing industry. The South, in the same intercourse, benefiting by the agency of the North, sees its agriculture grow and its commerce expand. Turning partly into its own channels the seamen of the North, it finds its particular navigation invigorated; and, while it contributes, in different ways, to nourish and increase the general mass of the national navigation, it looks forward to the protection of a maritime strength, to which itself is unequally adapted. The East, in a like intercourse with the West, already finds, and in the progressive improvement of interior communications by land and water, will more and more find a valuable vent for the commodities which it brings from abroad, or manufactures at home. The West derives from the East supplies requisite to its growth and comfort, and, what is perhaps of still greater consequence, it must of necessity owe the secure enjoyment of indispensable outlets for its own productions to the weight, influence, and the future maritime strength of the Atlantic side of the Union, directed by an indissoluble community of interest as one nation. Any other tenure by which the West can hold this essential advantage, whether derived from its own separate strength, or from an apostate and unnatural connection with any foreign power, must be intrinsically precarious.

While, then, every part of our country thus feels an immediate and particular interest in union, all the parts combined cannot fail to find in the united mass means and efforts greater strength, greater resource, proportionably greater security from external danger, a less frequent interruption of their peace by foreign nations; and, what is of inestimable value, they must derive from union an exemption from those broils and wars between themselves, which so frequently afflict neighboring countries not tied together by the same governments, which their own rival ships alone would be sufficient to produce, but which opposite foreign alliances, attachments, and intrigues would stimulate and embitter. Hence, likewise, they will avoid the necessity of those overgrown military establishments which, under any form of government, are inauspicious to liberty, and which are to be regarded as particularly hostile to republican liberty. In this sense it is that your union ought to be considered as a main prop of your liberty, and that the love of the one ought to endear to you the preservation of the other.

These considerations speak a persuasive language to every reflecting and virtuous mind, and exhibit the continuance of the Union as a primary object of patriotic desire. Is there a doubt whether a common government can embrace so large a sphere? Let experience solve it. To listen to mere speculation in such a case were criminal. We are authorized to hope that a proper organization of the whole with the auxiliary agency of governments for the respective subdivisions, will afford a happy issue to the experiment. It is well worth a fair and full experiment. With such powerful and obvious motives to union, affecting all parts of our country, while experience shall not have demonstrated its impracticability, there will always be reason to distrust the patriotism of those who in any quarter may endeavor to weaken its bands.

In contemplating the causes which may disturb our Union, it occurs as matter of serious concern that any ground should have been furnished for characterizing parties by geographical discriminations. Northern and Southern, Atlantic and Western; whence designing men may endeavor to excite a belief that there is a real difference of local interests and views. One of the expedients of party to acquire influence within particular districts is to misrepresent the opinions and aims of other districts. You cannot shield yourselves too much against the jealousies and heartburnings which spring from these misrepresentations; they tend to render alien to each other those who ought to be bound together by fraternal affection. The inhabitants of our Western country have lately had a useful lesson on this head; they have seen, in the negotiation by the Executive, and in the unanimous ratification by the Senate, of the treaty with Spain, and in the universal satisfaction at that event, throughout the United States, a decisive proof how unfounded were the suspicions propagated among them of a policy in the General Government and in the Atlantic States unfriendly to their interests in regard to the Mississippi; they have been witnesses to the formation of two treaties, that with Great Britain, and that with Spain, which secure to them everything they could desire, in respect to our foreign relations, towards confirming their prosperity. Will it not be their wisdom to rely for the preservation of these advantages on the Union by which they were procured? Will they not henceforth be deaf to those advisers, if such there are, who would sever them from their brethren and connect them with aliens?

To the efficacy and permanency of your Union, a government for the whole is indispensable. No alliance, however strict, between the parts can be an adequate substitute; they must inevitably experience the infractions and interruptions which all alliances in all times have experienced. Sensible of this momentous truth, you have improved upon your first essay, by the adoption of a constitution of government better calculated than your former for an intimate union, and for the efficacious management of your common concerns. This government, the offspring of your own choice, uninfluenced and unawed, adopted upon full investigation and mature deliberation, completely free in its principles, in the distribution of its powers, uniting security with energy, and containing within itself a provision for its own amendment, has a just claim to your confidence and your support. Respect for its authority, compliance with its laws, acquiescence in its measures, are duties enjoined by the fundamental maxims of true liberty. The basis of our political systems is the right of the people to make and alter their constitutions of government. But the **Constitution** which at any time exists, till changed by an explicit and authentic act of the whole people, is sacredly obligatory upon all. The very idea of the power and the right of the people to establish government presupposes the duty of every individual to obey the established government.

All obstructions to the execution of the laws, all combinations and associations, under whatever plausible character, with the real design to direct, control, counteract, or awe the regular deliberation and action of the constituted authorities, are destructive of this fundamental principle, and of fatal tendency. They serve to organize faction, to give it an artificial and extraordinary force; to put, in the place of the delegated will of the nation the will of a party, often a small but artful and enterprising minority of the community; and, according to the alternate triumphs of different parties, to make the public administration the mirror of the ill-concerted and incongruous projects of faction, rather than the organ of consistent and wholesome plans digested by common counsels and modified by mutual interests.

However, combinations or associations of the above description may now and then answer popular ends, they are likely, in the course of time and things, to become potent engines, by which cunning, ambitious, and unprincipled men will be enabled to subvert the power of the people and to usurp for themselves the reins of government, destroying afterwards the very engines which have lifted them to unjust dominion.

Towards the preservation of your government, and the permanency of your present happy state, it is requisite, not only that you steadily discountenance irregular oppositions to its acknowledged authority, but also that you resist with care the spirit of innovation upon its principles, however specious the pretexts. One method of assault may be to effect, in the forms of the **Constitution**, alterations which will impair the energy of the system, and thus to undermine what cannot be directly overthrown. In all the changes to which you may be invited, remember that time and habit are at least as necessary to fix the true character of governments as of other human institutions; that experience is the surest standard by which to test the real tendency of the existing constitution of a country; that facility in changes, upon the credit of mere hypothesis and opinion, exposes to perpetual change, from the endless variety of hypothesis and opinion; and remember, especially, that for the efficient management of your common interests, in a country so extensive as ours, a government of as much vigor as is consistent with the perfect security of liberty is indispensable. Liberty itself will find in such a government, with powers properly distributed and adjusted, its surest guardian. It is, indeed, little else than a name, where the government is too feeble to withstand the enterprises of faction, to confine each member of the society within the limits prescribed by the laws, and to maintain all in the secure and tranquil enjoyment of the rights of person and property.

I have already intimated to you the danger of parties in the State, with particular reference to the founding of them on geographical discriminations. Let me now take a more comprehensive view, and warn you in the most solemn manner against the baneful effects of the spirit of party generally.

This spirit, unfortunately, is inseparable from our nature, having its root in the strongest passions of the human mind. It exists under different shapes in all governments, more or less stifled, controlled, or repressed; but, in those of the popular form, it is seen in its greatest rankness, and is truly their worst enemy.

The alternative domination of one faction over another, sharpened by the spirit of revenge, natural to party dissension, which in different ages and countries has perpetrated the most horrid enormities, is itself a frightful despotism. But this leads at length to a more formal and permanent despotism. The disorders and miseries which result gradually incline the minds of men to seek security and repose in the absolute power of an individual; and sooner or later the chief of some prevailing faction, more able or more fortunate than his competitors, turns this disposition to the purposes of his own elevation, on the ruins of public liberty.

Without looking forward to an extremity of this kind (which nevertheless ought not to be entirely out of sight), the common and continual mischiefs of the spirit of party are sufficient to make it the interest and duty of a wise people to discourage and restrain it.

It serves always to distract the public councils and enfeeble the public administration. It agitates the community with ill-founded jealousies and false alarms, kindles the animosity of one part against another, foments occasionally riot and insurrection. It opens the door to foreign influence and corruption, which finds a facilitated access to the government itself through the channels of party passions. Thus, the policy and the will of one country are subjected to the policy and will of another.

There is an opinion that parties in free countries are useful checks upon the administration of the government and serve to keep alive the spirit of liberty. This within certain limits is probably true; and in governments of a monarchical cast, patriotism may look with indulgence, if not with favor, upon the spirit of party. But in those of the popular character, in governments purely elective, it is a spirit not to be encouraged. From their natural tendency, it is certain there will always be enough of that spirit for every salutary purpose. And there being constant danger of excess, the effort ought to be by force of public opinion, to mitigate and assuage it. A fire not to be quenched, it demands a uniform vigilance to prevent its bursting into a flame, lest, instead of warming, it should consume.

It is important, likewise, that the habits of thinking in a free country should inspire caution in those entrusted with its administration, to confine themselves within their respective constitutional spheres, avoiding in the exercise of the powers of one department to encroach upon another. The spirit of encroachment tends to consolidate the powers of all the departments in one, and thus to create, whatever the form of government, a real despotism. A just estimate of that love of power, and proneness to abuse it, which predominates in the human heart, is sufficient to satisfy us of the truth of this position. The necessity of reciprocal checks in the exercise of political power, by dividing and distributing it into different depositaries, and constituting each the guardian of the public weal against invasions by the others, has been evinced by experiments ancient and modern; some of them in our country and under our own eyes. To preserve them must be as necessary as to institute them. If, in the opinion of the people, the distribution or modification of the constitutional powers be in any particular wrong, let it be corrected by an amendment in the way which the **Constitution** designates. But let there be no change by usurpation; for though this, in one instance, may be the instrument of good, it is the customary weapon by which free governments are destroyed. The precedent must always greatly overbalance in permanent evil any partial or transient benefit, which the use can at any time yield.

Of all the dispositions and habits which lead to political prosperity, religion and morality are indispensable supports. In vain would that man claim the tribute of patriotism, who should labor to subvert these great pillars of human happiness, these firmest props of the duties of men and citizens. The mere politician, equally with the pious man, ought to respect and to cherish them. A volume could not trace all their connections with private and public felicity. Let it simply be asked: Where is the security for property, for reputation, for life, if the sense of religious obligation desert the oaths which are the instruments of investigation in courts of justice? An let us with caution indulge the supposition that morality can be maintained without religion. Whatever may be conceded to the influence of refined education on minds of peculiar structure, reason and experience both forbid us to expect that national morality can prevail in exclusion of religious principle.

It is substantially true that virtue or morality is a necessary spring of popular government. The rule, indeed, extends with more or less force to every species of free government. Who that is a sincere friend to it can look with indifference upon attempts to shake the foundation of the fabric?

Promote then, as an object of primary importance, institutions for the general diffusion of knowledge. In proportion as the structure of a government gives force to public opinion, it is essential that public opinion should be enlightened.

As a very important source of strength and security, cherish public credit. One method of preserving it is to use it as sparingly as possible, avoiding occasions of expense by cultivating peace, but remembering also that timely disbursements to prepare for danger frequently prevent much greater disbursements to repel it, avoiding likewise the accumulation of debt, not only by shunning occasions of expense, but by vigorous exertion in time of peace to discharge the debts which unavoidable wars may have occasioned, not ungenerously throwing upon posterity the burden which we ourselves ought to bear. The execution of these maxims belongs to your representatives, but it is necessary that public opinion should co-operate. To facilitate to them the performance of their duty, it is essential that you should practically bear in mind that towards the payment of debts there must be revenue; that to have revenue there must be taxes; that no taxes can be devised which are not more or less inconvenient and unpleasant; that the intrinsic embarrassment, inseparable from the selection of the proper objects (which is always a choice of difficulties), ought to be a decisive motive for a candid construction of the conduct of the government in making it, and for a spirit of acquiescence in the measures for obtaining revenue, which the public exigencies may at any time dictate.

Observe good faith and justice towards all nations; cultivate peace and harmony with all. Religion and morality enjoin this conduct; and can it be, that good policy does not equally enjoin it – It will be worthy of a free, enlightened, and at no distant period, a great nation, to give to mankind the magnanimous and too novel example of a people always guided by an exalted justice and benevolence. Who can doubt that, in the course of time and things, the fruits of such a plan would richly repay any temporary advantages which might be lost by a steady adherence to it? Can it be that Providence has not connected the permanent felicity of a nation with its virtue? The experiment, at least, is recommended by every sentiment which ennobles human nature. Alas! Is it rendered impossible by its vices?

In the execution of such a plan, nothing is more essential than that permanent, inveterate antipathies against particular nations, and passionate attachments for others, should be excluded; and that, in place of them, just and amicable feelings towards all should be cultivated. The nation which indulges towards another a habitual hatred or a habitual fondness is in some degree a slave. It is a slave to its animosity or to its affection, either of which is sufficient to lead it astray from its duty and its interest. Antipathy in one nation against another disposes each more readily to offer insult and injury, to lay hold of slight causes of umbrage, and to be haughty and intractable, when accidental or trifling occasions of dispute occur. Hence, frequent collisions, obstinate, envenomed, and bloody contests. The nation prompted by ill-will and resentment, sometimes impels to war the government , contrary to the best calculations of policy. The government sometimes participates in the national propensity, and adopts through passion what reason would reject; at other times it makes the animosity of the nation subservient to projects of hostility instigated by pride, ambition, and other sinister and pernicious motives. The peace often, sometimes perhaps the liberty, of nations, has been the victim.

So likewise, a passionate attachment of one nation for another produces a variety of evils. Sympathy for the favorite nation, facilitating the illusion of an imaginary common interest in cases where no real common interest exists, and infusing into one the enmities of the other, betrays the former into a participation in the quarrels and wars of the latter without adequate inducement or justification. It leads also to concessions to the favorite nation of privileges denied to others which is apt doubly to injure the nation making concessions; by unnecessarily parting with what ought to have been retained, and by exciting jealousy, ill-will, and a disposition to retaliate, in the parties from whom equal privileges are withheld. And it gives to ambitious, corrupted, or deluded citizens (who devote themselves to the favorite nation), facility to betray or sacrifice the interests of their own country, without odium, sometimes even with popularity; gilding, with the appearances of a virtuous sense of obligation, a commendable deference for public opinion, or a laudable zeal for public good, the base or foolish compliances of ambition, corruption, or infatuation.

As avenues to foreign influence in innumerable ways, such attachments are particularly alarming to the truly enlightened and independent patriot. How many opportunities do they afford to tamper with domestic factions, to practice the arts of seduction, to mislead public opinion, to influence or awe the public councils. Such an attachment of a small or weak towards a great and powerful nation dooms the former to be the satellite of the latter.

Against the insidious wiles of foreign influence (I conjure you to believe me, fellow-citizens) the jealousy of a free people ought to be constantly awake, since history and experience prove that foreign influence is one of the most baneful foes of republican government. But that jealousy to be useful must be impartial; else it becomes the instrument of the very influence to be avoided, instead of a defense against it. Excessive partiality for one foreign nation and excessive dislike of another cause those whom they actuate to see danger only on one side, and serve to veil and even second the art of influence on the other. Real patriots who may resist the intrigues of the favorite are liable to become suspected and odious, while its tools and dupes usurp the applause and confidence of the people, to surrender their interests.

The great rule of conduct for us in regard to foreign nations is in extending our commercial relations, to have with them as little political connection as possible. So far as we have already formed engagements, let them be fulfilled with perfect good faith. Here let us stop. Europe has a set of primary interests which to us have none; or a very remote relation. Hence, she must be engaged in frequent controversies, the causes of which are essentially

foreign to our concerns. Hence, therefore, it must be unwise in us to im-
plicate ourselves by artificial ties in the ordinary vicissitudes of her politics,
or the ordinary combinations and collisions of her friendships or enmities.

Our detached and distant situation invites and enables us to pursue a
different course. If we remain one people under an efficient government,
the period is not far off when we may defy material injury from external
annoyance; when we may take such an attitude as will cause the neutrality,
we may at any time resolve upon to be scrupulously respected; when belligerent nations, under the impossibility of making acquisitions upon us, will
not lightly hazard the giving us provocation; when we may choose peace or
war, as our interest, guided by justice, shall counsel.

Why forego the advantages of so peculiar a situation? Why quit our
own to stand upon foreign ground? Why, by interweaving our destiny with
that of any part of Europe, entangle our peace and prosperity in the toils of
European ambition, rivalship, interest, humor, or caprice?

It is our true policy to steer clear of permanent alliances with any portion of the foreign world; so far, I mean, as we are now at liberty to do it;
for let me not be understood as capable of patronizing infidelity to existing
engagements. I hold the maxim no less applicable to public than to private
affairs, that honesty is always the best policy. I repeat it, therefore, let those
engagements be observed in their genuine sense. But, in my opinion, it is
unnecessary and would be unwise to extend them.

Taking care always to keep ourselves by suitable establishments on a
respectable defensive posture, we may safely trust to temporary alliances
for extraordinary emergencies.

Harmony, liberal intercourse with all nations, are recommended by
policy, humanity, and interest. But even our commercial policy should hold
an equal and impartial hand; neither seeking nor granting exclusive favors
or preferences; consulting the natural course of things; diffusing and di-
versifying by gentle means the streams of commerce, but forcing nothing;
establishing (with powers so disposed, in order to give trade a stable course,
to define the rights of our merchants, and to enable the government to
support them) conventional rules of intercourse, the best that present circumstances and mutual opinion will permit, but temporary, and liable to
be from time to time abandoned or varied, as experience and circumstances

shall dictate; constantly keeping in view that it is folly in one nation to look for disinterested favors from another; that it must pay with a portion of its independence for whatever it may accept under that character; that, by such acceptance, it may place itself in the condition of having given equivalents for nominal favors, and yet of being reproached with ingratitude for not giving more. There can be no greater error than to expect or calculate upon real favors from nation to nation. It is an illusion, which experience must cure, which a just pride ought to discard.

In offering to you, my countrymen, these counsels of an old and affectionate friend, I dare not hope they will make the strong and lasting impression I could wish; that they will control the usual current of the passions, or prevent our nation from running the course which has hitherto marked the destiny of nations. But, if I may even flatter myself that they may be productive of some partial benefit, some occasional good; that they may now and then recur to moderate the fury of party spirit, to warn against the mischiefs of foreign intrigue, to guard against the impostures of pretended patriotism; this hope will be a full recompense for the solicitude for your welfare, by which they have been dictated.

How far in the discharge of my official duties I have been guided by the principles which have been delineated, the public records and other evidences of my conduct must witness to you and to the world. To myself, the assurance of my own conscience is, that I have at least believed myself to be guided by them.

In relation to the still subsisting war in Europe, my proclamation of the twenty-second of April, 1793, is the index of my plan. Sanctioned by your approving voice, and by that of your representatives in both houses of Congress, the spirit of that measure has continually governed me, uninfluenced by any attempts to deter or divert me from it.

After deliberate examination, with the aid of the best lights I could obtain, I was well satisfied that our country, under all the circumstances of the case, had a right to take, and was bound in duty and interest to take, a neutral position. Having taken it, I determined, as far as should depend upon me, to maintain it, with moderation, perseverance, and firmness.

The considerations which respect the right to hold this conduct, it is not necessary on this occasion to detail. I will only observe that, according to my understanding of the matter, that right, so far from being denied by any of the belligerent powers, has been virtually admitted by all.

The duty of holding a neutral conduct may be inferred , without anything more, from the obligation which justice and humanity impose on every nation, in cases in which it is free to act, to maintain inviolate the relations of peace and amity towards other nations.

The inducements of interest for observing that conduct will best be referred to your own reflections and experience. With me a predominant motive has been to endeavor to gain time to our country to settle and mature its yet recent institutions, and to progress without interruption to that degree of strength and consistency which is necessary to give it, humanly speaking, the command of its own fortunes.

Though, in reviewing the incidents of my administration, I am unconscious of intentional error, I am nevertheless too sensible of my defects not to think it probable that I may have committed many errors. Whatever they may be, I fervently beseech the Almighty to avert or mitigate the evils to which they may tend. I shall also carry with me the hope that my country will never cease to view them with indulgence; and that, after forty five years of my life dedicated to its service with an upright zeal, the faults of incompetent abilities will be consigned to oblivion, as myself must soon be to the mansions of rest.

Relying on its kindness in this as in other things, and actuated by that fervent love towards it, which is so natural to a man who views in it the native soil of himself and his progenitors for several generations, I anticipate with pleasing expectation that retreat in which I promise myself to realize, without alloy, the sweet enjoyment of partaking, in the midst of my fellow-citizens, the benign influence of good laws under a free government, the ever-favorite object of my heart, and the happy reward, as I trust, of our mutual cares, labors, and dangers.

//s// Geo Washington

6. LINCOLN'S INAUGURAL ADDRESS, MARCH 4, 1861

Fellow-Citizens of the United States:

In compliance with a custom as old as the Government itself, I appear before you to address you briefly and to take in your presence the oath prescribed by the Constitution of the United States to be taken by the President "before he enters on the execution of this office."
I do not consider it necessary at present for me to discuss those matters of administration about which there is no special anxiety or excitement.

Apprehension seems to exist among the people of the Southern States that by the accession of a Republican Administration their property and their peace and personal security are to be endangered. There has never been any reasonable cause for such apprehension. Indeed, the most ample evidence to the contrary has all the while existed and been open to their inspection. It is found in nearly all the published speeches of him who now addresses you. I do but quote from one of these speeches when I declare that –

"I have no purpose, directly or indirectly, to interfere with the institution of slavey in the States where it exists. I believe I have no lawful right to do so, and I have no inclination to do so."

Those who nominated and elected me did so with full knowledge that I had made this and many similar declarations and had never recanted them; and more than this, they placed in the platform for my acceptance, and as a law to themselves and to me, the clear and emphatic resolution which I now read:

Resolved, That the maintenance inviolate of the rights of the States, and especially the right of each State to order and control its own domestic institutions according to its own judgement exclusively, is essential to that balance of power on which the perfection and endurance of our political fabric depend; and we denounce the lawless invasion by armed force of the soil of any State or Territory, no matter what pretext, as among the gravest of crimes.

I now reiterate these sentiments, and in doing so I only press upon the public attention the most conclusive evidence of which the case is susceptible that the property, peace, and security of no section are to be in any wise endangered by the now incoming Administration. I add, too, that all the protection which, consistently with the Constitution and the laws, can be given will be cheerfully given to all the States when lawfully demanded, for whatever cause – as cheerfully to one section as to another.

There is so much controversy about the delivering up of fugitives from service or labor. The clause I now read is as plainly written in the Constitution as any other of its provisions:

"No person held to service or labor in one State, under the laws thereof, escaping into another, shall in consequence of any law or regulation therein be discharged from such service or labor, but shall be delivered up on claim of the party to whom such service or labor may be due."

It is scarcely questioned that this provision was intended by those who made it for the reclaiming of what we call fugitive slaves; and the intention of the lawgiver is the law. All members of Congress swear their support to the whole Constitution – to this provision as much as to any other. To the proposition, then, that slaves whose cases come within the terms of this clause "shall be delivered up" their oaths are unanimous. Now, if they would make the effort in good temper, could they not with nearly equal unanimity frame and pass a law by means of which to keep good that unanimous oath?

There is some difference of opinion whether this clause should be enforced by national or by State authority, but surely that difference is not a very material one. If the slave is to be surrendered, it can be of but little consequence to him or to others by which authority it is done. And should anyone in any case be content that his oath shall go unkept on a merely unsubstantial controversy as to *how* it shall be kept.

Again: In any law upon this subject ought not all the safeguards of liberty known in civilized and humane jurisprudence to be introduced, so that a free man be not in any case surrendered as a slave? And might it not be well at the same time to provide by law for the enforcement of that clause in the Constitution which guarantees that "the citizens of each State shall be entitled to all privileges and immunities of citizens in the several States?"

I take the official oath to-day with no mental reservations and with no purpose to construe the Constitution or laws by any hypercritical rules; and while I do not choose now to specify particular acts of Congress as proper to be enforced, I do suggest that it will be much safer for all, both in official and private stations, to conform to and abide by all those acts which stand unrepealed than to violate any of them trusting to find impunity in having them held to be unconstitutional.

It is seventy-two years since the first inauguration of a President under our National Constitution. During that period fifteen different and greatly distinguished citizens have in succession administered the executive branch of the Government. They have conducted it through many perils, and generally with great success. Yet, with all this scope of precedent, I now enter upon the same task for the brief constitutional term of four years under great and peculiar difficulty. A disruption of the Federal Union, heretofore only menaced, is now formidably attempted.

I hold that in contemplation of universal law and of the Constitution the Union of these States is perpetual. Perpetuity is implied, if not expressed, in the fundamental law of all national governments. It is safe to assert that no government proper ever had a provision in its organic law for its own termination. Continue to execute all the express provisions of our National Constitution, and the Union will endure forever, it being impossible to destroy it except by some action not provided for in the instrument itself.

Again: If the United States be not a government proper, but an association of States in the nature of contract merely, can it, as a contract, be peaceably unmade by less than all the parties who made it? One party to a contract may violate it – break it, so to speak – but does it not require all to lawfully rescind it?

Descending from these general principles, we find the proposition that in legal contemplation the Union is perpetual confirmed by the history of the Union itself. The Union is much older than the Constitution. It was formed, in fact, by the Articles of Association in 1774. It was matured and continued by the Declaration of Independence in 1776. It was further matured, and the faith of all the then thirteen States expressly plighted and engaged that it should be perpetual, by the Articles of Confederation in 1778. And finally, in 1787, one of the declared objects for ordaining and establishing the Constitution was "to form a more perfect Union."

But if destruction of the Union by one or by a part only of the States be lawfully possible, the Union is *less* perfect than before the Constitution, having lost the vital element of perpetuity.

It follows from these views that no State upon its own mere motion can lawfully get out of the Union; that *resolves* and *ordinances* to that effect are legally void, and that acts of violence within any State or States against the authority of the United States are insurrectionary or revolutionary, according to circumstances.

I therefore consider that in view of the Constitution and the laws the Union is unbroken, and to the extent of my ability, I shall take care, as the Constitution itself expressly enjoins upon me, that the laws of the Union be faithfully executed in all the States. Doing this I deem to be only a simple duty on my part, and I shall perform it so far as practicable unless my rightful masters, the American people, shall withhold the requisite means or in some authoritative manner direct the contrary. I trust this will not be regarded as a menace, but only as the declared purpose of the Union that it will constitutionally defend and maintain itself.

In doing this there needs to be no bloodshed or violence, and there shall be none unless it be forced upon the national authority. The power confided to me will be used to hold, occupy, and possess the property and places belonging to the Government and to collect the duties and imposts; but beyond what may be necessary for these objects, there will be no invasion, no using of force against or among the people anywhere. Where hostility to the United States in any interior locality shall be so great and universal as to prevent competent resident citizens from holding the Federal offices, there will be no attempt to force obnoxious strangers among the people for that object. While the strict legal right may exist in the Government to enforce the exercise of these offices, the attempt to do so would be so irritating and so nearly impracticable withal that I deem it better to forego for the time the uses of such offices.

The mails, unless repelled, will continue to be furnished in all parts of the Union. So far as possible the people everywhere shall have that sense of perfect security which is most favorable to calm thought and reflection. The course here indicated will be followed unless current events and experience shall show a modification or change to be proper, and in every case and exigency my best discretion will be exercised, according to circumstances actually existing and with a view and a hope of a peaceful solution of the national troubles and the restoration of fraternal sympathies and affections.

That there are persons in one section or another who seek to destroy the Union at all events and are glad of any pretext to do it I will neither affirm nor deny; but if there be such, I need address no word to them. To those, however, who really love the Union may I not speak?

Before entering upon so grave a matter as the destruction of our national fabric, with all its benefits, its memories, and its hopes, would it not be wise to ascertain precisely why we do it? Will you hazard so desperate a step while there is any possibility that any portion of the ills you fly from have no real existence? Will you, while the certain ills you fly to are greater than all the real ones you fly from, will you risk the commission of so fearful a mistake?

All profess to be content in the Union if all constitutional rights can be maintained. Is it true, then, that any right plainly written in the Constitution has been denied? I think not. Happily the human mind is so constituted that no party can reach to the audacity of doing this. Think, if you can, of a single instance in which a plainly written provision of the Constitution has ever been denied. If by the mere force of numbers a majority should deprive a minority of any clearly written constitutional right, it might in a moral point of view justify revolution; certainly would if such right were a vital one. But such is not our case. All the vital rights of minorities and of individuals are so plainly assured to them by affirmations and negations, guaranties and prohibitions, in the Constitution that controversies never arise concerning them. But no organic law can ever be framed with a provision specifically applicable to every question which may occur in practical administration. No foresight can anticipate nor any document of reasonable length contain express provisions for all possible questions. Shall fugitives from labor be surrendered by national or by State authority? The Constitution does not expressly say. *May* Congress prohibit slavery in the Territories? The Constitution does not expressly say. *Must* Congress protect slavery in the Territories? The Constitution does not expressly say.

From questions of this class spring all our constitutional controversies, and we divide upon them into majorities and minorities. If the minority will no acquiesce, the majority must, or the Government must cease. There is no other alternative, for continuing the Government is acquiescence on one side or the other. If a minority in such case will secede rather than acquiesce, they make a precedent which in turn will divide and ruin them, for a minority of their own will secede from them whenever a majority refuses to be controlled by such minority. For instance, why may not any portion of a new confederacy a year or two hence arbitrarily secede again, precisely as portions of the present Union now claim to secede from it? All who cherish disunion sentiments are now being educated to the exact temper of doing this.

Is there such perfect identity of interests among the States to compose a new union as to produce harmony only and prevent renewed secession?

Plainly the central idea of secession is the essence of anarchy. A majority held in restraint by constitutional checks and limitations, and always changing easily with deliberate changes of popular opinions and sentiments, is the only true sovereign of a free people. Whoever rejects it does of necessity fly to anarchy or despotism. Unanimity is impossible. The rule of a minority, as a permanent arrangement, is wholly inadmissible; so that, rejecting the majority principle, anarchy or despotism in some form is all that is left.

I do not forget the position assumed by some that constitutional questions are to be decided by the Supreme Court, nor do I deny that such decisions must be binding in any case upon the parties to a suit as to the object of that suit, while they are also entitled to very high respect and consideration in all parallel cases by all other departments of the Government. And while it is obviously possible that such decision may be erroneous in any given case, still the evil effect following it, being limited to that particular case, with the chance that it may be overruled and never become a precedent for other cases, can better be borne than could the evils of a different practice. At the same time, the candid citizen must confess that if the policy of the Government upon vital questions affecting the whole people is to be irrevocably fixed by decisions of the Supreme Court, the instant they are made in ordinary litigation between parties in personal actions the people will have ceased to be their own rulers, having to that extent practically resigned their Government into the hands of that eminent tribunal. Nor is there in this view any assault upon the court or the judges. It is a duty from which they may not shrink to decide cases properly brought before them, and it is no fault of theirs if others seek to turn their decisions to political purposes.

One section of our country believes slavery is *right* and ought to be extended, while the other believes it is *wrong* and ought not to be extended. This is the only substantial dispute. The fugitive – slave clause of the Constitution and the law for the suppression of the foreign slave trade are each as well enforced, perhaps, as any law can ever be in a community where the moral sense of the people imperfectly supports the law itself. The great body of the people abide by the dry legal obligation in both cases, and a few break over in each. This, I think, can not be perfectly cured, and it would be worse in both cases *after* the separation of the sections than before. The foreign slave trade, now imperfectly suppressed, would be ultimately revived without restriction in one section, while fugitive slaves, now only partially surrendered, would not be surrendered at all by the other.

Physically speaking, we can not separate. We can not remove our respective sections from each other nor build an impassable wall between them. A husband and wife may be divorced and go out of the presence and beyond the reach of each other, but the different parts of our country can not do this. They can not but remain face to face, and intercourse, either amicable or hostile, must continue between them. Is it possible, then, to make that intercourse more advantageous or more satisfactory *after* separation than *before*? Can aliens make treaties easier than friends can make laws? Can treaties be more faithfully enforced between aliens than laws among friends? Suppose you go to war, you can not fight always; and when, after much loss on both sides and no gain on either, you cease fighting, the identical old questions, as to terms of intercourse, are again upon you.

This country, with its institutions, belongs to the people who inhabit it. Whenever they shall grow weary of the existing Government, they can exercise their *constitutional* right of amending it or their *revolutionary* right to dismember or overthrow it. I can not be ignorant of the fact that many worthy and patriotic citizens are desirous of having the National Constitution amended. While I make no recommendation of amendments, I fully recognize the rightful authority of the people over the whole subject, to be exercised in either of the modes prescribed in the instrument itself; and I should, under existing circumstances, favor rather than oppose a fair opportunity being afforded the people to act upon it. I will venture to add that to me the convention mode seems preferable, in that it allows amendments to originate with the people themselves, instead of only permitting them to take or reject propositions originated by others, not especially chosen for the purpose, and which might not be precisely such as they would wish to either accept or refuse. I understand a proposed amendment to the Constitution – which amendment , however, I have not seen – has passed Congress, to the effect that the Federal Government shall never interfere with the domestic institutions of the States, including that of persons held to service. To avoid misconstruction of what I have said, I depart from my promise not to speak of particular amendments so far as to say that, holding such a provision to now be implied constitutional law, I have no objection to its being made express and irrevocable.

The Chief Magistrate derives all his authority from the people, and they have referred none upon him to fix terms for the separation of the States. The people themselves can do this if also they choose, but the Executive as such has nothing to do with it. His duty is to administer the present Government as it came into his hands and to transmit it unimpaired by him to his successor.

Why should there not be a patient confidence in the ultimate justice of the people? Is there any better or equal hope in the world? In our present differences, is either party without faith of being in the right? If the Almighty Ruler of Nations, with His eternal truth and justice, be on your side of the North or on yours of the South, that truth and that justice will surely prevail by the judgement of this great tribunal of the American people.

By the frame of the Government under which we live this same people have wisely given their public servants but little power for mischief, and have with equal wisdom provided for the return of that little to their own hands at very short intervals. While the people retain their virtue and vigilance no Administration by any extreme of wickedness or folly can very seriously injure the Government in the short space of four years.

My countrymen, one and all, think calmly and *well* upon this whole subject. Nothing valuable can be lost by taking time. If there be an object to *hurry* any of you in hot haste to a step which you would never take *deliberately*, that object will be frustrated by taking time; but no good object can be frustrated by it. Such of you as are now dissatisfied still have the old Constitution unimpaired, and, on the sensitive point, the laws of your own framing under it; while the new Administration will have no immediate power, if it would, to change either. If it were admitted that you who are dissatisfied hold the right side in the dispute, there still is no single good reason for precipitate action. Intelligence, patriotism, Christianity, and a firm reliance on Him who has never yet forsaken this favored land are still competent to adjust in the best way all our present difficulty.

In *your* hands, my dissatisfied fellow-countrymen, and not in *mine*, is the momentous issue of civil war. The Government will not assail *you*. You can have no conflict without being yourselves the aggressors. *You* have no oath registered in heaven to destroy the Government, while *I* shall have the most solemn one to "preserve, protect, and defend it."

I am loath to close. We are not enemies, but friends. We must not be enemies. Though passion may have strained it must not break our bonds of affection. The mystic chords of memory, stretching from every battlefield and patriot grave to every living heart and hearthstone all over this broad land, will yet swell the chorus of the Union, when again touched, as surely they will be, by the better angels of our nature.

7. WASHINGTON'S NEWBURGH ADDRESS, MARCH 15, 1783

In contrast to his Inaugural Address, these words are in Washington's own hand, indicating they were not prepared by a professional secretary or advisor. The document shows his distinctive spellings, abbreviations, and punctuation, as well as displaying typical 18ᵗʰ century vocabulary. He planned that no one knew that he would attend, much less speak — until the moment he appeared.

Head Quarters Newburgh 15ᵗʰ of March 1783

Gentlemen,

By an anonymous summons, an attempt has been made to convene you together - how inconsistent with the rules of propriety! how unmilitary! And how subversive of all order and discipline - let the good sense of the Army decide.

In the moment of this summons, another anonymous production was sent into circulation; addressed more to the feelings & passions, than to the reason & judgment of the Army. The Author of the piece, is entitled to much credit for the goodness of his Pen: and I could wish he had as much credit for the rectitude of his Heart -- for, as Men see thro' different Optics, and are induced by the reflecting faculties of the Mind, to use different means to attain the same end; the Author of the Address, should have had more charity, than to mark for Suspicion, the Man who should recommend Moderation and longer forbearance -- or, in other words, who should not think as he thinks, and act as he advises. But he had another plan in view, in which candor and liberality of Sentiment, regard to justice, and love of

Country, have no part; and he was right, to insinuate the darkest suspicion, to effect the blackest designs.

The Address is drawn with great art, and is designed to answer the most insidious purposes. That it is calculated to impress the Mind, with an idea of premeditated injustice in the Sovereign power of the United States, and rouse all those resentments which must unavoidably flow from such a belief. That the secret Mover of this Scheme (whoever he may be) intended to take advantage of the passions, while they were warmed by the recollection of past distresses, without giving time for cool, deliberative thinking, & that composure of Mind which is so necessary to give dignity & stability to measures, is rendered too obvious, by the mode of conducting the business, to need other proof than a reference to the proceeding.

Thus much, Gentlemen, I have thought it incumbent on me to observe to you, to shew upon what principles I opposed the irregular and hasty meeting which was proposed to have been held on Tuesday last: and not because I wanted a disposition to give you every opportunity consistent with your own honor, and the dignity of the Army, to make known your grievances. If my conduct heretofore, has not evinced to you, that I have been a faithful friend to the Army; my declaration of it at this time wd be equally unavailing & improper --But as I was among the first who embarked in the cause of our common Country -- As I have never left your side one moment, but when called from you, on public duty -- As I have been the constant companion & witness of your Distresses, and not among the last to feel, & acknowledge your Merits -- As I have ever considered my own Military reputation as inseparably connected with that of the Army -- As my Heart has ever expanded with joy, when I have heard its praises -- and my indignation has arisen, when the Mouth of detraction had been opened against it -- it can <u>scarcely be supposed</u>, at this late stage of the War, that I am indifferent to its interests.

But – how are they to be promoted? The way is plain, says the anonymous Addresser -- If War continues, remove into the unsettled Country -- there establish yourselves, and leave an ungrateful Country to defend itself --But who are they to defend? Our Wives, our Children, our Farms, and other property which we leave behind us. Or --in this state of hostile separation, are we take the two first (the latter cannot be removed) to perish in a Wilderness, with hunger, cold, & nakedness? If Peace takes place, never sheath your Sword says he until you have obtained full and ample Justice --this dreadful alternative, of either deserting our Country in the extremest hour of her distress, or turning our Army against it, (which is the apparent object, unless Congress can be compelled into an instant compliance) has something so shocking in it, that humanity revolts at the idea. My God! What can this Writer have in view, by recommending such measures? Can he be a friend to the Army? Can he be a friend to this Country? Rather, is he not an insidious Foe? Some Emissary, perhaps, from New York, plotting the ruin of both, by sowing the seeds of discord & separation between the Civil & Military powers of the Continent? And what a Compliment does he pay to our understandings, when he recommends measures in either alternative, impracticable in their nature?

But here, Gentlemen, I will drop the curtain; because it wd be as imprudent in me to assign my reasons for this opinion, as it would be insulting to your conception, to suppose you stood in need of them. A moment's reflection will convince every dispassionate Mind of the physical impossibility of carrying either proposal into execution.

There might, Gentlemen, be an impropriety in my taking notice, in this Address to you, of an anonymous production -- but the manner in which that performance has been introduced to the Army -- the effect it was intended to have, together with some other circumstances, will amply justify my observations on the tendency of that Writing. With respect to the advice given by the Author, to suspect the Man, who shall recommend moderate measures and longer forbearance -- I spurn it -- as every Man, who regards that liberty, & reveres that Justice for which we contend, undoubtable must -- for if Men are to be precluded from offering their sentiments on a matter, which may involve the most serious and alarming consequences, that can invite the consideration of Mankind, reason is of no use to us -- the freedom of Speech may be taken away -- and dumb & silent we may be led, like sheep, to the Slaughter.

I cannot, in justice to my own belief, & what I have great reason to conceive is the intention of Congress, conclude this Address, without giving it as my decided opinion; that that Honble (abbreviation) Body, entertain exalted sentiments of the Services of the Army; and, from a full conviction of its Merits & sufferings, will do it compleat Justice: That their endeavors, to discover & establish funds for this purpose, have been unwearied, and will not cease, till they have succeeded, I have not a doubt. But, like all other large Bodies, where there is a variety of different Interests to reconcile, their deliberations are slow. Why then should we distrust them? and, in consequence of that distrust, adopt measures, which may cast a shade over that glory which, has been so justly acquired; and tarnish the reputation of an Army which is celebrated thro' all Europe, for its fortitude and Patriotism? and for what is this done? to bring the object we seek for nearer? No! most certainly, in my opinion, it will cast it at a greater distance.

For myself (and I take no merit in giving the assurance, being induced to it from principles of gratitude, veracity, and justice) -- a grateful sense of the confidence you have ever placed in me -- a recollection of the Cheerful assistance, & prompt obedience I have experienced from you, under every vicisitude (sic) of Fortune, and the sincere affection I feel for an Army, I have so long had the honor to Command, will oblige me to declare, in this public & solemn manner, that, in the attainment of compleat justice for all your toils & dangers, and in the gratification of every wish, so far as may be done consistently with the great duty I owe my Country, and those powers we are bound to respect, you may freely command my services to the utmost of my abilities.

While I give you these assurances, and pledge my self in the most unequivocal manner, to exert whatever ability I am possessed of, in your favor -- let me entreat you, Gentlemen, on your part, not to take any measures, which, viewed in the calm light of reason, will lessen the dignity, & sully the glory you have hitherto maintained -- let me request you to rely on the plighted faith of your Country, and place a full confidence in the purity of the intentions of Congress; that previous to your dissolution as an Army they will cause all your Accts to be fairly liquidated, as directed in their resolutions, which were published to you two days ago -- and that they will adopt the most effectual measures in their power, to render ample justice to you, for your faithful and meritorious Services. And let me conjure you, in the name of our common Country -- as you value your sacred honor -- as you respect the rights of humanity, & as you regard the Military and national character of America, to express your utmost horror & detestation of the

Man who wishes, under any specious pretences, to overturn the liberties of our Country, & who wickedly attempts to open the flood Gates of Civil discord, and deluge our rising Empire in Blood.

By thus determining--& thus acting, you will pursue the plain & direct Road to the attainment of your wishes. You will defeat the insidious designs of our Enemies, who are compelled to resort from open force to secret Artifice. You will give one more distinguished proof of unexampled patriotism & patient virtue, rising superior to the pressure of the most complicated sufferings; And you will, by the dignity of your Conduct, afford occasion for Posterity to say, when speaking of the glorious example you have exhibited to man kind, "had this day been wanting, the World had never seen the last stage of perfection to which human nature is capable of attaining.

//s// Go: Washington

To the General, Field, & other Officers Assembled at the New Building pursuant to the General Order of the 11ᵗʰ Instant March

8. LINCOLN'S LAST PUBLIC ADDRESS, APRIL 11, 1865 ON LIMITED ENFRANCHISEMENT

A crowd of several thousand gathered outside the White House, still celebrating the surrender of Robert E Lee's Army of Northern Virginia to U.S. Grant and the main Federal Army, the Army of the Potomac, effectively ending the war. Unfortunately, this speech also was presented only three days before Lincoln's assassination. The speech marked Lincoln's first public statement to start the process of giving the right for Black People to vote, receiving full citizenship rights. He delivered it from a second-floor window at the White House.

We meet this evening, not in sorrow, but in gladness of heart. The evacuation of Petersburg and Richmond, and the surrender of the principal insurgent army, give hope of a righteous and speedy peace whose joyous expression can not be restrained. In the midst of this, however, He from whom all blessings flow, must not be forgotten. A call for a national thanksgiving is being prepared, and will be duly promulgated. Nor must those whose harder part gives us the cause of rejoicing, be overlooked. Their honors must not be parcelled (sic) out with others. I myself was near the front, and had the high pleasure of transmitting much of the good news to you; but no part of the honor, for plan or execution, is mine. To Gen Grant, his skillful officers and brave men, all belongs. The gallant Navy stood ready, but was not in reach to take active part.

By these recent successes the re-inauguration of the national authority – reconstruction – which has had a large share of thought from the first, is pressed much more closely upon our attention. It is fraught with great difficulty. Unlike a case of a war between independent nations, there is no authorized organ for us to treat with. No one man has authority to give up the rebellion for any other man. We simply must begin with, and mould from, disorganized and discordant elements. Nor is it a small additional embarrassment that we, the loyal people, differ among ourselves as to the mode, manner, and means of reconstruction.

As a general rule, I abstain from reading the reports of attacks upon myself, wishing not to be provoked by that to which I can not properly offer an answer. In spite of this precaution, however, it comes to my knowledge that I am much censured for some supposed agency in setting up, and seeking to sustain, the new State government of Louisiana. In this I have done just so much as, and no more than, the public knows. In the Annual Message of Dec.1863 and accompanying Proclamation, I presented a plan of re-construction (as the phrase goes) which, I promised, if adopted by any State, should be acceptable to, and sustained by, the Executive government of the nation. I distinctly stated that this was not the only plan which might possibly be acceptable; and I also distinctly protested that the Executive claimed no right to say when, or whether members should be admitted to seats in Congress from such States. This plan was, in advance, submitted to the then Cabinet, and distinctly approved by every member of it. One of them suggested that I should then, and in that connection, apply the Emancipation Proclamation to the theretofore excepted parts of Virginia and Louisiana; that I should drop the suggestion about apprenticeship for freed-people, and that I should omit the protest against my own power, in regard to the admission of members to Congress; but even he approved every part and parcel of the plan which has since been employed or touched by the action of Louisiana. The new constitution of Louisiana, declaring emancipation for the whole State, practically applies the Proclamation to the part previously excepted. It does not adopt apprenticeship for freed-people; and it is silent, as it could not well be otherwise, about the admission of members to Congress. So that, as it applies to Louisiana, every member of the Cabinet fully approved the plan. The message went to Congress, and I received many commendations of the plan, written and verbal; and not a single objection to it, from any professed emancipationist, came to my knowledge, until after the news reached Washington that the people of

Louisiana had begun to move in accordance with it. From about July 1862, I had corresponded with different persons, supposed to be interested, seeking a reconstruction of a State government for Louisiana. When the message of 1863, with the plan before mentioned, reached New Orleans, Gen. Banks wrote me that he was confident the people, with his military co-operation, would reconstruct, substantially on that plan. I wrote him, and some of them to try it; they tried it, and the result is known. Such only has been my agency in getting up the Louisiana government. As to sustaining it, my promise is out, as before stated. But, as bad promises are better broken than kept, I shall treat this as a bad promise, and break it, whenever I shall be convinced that keeping it is adverse to the public interest. But I have not yet been so convinced.

I have been shown a letter on this subject, supposed to be an able one, in which the writer expresses regret that my mind has not seemed to be definitely fixed on the question whether the seceding States, so called, are in the Union or out of it. It would perhaps, add astonishment to his regret, were he to learn that since I have found professed Union men endeavoring to make that question, I have *purposely* forborne any public expression upon it. As appears to me that question has not been, nor yet is, a practically material one, and that any discussion of it, while it thus remains practically immaterial, could have no effect other than the mischievous one of dividing our friends. As yet, whatever it may hereafter become, that question is bad, as the basis of a controversy, and good for nothing at all – a merely pernicious abstraction.

We all agree that the seceded States, so called, are out of their proper relation with the Union; and that the sole object of the government, civil and military, in regard to those States is to again get them into that proper practical relation. I believe it is not only possible, but in fact, easier to do this, without deciding, or even considering, whether these States have ever been out of the Union, than with it. Finding themselves safely at home, it would be utterly immaterial whether they had ever been abroad. Let us all join in doing the acts necessary to restoring the proper practical relations between these States and the Union; and each forever after, innocently indulge his own opinion whether, in doing the acts, he brought the States from without, into the Union, or only gave them proper assistance, they never having been out of it.

The amount of constituency, so to speak, on which the new Louisiana government rests, would be more satisfactory to all, if it contained fifty, thirty, or even twenty thousand, instead of only about twelve thousand, as it does. It is also unsatisfactory to some that the elective franchise is not given to the colored man. I would myself prefer that it were now conferred on the very intelligent, and on those who serve our cause as soldiers. Still the question is not whether the Louisiana government, as it stands, is quite all that is desirable. The question is, "Will it be wiser to take it as it is, and help to improve it; or to reject, and disperse it?" "Can Louisiana be brought into proper practical relation with the Union *sooner* by *sustaining*, or by *discarding* her new State government?"

Some twelve thousand voters in the heretofore slave-state of Louisiana have sworn allegiance to the Union, assumed to be the rightful political power of the State, held elections, organized a State government, adopted a free-state constitution, giving the benefit of public schools equally to black and white, and empowering the Legislature to confer the elective franchise upon the colored man. Their Legislature has already voted to ratify the constitutional amendment recently passed by Congress, abolishing slavery throughout the nation. These twelve thousand persons are thus fully committed to the Union, and to perpetual freedom in the state – committed to the very things, and nearly all the things the nation wants – and they ask the nation's recognition and it's assistance to make good their committal. Now, if we reject, and spurn them, we do our utmost to disorganize and disperse them. We in effect say to the white men "You are worthless, or worse – we will neither help you, nor be helped by you." To the blacks we say "This cup of liberty which these, your old masters, hold to your lips, we will dash from you, and leave you to the chances of gathering the spilled and scattered contents in some vague and undefined when, where, and how." If this course, discouraging and paralyzing both white and black, has any tendency to bring Louisiana into proper practical relations with the Union, I have, so far, been unable to perceive it. If, on the contrary, we recognize, and sustain the new government of Louisiana the converse of all this is made true. We encourage the hearts, and nerve the arms of the twelve thousand to adhere to their work, and argue for it, and proselyte for it, and fight for it, and feed it, and grow it, and ripen it to a complete success. The colored man too, in seeing all united for him, is inspired with vigilance, and energy, and daring, to the same end. Grant that he desires the elective franchise, will he not attain it sooner by saving the already advanced steps toward it, than by running backward over them? Concede that the new government of Louisiana is only to what it should be as the egg is to the fowl, we shall sooner have the fowl by hatching the egg than by smashing it? Again, if we reject Louisiana, we also reject one vote in favor of the proposed amendment to the national Constitution. To meet this proposition, it has been argued that no more than three fourths of those States which have not attempted secession are necessary to validly ratify the amendment. I do not commit myself against this, further than to say that such a ratification would be questionable, and sure to be persistently questioned; while a ratification by three-fourths of all the States would be unquestioned and unquestionable.

I repeat the question, "Can Louisiana be brought into proper practical relation with the Union *sooner* by *sustaining* or by *discarding* her new State Government?"

What has been said of Louisiana will apply generally to other States. And yet so great peculiarities pertain to each state, and such important and sudden changes occur in the same state; and withal, so new and unprecedented is the whole case, that no exclusive, and inflexible plan can be safely prescribed as to details and colatterals [sic]. Such exclusive, and inflexible plan, would surely become a new entanglement. Important principles may, and must, be inflexible.

In the present "*situation*" as the phrase goes, it may be my duty to make some new announcement to the people of the South. I am considering, and shall not fail to act, when satisfied that action will be proper.

9. A SUMMARIZED VERSION OF THE 12 ACTS OF ACCUSATION - THE CHARGES AND JOAN'S RESPONSES.

Accusation	Response
1. Heresy – Joan claims she had direct communication with God and his saints	1. She accepted her visions are St. Michael, St. Gabriel, St. Catherine, and St. Margaret, have sent been sent by God, and will not defer or submit to the Church (Militant).
2. Heresy – Joan claims a saint gave her a sign	2. She stated to Charles that she had a sign from St. Michael to have him crowned king of France
3. Heresy – Joan claims to have visits with saints	3. She stated she received visits from St. Michael, St. Catherine, and St. Margaret.
4. Sorcery – Joan communes with the devil	4. She prophesized that France will perform great exploits under her guidance.
5. Apostasy – By dressing in men's attire she violates Church law	5. She wore men's dress and stated it is from God's command.
6. Heresy – Joan, again, claims to have direct communication and instructions from God and his saints	6. She stated that she did no acts except under instruction from revelation and the order of God, including having the banner with "Jhesus Maria" written on it and the sign of the cross.
7. Apostasy – violation of Church law	7. She abandoned her parents at age 17 to seek a knight (de Baudricourt of Vaucouleurs) under the saints' instructions.
8. Apostasy – violation of Church law – attempted suicide	8. She threw herself from a "very high tower" – in order to escape.
9. Sorcery – Joan communes with the devil	9. If she stayed virgin/pure in body and soul, St. Catherine and St. Margaret promised her she would go to Paradise.

10. Apostacy and Heresy – Joan claims she knows what God favors and communicates with him	10. God loves Charles and the French, speaks French and not English, and does not favor either the English or Burgundians.
11. Heresy – Joan claims she knows the difference between saints and the devil	11. She stated that she knows that St. Michael, St. Gabriel, St. Catherine, and St. Margaret come from God and are not evil.
12. Schism – Joan refuses to consent to Church authorities	12. If the Church wishes her to do something and it is contrary to the orders she states comes from God, she will not consent to the Church's instructions.

These were distilled from the 70 original Acts of Accusation drafted April 5, 1431 and formally delivered to her on May 2, 1431. In summary, she was accused of being "a heretic, sorceress, schismatic and apostate."

The original text of the 12 Accusations runs to five pages of lengthy, medieval French. Written by ecclesiastical and legal experts, a summary is clearly warranted.

10. MARK TWAIN'S OBSERVATIONS ON JOAN OF ARC FROM HIS BOOK, *PERSONAL RECOLLECTIONS OF JOAN OF ARC*, 1896

Mark Twain is arguably America's most famous author, as well as the writer who most personifies what it meant to be an American in the late 19th century. His stories – and views – resonate today as they did then. Stories like Tom Sawyer and Huck Finn are staples of not just juvenile readings and film, but still read as classics for literature. Twain was noted for his denunciation of slavery and racism, opposition to imperialism, and support of women's rights, labor rights, and political accountability. His standpoints made him a target for lifelong abuse and represented only a tiny minority of popular opinion.

His historical novel, Personal Recollections of Joan of Arc, has been seldom printed or even known today, compared to many of his other works. However, it was not only Twain's favorite book, but the one that he spent the most time on – twelve years. His efforts to research the details as accurately as possible led him to review the transcripts of Joan's trials and investigations. Further, he cross-checked details of her life and times with the period's leading experts, as referenced after the title page. It was also the last full novel he wrote (1896). To ensure the book was evaluated based on its merits rather than being connected to his famous name, he published it anonymously with the author listed as the Sieur Louis de Conte (Joan's page and secretary).

When asked about his accuracy on the events portrayed, the famous satirist and humorist responded, "I never attributed an act to the Maid herself that was not strictly historical, and I never put a sentence in her mouth which she had not uttered." With Joan, Mark Twain was completely serious.

Perhaps more than anything else that Twain produced in his life, his work on Joan epitomized his genius and passion for writing. He poured himself into Joan's life because he believed that she was "the most noble life that was ever born into this world save only One." Twain was known as a religious skeptic and critic of established churches. The reader is therefore immediately struck by the sense of awe and wonder he felt for his subject. From start to finish, he was inspired by her personal achievements and held her in reverence.

Twain's preface for the "Recollections" not only outlines his views on Joan, but remains relevant to this day. Some elements of modern society delight in tearing apart the efforts and achievements of historic figures, whom they judge as failing to meet today's more exacting standards and mores. Their condemnation is directed at Joan, George Washington, Abraham Lincoln, and any other person of renown whose motives and actions are re-interpreted by values divorced from the situations under which they labored. Twain's thoughts bear repeating in total and are worthy of our reflection:

To arrive at a just estimate of a renowned man's character one must judge it by the standards of his time, not ours. Judged by the standards of one century, the noblest characters of an earlier one lose much of their luster; judged by the standards of to-day, there is probably no illustrious man of four or five centuries ago whose character could meet the test at all points. But the character of Joan of Arc is unique. It can be measured by the standards of all times without misgiving or apprehension as to the result. Judged by any of them, judged by all of them, it is still flawless, it is still ideally perfect; it still occupies the loftiest place possible to human attainment, a loftier one than has been reached by any other mere mortal.

When we reflect that her century was the brutalest, the wickedest, the rottenest in history since the darkest ages, we are lost in wonder at the miracle of such a product from such a soil. The contrast between her and her century is the contrast between day and night. She was truthful when lying was the common speech of men; she was honest when honesty was become a lost virtue; she was a keeper of promises when the keeping of a promise was expected of no one; she gave her great mind to great thoughts and great purposes when other great minds wasted themselves on pretty fancies or upon poor ambitions; she was modest, and fine, and delicate when to be loud and coarse might be said to be universal; she was full of pity when a merciless cruelty was the rule; she was steadfast when stability was unknown, and honorable in an age which had forgotten what honor was; she was a rock of convictions in a time when men believed in nothing and scoffed at all things; she was unfailingly true in an age that was false to the core; she maintained her personal dignity unimpaired in an age of fawnings and servilities; she was of a dauntless courage when hope and courage had perished in the hearts of her nation; she was spotlessly pure in mind and body when society in the highest places was foul in both – she was all these things in an age when crime was the common business of lords and princes, and when the highest personages in Christendom were able to astonish even that infamous era and make it stand aghast at the spectacle of their atrocious lives black with unimaginable treacheries, butcheries, and beastialities.

She was perhaps the only entirely unselfish person whose name has a place in profane history. No vestige or suggestion of self-seeking can be found in any word or deed of hers. When she had rescued her King from his vagabondage, and set his crown upon his head, she was offered rewards and honors, but she refused them all, and would take nothing. All she would take for herself – if the King would grant it – was leave to go back to her village home, and tend her sheep again, and feel her mother's arms about her, and to be her housemaid and helper. The selfishness of this unspoiled general of victorious armies, companion of princes, and idol of applauding and grateful nation, reached but that far and no further.

The work wrought by Joan of Arc may fairly be regarded as ranking any recorded in history, when one considers the conditions under which it was undertaken, the obstacles in the way, and the means at her disposal. Caesar carried conquest far, but he did it with the trained and confident veterans of Rome, and was a trained soldier himself; and Napoleon swept away the disciplined armies of Europe, but he also was a trained soldier, and he began his work with patriot battalions inflamed and inspired by the miracle-working new breath of Liberty breathed upon them by the Revolution – eager young apprentices to the splendid trade of war, not old and broken men-at-arms, despairing survivors of an age-long accumulation of monotonous defeats; but Joan of Arc, a mere child in years, ignorant, unlettered, a poor village girl unknown and without influence, found a great nation lying in chains, helpless and hopeless under an alien domination, its treasury bankrupt, its soldiers disheartened and dispersed, all spirit torpid, all courage dead in the hearts of the people through long years of foreign and domestic outrage and oppression, their King cowed, resigned to its fate, and preparing to fly the country; and she laid her hand upon this nation, this corpse, and it rose and followed her. She led it from victory to victory, she turned back the tide of the Hundred Years' War, she fatally crippled the English power, and died with the earned title of DELIVERER OF FRANCE, which she bears to this day.

And for all reward, the French King, whom she had crowned, stood supine and indifferent, while French priests took the noble child, the most innocent, the most lovely, the most adorable the ages have produced, and burned her alive at the stake.

11. LINCOLN'S GETTYSBURG ADDRESS, NOVEMBER 19, 1863

A final appendix is Abraham Lincoln's Gettysburg Address. Though only 271 words long and taking about two minutes to read, this address is remembered as perhaps the greatest speech in American history. For generations, school children were taught it and often asked to recite it formally in front of fellow students, teachers, and parents. This brief speech captures all that is great that America is supposed to be – and was trying to be – a new type of nation that was free, equal, dedicated, showed honor, maintained faith, and gave hope. Discussing America in 2020, Lincoln's words of common sense are a fitting conclusion to these descriptions of character, statesmanship, faith, and opportunity for today

Of five known copies of Lincoln's speech, all are slightly different. One version, given to George Bancroft, is noted as the "Bliss copy," and it was the second copy given to Bancroft. In contrast to the others, it was actually signed by Lincoln. It is the copy kept at the White House today.

Four score and seven years ago our fathers brought forth on this continent, a new nation, conceived in Liberty, and dedicated to the proposition that all men are created equal.

Now we are engaged in a great civil war, testing whether that nation, or any nation so conceived and so dedicated, can long endure. We are met on a great battle-field of that war. We have come to dedicate a portion of that field, as a final resting place for those who here gave their lives that that nation might live. It is altogether fitting and proper that we should do this.

But, in a larger sense, we can not dedicate – we can not consecrate – we can not hallow – this ground. The brave men, living and dead, who struggled here, have consecrated it, far above our poor power to add or detract. The world will little note, nor long remember what we say here, but it can never forget what they did here. It is for us the living, rather, to be dedicated here to the unfinished work which they who fought here have thus far so nobly advanced. It is rather for us to be here dedicated to the great task remaining before us – that from these honored dead we take increased devotion to that cause for which they gave the last full measure of devotion – that we here highly resolve that these dead shall not have died in vain – that this nation, under God, shall have a new birth of freedom – and that government of the people, by the people, for the people, shall not perish from the earth."

Abraham Lincoln //s//

12. PRESIDENT BIDEN'S INAUGURAL ADDRESS, JANUARY 20, 2021 [143]

This is America's day. This is democracy's day. A day of history and hope, of renewal and resolve. Through a crucible for the ages, America has been tested anew and America has risen to the challenge. Today we celebrate the triumph not of a candidate but of a cause, a cause of democracy. The people – the will of the people – has been heard and the will of the people has been heeded.

We've learned again that democracy is precious, democracy is fragile and, at this hour my friends, democracy has prevailed. So now on this hallowed ground where just a few days ago violence sought to shake the Capitol's very foundations, we come together as one nation under God – indivisible – to carry out the peaceful transfer of power as we have for more than two centuries.

I've just taken a sacred oath each of those patriots have taken. The oath first sworn by George Washington. But the American story depends not on any one of us, not on some of us, but on all of us. On we the people who seek a more perfect union. This is a great nation; we are good people. And over the centuries through storm and strife in peace and in war we've come so far. But we still have far to go.

We'll press forward with speed and urgency for we have much to do in this winter of peril and significant possibility. Much to do, much to heal, much to restore, much to build and much to gain. Few people in our nation's history have been more challenged or found a time more challenging or difficult than the time we're in now. A once in a century virus that silently stalks the country has taken as many lives in one year as in all of World War Two.

---

143   The speech as presented, rather than the officially released version.

Millions of jobs have been lost. Hundreds of thousands of businesses closed. A cry for racial justice, some 400 years in the making, moves us. The dream of justice for all will be deferred no longer. A cry for survival comes from the planet itself, a cry that can't be any more desperate or any more clear now. The rise of political extremism, white supremacy, domestic terrorism, that we must confront and we will defeat.

To overcome these challenges, to restore the soul and secure the future of America, requires so much more than words. It requires the most elusive of all things in a democracy – unity. In another January on New Year's Day in 1863 Abraham Lincoln signed the Emancipation Proclamation. When he put pen to paper the president said, and I quote, "if my name ever goes down in history, it'll be for this act, and my whole soul is in it."

My whole soul is in it today, on this January day. My whole soul is in this. Bringing America together, uniting our people, uniting our nation. And I ask every American to join me in this cause. Uniting to fight the foes we face – anger, resentment, and hatred. Extremism, lawlessness, violence, disease, joblessness, and hopelessness.

With unity we can do great things, important things. We can right wrongs, we can put people to work in good jobs, we can teach our children in safe schools. We can overcome the deadly virus, we can rebuild work, we can rebuild the middle class and make work secure, we can secure racial justice and we can make America once again the leading force for good in the world.

I know speaking of unity can sound to some like a foolish fantasy these days. I know the forces that divide us are deep and they are real. But I also know they are not new. Our history has been a constant struggle between the American ideal, that we are all created equal, and the harsh ugly reality that racism, nativism, and fear have torn us apart. The battle is perennial and victory is never secure.

Through civil war, the Great Depression, World War, 9/11, through struggle, sacrifice, and setback, our better angels have always prevailed. In each of our moments enough of us have come together to carry all of us forward and we can do that now. History, faith, and reason show the way. The way of unity.

We can see each other not as adversaries but as neighbors. We can treat each other with dignity and respect. We can join forces, stop the shouting and lower the temperature. For without unity there is no peace, only bitterness and fury, no progress, only exhausting outrage. No nation, only a state of chaos. This is our historic moment of crisis and challenge. And unity is the path forward. And we must meet this moment as the United States of America.

If we do that, I guarantee we will not failed [sic]. We have never, ever, ever failed in American when we've acted together. And so today at this time in this place, let's start afresh, all of us. Let's begin to listen to one another again, hear one another, see one another. Show respect to one another. Politics doesn't have to be a raging fire destroying everything in its path. Every disagreement doesn't have to be a cause for total war and we must reject the culture in which facts themselves are manipulated and even manufactured.

My fellow Americans, we have to be different than this. We have to be better than this and I believe America is so much better than this. Just look around. Here we stand in the shadow of the Capitol dome. As mentioned earlier, completed in the shadow of the Civil War. When the union itself was literally hanging in the balance. We endure, we prevail. Here we stand looking out on the great Mall, where Dr King spoke of his dream.

Here we stand, where 108 years ago at another inaugural, thousands of protesters tried to block brave women marching for the right to vote. And today we mark the swearing in of the first woman elected to national office, Vice President Kamala Harris. Don't tell me things can't change. Here we stand where heroes who gave the last full measure of devotion rest in eternal peace.

And here we stand just days after a riotous mob thought they could use violence to silence the will of the people, to stop the work of our democracy, to drive us from this sacred ground. It did not happen, it will never happen, not today, not tomorrow, not ever. Not ever. To all those who supported our campaign, I'm humbled by the faith you placed in us. To all those who did not support us, let me say this. Hear us out as we move forward. Take a measure of me and my heart.

If you still disagree, so be it. That's democracy. That's America. The right to dissent peacefully. And the guardrail of our democracy is perhaps our nation's greatest strength. If you hear me clearly, disagreement must not lead to disunion. And I pledge this to you. I will be a President for all Americans, all Americans. And I promise you I will fight for those who did not support me as for those who do.

Many centuries ago, St Augustine – the saint of my church – wrote that a people was (sic) a multitude defined by the common objects of their love. Defined by the common objects of their love. What are the common objects we as Americans love, that define us as Americans? I think we know. Opportunity, security, liberty, dignity, respect, honor, and yes, the truth.

Recent weeks and months of have taught us a painful lesson. There is a truth and there are lies. Lies told for power and for profit. And each of us has a duty and a responsibility as citizens as Americans and especially as leaders. Leaders who are pledged to honor our Constitution to protect our nation. To defend the truth and defeat the lies.

Look, I understand that many of my fellow Americans view the future with fear and trepidation. I understand they worry about their jobs. I understand like their dad they lay in bed at night staring at the ceiling thinking: 'Can I keep my healthcare? Can I pay my mortgage?' Thinking about their families, about what comes next. I promise you; I get it. But the answer's not to turn inward. To retreat into competing factions. Distrusting those who don't look like you, or worship the way you do, who don't get their news from the same source as you do.

We must end this uncivil war that pits red against blue, rural versus urban, conservative versus liberal. We can do this if we open our souls instead of hardening our hearts, if we show a little tolerance and humility, and if we're willing to stand in the other person's shoes, as my mom would say. Just for a moment, stand in their shoes.

Because here's the thing about life. There's no accounting for what fate will deal you. Some days you need a hand. There are other days when we're called to lend a hand. That's how it has to be, that's what we do for one another. And if we are that way our country will be stronger, more prosperous, more ready for the future. And we can still disagree.

My fellow Americans, in the work ahead of us we're going to need each other. We need all our strength to persevere through this dark winter. We're entering what may be the darkest and deadliest period of the virus. We must set aside politics and finally face this pandemic as one nation, one nation. And I promise this, as the Bible says, 'Weeping may endure for a night, joy cometh in the morning.' We will get through this together. Together.

Look folks, all my colleagues I serve with in the House and the Senate up here, we all understand the world is watching. Watching all of us today. So, here's my message to those beyond our borders. America has been tested and we've come out stronger for it. We will repair our alliances, and engage with the world once again. Not to meet yesterday's challenges but today's and tomorrow's challenges. And we'll lead not merely by the example of our power but the power of our example.

Fellow Americans, moms, dads, sons, daughters, friends, neighbors and co-workers. We will honor them by becoming the people and the nation we can and should be. So, I ask you let's say a silent prayer for those who lost their lives, for those left behind and for our country. Amen.

Folks, it's a time of testing. We face an attack on our democracy, and on truth, a raging virus, a stinging inequity, systematic racism, a climate in crisis, America's role in the world. Any one of these would be enough to challenge us in profound ways. But the fact is we face them all at once, presenting this nation with one of the greatest responsibilities we've had. Now we're going to be tested. Are we going to step up?

It's time for boldness for there is much to do. And this is certain, I promise you. We will be judged, you and I, by how we resolve these cascading crises of our era. We will rise to the occasion. Will we master this rare and difficult hour? Will we meet our obligations and pass along a new and better world to our children? I believe we must and I'm sure you do as well. I believe we will, and when we do, we'll write the next great chapter in the history of the United States of America. The American story.

A story that might sound like a song that means a lot to me; it's called American Anthem. And there's one verse that stands out at least for me and it goes like this:

'The work and prayers of centuries have brought us to this day, which shall be our legacy, what will our children say?

Let me know in my heart when my days are through, America, America, I gave my best to you.'

Let us add our own work and prayers to the unfolding story of our great nation. If we do this, then when our days are through, our children and our children's children will say of us: 'They gave their best, they did their duty, they healed a broken land.'

My fellow Americans I close the day where I began, with a sacred oath. Before God and all of you, I give you my word. I will always level with you. I will defend the Constitution; I'll defend our democracy.

I'll defend America and I will give all – all of you – keep everything I do in your service. Thinking not of power but of possibilities. Not of personal interest but of public good.

And together we will write an American story of hope, not fear. Of unity not division, of light not darkness. A story of decency and dignity, love and healing, greatness and goodness. May this be the story that guides us. The story that inspires us. The story that tells ages yet to come that we answered the call of history. We met the moment. Democracy and hope, truth and justice, did not die on our watch but thrive.

That America secured liberty at home and stood once again as a beacon to the world. That is what we owe our forbearers, one another, and generations to follow.

So, with purpose and resolve, we turn to those tasks of our time. Sustained by faith, driven by conviction and devoted to one another and the country we love with all our hearts. May God bless America and may God protect our troops.

13. COMMON SENSE IN THE YEAR 2020 AS IT MIGHT HAVE BEEN

This book was originally planned for release by late summer 2020. At the time, the author intended this essay to be Chapter 10. Unfortunately, much of the content was out-of-date by the election of November 3, 2020.

The essential need to rebuild American unity transcends all other issues. Without national unity, many, if not all, of the other challenges facing the country may only be partially resolved or perhaps even prove incapable of being addressed prior to the next election cycle. As pointed out in Chapter 5, Lincoln stated: "A house divided against itself cannot stand." The purpose of this appendix is to outline some of the other secondary challenges, outside of Chapter 10, that face the USA and how, with unity, they may possibly be resolved.

Indeed, beyond solving specific problems, the approaches suggested below are potential opportunities to build national unity and long-term economic prosperity. An added benefit of these suggestions is that they would produce similar spillover benefits for other democracies. Intentionally, the most divisive or emotional issues are not addressed; it is best to focus on what is possible first and build momentum before tackling the most vexing challenges.

Yet, success in any of these issues can only happen if President Biden has the ability to convince the majority of the nation to think of themselves as Americans first, rather than Republicans or Democrats – or any other polarizing group identity. And he must convince both parties of Congress to work with each other and him. The reader may notice that parts of this appendix overlap with Chapter 10, its replacement. However, several sections have been revised to minimize duplication while preserving the key points. Further, minor changes have been added to bring it up-to-date since November 2020, such as identifying President Biden by name and the roll-out of Covid vaccines.

What if?
Common Sense in the Year 2020 – an Extended Essay

"These are the times that try men's souls. The summer soldier and sunshine patriot will, in this crisis, shrink from the service of his country; but he that stands it NOW, deserves the love and thanks of man and woman." Thomas Paine's words of long ago once again bring to focus the challenges of today's world. His words ring as true today as when written. Everyone can identify multiple problems that currently plague the world.

Granted, there are always naysayers and those who disagree with the status quo. But today, consensus has grown on the primary challenges that disturb the vast majority of people – not only in the United States, but across a world of nearly 8 billion. Now is not the time to sit back, watch, and wait; it is time to act, as the leaders profiled in this book did – leaving us examples of the way forward.

Major political issues today contrast markedly with those of the past. Rather than reacting to a direct attack that threatens the existence of the country or a disaster that requires an immediate response, current crises are contemplated from the comfort of one's living room – or smartphone. The United States stands not as the weak, undeveloped country of the Constitutional days or a developing, self-absorbed young nation of the mid-19th century. The country ended the 20th century and began the 21st as the world's foremost power.

Presently, the country has the highest standard of living in history, no enemies capable of invading, and a culture of freedom and rights that provide opportunities unmatched any time in history. It remains easy to believe this situation will continue indefinitely. And when elected political leaders assure citizens that there is no need to make sacrifices or change the way society operates, the willingness to look beyond the horizon continues to be limited. Yet, that viewpoint is merely an illusion.

Elected leaders have long ignored the obvious. Obstacles ahead, if left unattended, have the potential to rival the social disruptions of the Revolution, the Civil War, or the surprise attack on Pearl Harbor that resulted in the U.S. entry into the Second World War. At those moments, national leaders stepped up, directly faced the challenges, and honestly exhorted the country to make the efforts and sacrifices essential to overcome them. Accordingly, the necessary actions were taken, and success happened. The difference today is that bitter partisan politics reign and inertia results. Partisanship predominates as the rule of the land just as Washington feared – and warned of in his Farewell Address.

Addressing challenges systematically do not happen by anyone or any single institution working alone – the president, Congress, the United Nations, or any influential overseas political leader. The problems are considered so big, so difficult, and require so much effort that elected officials with the requisite responsibility and authority do not know where to start. The typical responses are to ignore the problems or address only the margins of an issue for re-election purposes.

Consequently, many challenges remain unresolved, and the root causes persist. The causes or faults are irrelevant, as the challenges multiply and become increasingly knotty. In the meantime, elected leaders blame political opponents for inaction or incorrect solutions while doing little themselves when they assume authority. Whether one considers slavery in the U.S., or the rise of totalitarian states in the 1930s, there are many examples where failure to act on new, obvious problems required far greater expenditures of lives and treasure to solve when action finally was undertaken.

The clearest example of leadership failure in American history was the primary unsettled issue since independence – slavery. Elected leaders were unable or unwilling to cooperate to peacefully resolve slavery, directly precipitating the U.S. Civil War. Presidents and legislators between the Missouri Compromise of 1820 and forty years later showed themselves to be, regrettably, all too similar to their counterparts facing today's political situation. As with many of my generation, I often gain a valuable, different perspective by discussing current events with my children. My daughter discusses recent U.S. political leaders as having chosen "willful ignorance," consciously turning blind eyes to the considerable quandaries facing the country and her American future.

The brief episodes this book relates to George Washington, Abraham Lincoln, and Joan of Arc plainly demonstrate that they confronted nearly impossible obstacles at both the personal and national level. These challenges were every bit as daunting as anything facing America today. Yet, they conducted themselves differently than elected officials of the present.

Each firmly fronted and openly addressed difficult challenges head on. They focused on the essential and let the extraneous fall in place when or if it did not interfere with the central need. Personal experiences had already developed their character; their actions when "men's souls" were tried only continued to further test and strengthen them. These three, as have others – before and since – did not shirk from toiling step by step, even when working alone.

Rather, they built support, unity, and momentum because they knew what was the right thing to do. They refused to procrastinate, but instead welcomed and accepted responsibility, shared their visions, and used whatever tools they could muster exerting willpower to bring change and achieve a goal. And none of them ever encountered an easy road. Their beliefs were sorely tried; many were the opportunities to just give up. Yet, they were not summer soldiers or sunshine patriots. Even at the risk of their lives (which, indeed, two of them lost for their causes), they continued forward with their very last efforts – and breaths – to see their convictions acted upon.

One basic theme encapsulates exactly what Washington, Lincoln, and Joan accomplished to realize their goals. This trio created unity. They kept their mission simple and focused. [144]

Washington twice convinced diverse groups of colonists – first to become soldiers to take on the most powerful army in the world and later to become citizens of a democratic, united country.

Lincoln inherited a nation that had broken apart after decades of acrimonious infighting and simmering hostilities. He inspired its citizens not only to reunite following a horrific civil war, but to open the road to equality for all its citizens.

Joan came out of nowhere and performed astonishing miracles unimagined before her arrival. In a few short months, she had the former Dauphin crowned King of France after leading his newly assembled army to a series of victories over a previously unbeaten English army in France.

---

144 Today's popular business and military acronym, KISS, captures the same concept – keep it short and simple.

She set Charles VII on a trajectory that would liberate France and see him rule for over 30 years.

Unity — the ability to lead a large group to focus on one simple, clear goal stands as that indispensable prerequisite for all great deeds. These three each displayed strength of character, ironclad belief in the justice of their cause, and the skill to mobilize every possible resource to bring lofty ideals to reality. Consequently, they — with their inspired supporters — overcame and moved forward.

The challenge of unity is what President Biden discussed as his primary goal in his Inauguration Address. He recognizes the same necessity as our subjects did; now the question before him and the country is how he will confront this primary challenge.

Compounding the president's task is the need to address many of these deep-rooted secondary issues, any of which could alone be overwhelming. None has arisen recently; too long has been the time that people in authority have neglected, temporized, or equivocated rather than taking advantage of the circumstances available.

Consequently, the situations grow ever more complicated. Worse, since September 11, 2001, the world appears to be accelerating into chaos with the side-effects of this willing ignorance — endless wars, terrorism, mass migrations and pandemics. The U.S. and other governments have ignored the perils of inaction — and disunity. Should it be business as usual or are we selfishly dropping the burden which current citizens ought to bear? Stated simply, the Road to Hell is lined with good intentions — unless President Biden makes decisive choices for action and resolution.

The following is a partial list of enduring challenges that applies not only to the United States, but also to much of the rest of the world. Yet without American leadership, major global initiatives that are in accord with our beliefs and priorities are quite unlikely. Our country has the opportunity to lead a united response, nationally and internationally just as we have before, rather than proceeding along a path of complacency.

This moment in time also provides the potential for the country to regain many of the best attributes of our national past, moral and economic — once they are addressed. As with the secondary challenges described in Chapter 10, resolution of these can contribute to building national unity and providing a new foundation for directing our attention to the rapidly evolving future.

Still, the primary effort must be focused on American unity. The country needs to speak with one voice, one that includes the majority of citizens from all parties and beliefs. At the same time, dissenting voices have to be acknowledged. Otherwise, no chance exists to lead a national response to address any long-term challenges. Further, no change is possible, even if the vast majority of citizens support the president, unless the president proves capable of convincing *both* parties in Congress to support his and their *joint* initiatives.

To make progress, the unity that Washington and Lincoln brought has to return. Unity will occur far faster if the president combines a drive for unity with control of the pandemic and economic development. Succeeding with these measures will allow America to set our affairs into reasonable order. With that base established, America can begin to rectify other pressing challenges that have the potential to be turned into opportunities for continued unity.

Accordingly, a short listing of many of the key persisting, secondary challenges is appropriate. These items noted are not the fiery emotional issues, but are suggested for resolution because they have the most scope for potential solutions if Congress and the executive work together. [145]

Therefore, the list is not intended to be an inclusive compilation of every challenge nor a debate on the arguments about scope or priority. The concept is simple and to the point: issues and questions exist with all of these areas. They are incapable of being solved by narrow, fleeting majorities in one or both elected branches. Addressing them with a broad coalition will provide either the possibility of a consensus solution, or evidence that what is possible is not worth the cost or effort. Or in other words, making common sense decisions.

---

145 The author will therefore not attempt to address the nation's most "red-hot," divisive, or polarizing issues including: abortion, gun control, judicial reform, Supreme Court expansion or reconfiguration, sexual harassment, reparations for slavery, D.C. statehood, social media censorship, the bias/ fairness and responsibility of the press, or others raising similar passions. The strongly opposing viewpoints these issues bring about renders them quite unlikely for near-term cooperation and unity. However, with progress on other secondary issues, the same may occur with these.

To simplify the approach, the author will present challenges in two different groups of problems. One group is related to Americans' – and humanity's – physical presence on planet Earth. Solutions to these can be technical and objective based on science and programs that already work.

The second group is related to policies that affect politics, economics, and society. Many of the words and phrases that define the issues carry so much meaning, incite so much emotion, and so motivate special interests that they have often been confined to the "too hard" basket at the political level. Resolution or attempting to systematically tackle them has not occurred. The solutions to this group are subjective and require cooperation, compromise, and consensus to support real change. Those outcomes can result only from decentralized efforts across the country and provide time to implement rather than directives from aloof people sitting in distant seats at the nation's capital.

Group one issues include: population, extinction of species and diseases, energy, water, and consumer needs and infrastructure. Intentionally left unsaid is the divisive issue of climate change. If measures are implemented on the above issues, they will impact existing man-induced changes far more quickly and effectively than any bureaucratic agreement that does not include all parties or address the commercial and cultural impacts of change. The genius of America has always stepped up when necessity demands. Now is such a time.

Group two issues, enumerated below, concern policies that affect how we live: population, employment and the economy, government funding (specifically: taxes, budgets, and donations/ lobbyists), education, national service, public services (police and medical), immigration, racism, and foreign affairs. Finally, as George Washington emphasized, foreign relationships should focus on maximizing commerce, minimizing involvement in others' politics, and yet maintaining our *moral* leadership

A concise list, summarizing each group of issues, follows along with some context and concludes with a synopsis of potential solutions.

Population. In 1960, the U.S. population numbered under 180 million people; today, it totals over 330 million. Within a lifetime, the amount has almost doubled. Worldwide, it had just hit 3 billion by 1960; today, it has grown to nearly 8 billion, closer to tripling. Though not possible to quantify even in America, in 1960 the average family had far fewer of today's modern conveniences. Consequently, growth over the past 60 years means not merely a near doubling of resources needed to sustain the country, it means consumption and the resources required are several times higher.

Whereas the majority of the world lived at a subsistence level in 1960, today's world contains a "middle class" of billions and only a much smaller percentage of society making a minimal impact on resources. Finally, with current trends America's and the world's population will only get larger in the short-term.

Even if technology and innovation can continue to support a growing population, real questions concerning our quality of life – infrastructure, schools, medical, traffic, houses versus apartments – need to be asked to determine what is optimal. Lastly, officials should question how this increasing stress of crowding will affect societies and their competition for resources.

Extinction. Human population levels directly pertain to our ability to live alongside the rest of the world's species amid our ever-increasing demands for a finite group of shared resources. Other than domestic or farm animals, it is certain that nearly all large mammals are disappearing from the wild. Large, open spaces capable of supporting interconnected communities of large mammals are required for survival, let alone the ability to thrive. These conditions existed long before mankind expanded to billions, but simply do not remain, anywhere. This was different as recently as the 1960s.

The same can be said for birds, amphibians, reptiles, key insects like bumblebees – which directly support plant life and humanity, and many other invertebrates – in other words, complete ecosystems. In the oceans, despite varied small-scale efforts to set up reserves, the high-tech fishing fleets of this country and the world scour more and more of the oceans, seas, and rivers. Some species have been fished out in a short span of time.

There are indications that the bedrock species of the oceans, corals and plankton, have begun a downward spiral due to the pressure on their ecosystems. If, or once, they disappear, it is impossible to predict with any accuracy what that may mean for the rest of the world. Nearly all ocean life depends on both to flourish; without them over 70% of the Earth's surface will be very different.

A subsection of extinction also relates directly to humanity, **epidemic diseases**. One can safely predict that as animals and people live closer together, events like Covid-19, SARS, Ebola, and AIDs will become more frequent – and could be much worse as the Black Death proved to be. [146]. Today's series of epidemics beginning with AIDs in the 1980s indicate this progression is underway already despite our advances in medicine – and whether coincidence or not with our rapidly growing populations and demand for resources. Common sense suggests more than a coincidence.

Energy. Since the 1973 energy crisis, companies and nations have invested heavily in "clean" energy, like wind, solar, geothermal, tidal, and nuclear. Their total output increases and slowly grows as a percentage of overall power usage.

However, since the Industrial Revolution began more than two hundred years ago, the demands for the three key drivers of power: coal, oil, and natural gas, also continue to rise, but at a higher rate. Coal usage has doubled since 1960 and tripled since 1920. In the same periods, oil use has tripled and climbed a factor of ten over the past century. Natural gas has quadrupled and soared by close to a factor of twenty over this last hundred years.

Hydro power has risen fourfold since the 1960s, but has issues with degradation of the local environments and may have reached its practical capacity.

Nuclear power has had no real growth in the past decades as the Three Mile Island and Chernobyl incidents virtually ended all new development.

---

146 Though little remembered, the Black Death pandemic swept through Europe, North Africa, and much of Asia beginning in 1346. The one constant throughout these outbreaks was that they occurred not only in crowded cities but also in rural areas. Other plagues throughout history have done the same. All too often, they were accompanied by additional tragedies like natural disasters, starvation, and social upheavals due to the inability of societies to react once stability was upset. A consistent characteristic that compounds such disasters are too many people on too much marginal land. Today, disasters with wildfires, hurricanes, floods, or pandemics occur more frequently than ever despite our ability to be better prepared and may be a harbinger for a crowded, interconnected world. The second note in Chapter 9 recounts more detail – and horrors – of this medieval pandemic.

Politically, it is difficult to envision that the fears of its disadvantages will outweigh its useful possibilities.

The other renewable sources remain uncompetitive commercially and generally useful only as a supplement rather than a reliable source day in and day out. The summary is simple. Fossil fuel usage escalates every year, while renewables generate barely a total 10% of power generation. Greater population and more middle-class consumers will mean increased demand for the immediate future.

Water. The one indispensable natural resource that all animals and humans require is water. Over 96% of the Earth's water remains locked in the oceans and seas – salt water. That is great for ocean dwelling fish, mammals, and invertebrates, but not so good for human consumption or farming. Of the less than 4% that exists as fresh water, over half of that is held in the polar ice caps and world's glaciers.

Well under 2% of planetary water flows in all the rivers, lakes, and aquifers on the planet. As any Midwestern farmer knows, the great aquifers underlying the U.S. have shrunk dramatically in both size and quality over the past few decades. Former great rivers like the Colorado and Rio Grande often fail to reach the sea now due to over-extraction. With more demand for crops, more need for irrigation, the need to replenish rivers, lakes, and aquifers, while keeping in mind the vagaries of weather, means we are never able to replace what we remove.

And the U.S. is lucky. Its population has experienced a lower rate of increase than the rest of the world and has far more technical resources and climate advantages that minimize waste and loss. Much of the rest of the world, especially in places that have marginal or unsuitable climates for farming, have had massive increases in population, especially their cities and middle classes. Water already occupies a critical element in the disagreements between nation-states and the demand for more will only increase. The water wars depicted in old cowboy movies give an indication of what happened 150 years ago, as well as what can eventuate if the population involved measures not in the hundreds, but in millions. A recent example of failed stewardship is the freshwater Aral Sea in central Asia which has lost more than 90% of its volume since the 1960s and is largely composed of desert now.

Three more pieces of the puzzle that form part of our human race's footprint involve what we now require to support ourselves above and beyond food and water. An accurate set of terms would be consumer needs, infrastructure, and the resulting pollution of our environment.

Consumer needs can be defined as contents of one's house, yard, personal transportation, and the places visited for entertainment. **Infrastructure** would be housing, businesses, roads, bridges, and the planes and ships that connect points together. Two or three generations ago, mankind's effect in these areas stayed relatively minor. Part was due to our much smaller population. Further, most personal items were reused and capable of regenerating back into the earth. Infrastructure was rarely permanent and when it was, it covered a relatively small part of the planet – due to fewer people and a simpler lifestyle.

That is not the case today. Most consumer items consist of only a tiny percentage that is reusable or repairable. They are far more complicated, requiring more effort to source raw materials and manufacture them. Fragility and obsolescence mean these items have relatively short lifespans. Development sees them consumed by an expanding percentage of mankind's ever-increasing numbers. Globalization has connected the world, raised billions out of poverty, and allowed every country, no matter how small or poor, to have more of the inventions that raise the standards of living and life expectancy.

But evidence of humanity's hand is everywhere. [147] One can fly in an airplane around the world and whether day or night, summer or winter, see that mankind's effect on the land is never far away. And even when walking away from cities in "nature," it is difficult to not see man's impact with every stride taken.

Recent research continues to attest, the 70% of Earth covered in water also displays the residue of our lifestyles in tropical seas, uninhabited polar regions, and along the surface and depths of the oceans and highest

---

147 See satellite photos of North America at night and day.

mountains. Mankind does not pick up after itself; the **pollution** we leave behind on land, water, and air affects all life on our planet. We are the dominant species on earth.

It does not take the president of the United States, the Secretary General of the United Nations, or a learned and respected scientist to state what is plainly obvious – mankind has a responsibility to steward the planet for all species. And our efforts do not bear out that obligation. In other words, common sense has been abandoned in our drive for comfort – or is it dominance?

If inaction persists, these material issues have the potential to seriously transform our habitats and civilizations.

Likely repercussions include increasingly volatile weather, inconsistent food production, and loss of a significant percentage of other life forms. Other far more dire forecasts are also predicted, some of which are supported by the vast majority of professional scientists and their research.

Yet, those results represent just the physical nature of these issues; the social effects on people and countries will be every bit as substantial – again, without action. At best, people would have fewer viable options on where to live, prospects for resource-based conflict will escalate, and the pace of change will only accelerate, unless all the above problems shrink promptly. Again, it comes down to common sense.

More people mean greater demand for food, energy, water, consumer items, and infrastructure, as well as the eventual disposal once past their use, whether as large as container ships or microscopic pieces of plastic that have been found in every environment on earth. The increased likelihood of new, more virulent diseases and loss of biodiversity must also be anticipated. Consequently, all these issues will put pressure on a finite environment and our quality of life. They will continue to increase, and eventually, have a negative impact. One day, we will have to deal with them. Better now, than too late. Lost time can never be made up. In contrast, developing wonder products or figuring costs – and profits – required that are prepared in advance represent a more intelligent way to address issues. [148]

DAY - SATELLITE PHOTO OF NORTH AMERICA – LOOKING BENIGN AND UNSPOILED.

---

148 Numbers and percentages are all open-source figures available on multiple sites for each issue listed, whether via national or international government sites or the companies that use the materials outlined. I leave it to the reader to consult any reputable source as desired. With energy sources, both fossil fuel companies and NGOs that track the energy business, have comparable numbers.

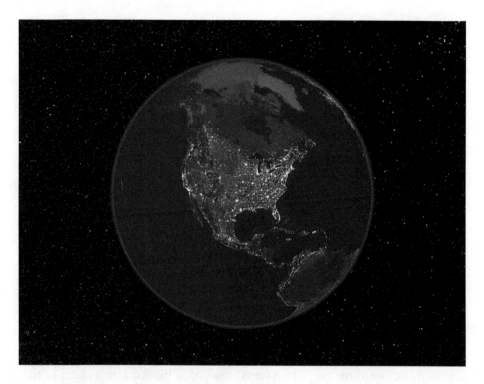

NIGHT - SATELLITE PHOTO OF NORTH AMERICA – SHOWING THE PRESENCE OF
MANKIND EVERYWHERE BUT THE HIGHEST MOUNTAINS AND THE ARCTIC.

The above preceding paragraphs, not so optimistically, give descriptions of what is only Part 1, our physical presence. Part 2 is how we live.

To put that picture in a better perspective one needs to go back to the mid-20th century. After the Second World War, the successful "Great Powers" agreed, unanimously, that the world could not undergo another such catastrophe. With the support of every other country, including the defeated aggressors who joined later, the United Nations (UN) was established to ensure that our future would be different.

Major geopolitical problems would be sorted by the five primary victors of the Second World War, the U.S., the Soviet Union, China, Britain, and France – as permanent members of the Security Council, augmented by ten other nations on seats rotated among countries drawn from the balance of the UN's general membership. [149] The basic concepts were that peace was preferable to war, and that the UN would work together to ensure the world stayed that way. Further, the Great Powers also agreed to support colonies' efforts to achieve self-determination in accordance with the 1941 Atlantic Charter. The UN also agreed to support global improvement of political, economic, and social conditions. [150]

There has never been a third World War and the vast majority of the world has succeeded in achieving political self-determination. Yet, the UN's great powers and Security Council have seldom proved capable of working together to achieve improved conditions for all people everywhere. Overall improvements have come to pass, but not due to any coordinated plan or actions. Generally, at the UN, one or a block of nations veto actions by another, whether due to self-interest or lack of trust. The Great Powers, themselves, have waged aggressive wars and both supported, or fought to thwart insurgencies.

Political freedoms, economic development, and progressive social movements continue to be inconsistent. Progress in these is frequently marked by one step backward for every two steps forward. This remains as true in the United States as it does in the rest of the world. Despite general advancement, social problems like oppression, inequality, and intolerance have not disappeared. All too often, these have led to setbacks throughout much of the past 75 years.

Smaller, more narrowly focused organizations have been established to work around the UN's inability to adhere to or enforce its charter. NATO, the Warsaw Pact, G-7/20, and other multinational organizations have also failed to compensate for the inability to achieve broad cooperation. The collapse of the bi-polar Cold War era has led to the rise of a number of rogue states. They have chosen to stay outside the bounds of international

---

149   In 1971 the UN General Assembly recognized the People's Republic of China (Beijing) as China's rightful representative, replacing the Republic of China (Taiwan). In 1991 Russia was recognized as the successor to the USSR's seat.

150   The Atlantic Charter was issued on August 14, 1941 by President Franklin Roosevelt and British Prime Minister Winston Churchill. It stated peoples of the world had the right to self-determination, territories would not be seized, and that the rule of law would govern economic and social situations with cooperation to minimize force and want. The UN charter is based on this document.

law and all else that the UN is supposed to stand for and support. These rogues use overt aggression or subversion against their perceived foes. The UN has seldom succeeded to coerce or force such renegades into following the charter's principles of law, order, and justice. Periodically, the U.S. has tried either on its own or with a small group of allies to fix such problems; the results tally as a mixed bag of successes and disasters.

Disappointingly, many countries represented in the UN have limited political freedom, or less. Dictatorships and oligarchies still flourish. Economic choices by the leaders in such countries mean huge inequalities in wealth and standard of living. Basic freedoms guaranteed in the U.S. Bill of Rights, such as Freedoms of Speech, Religion, Assembly, Press, Jury Trial, Voting, and protection against unreasonable searches or arrest are limited or nonexistent. [151]

With globalization and communications technology, nearly everyone in the world is conscious of the safest countries that provide the most opportunity for freedom and wellbeing. People are not stupid. If they can figure out how to reach a better location, as mankind has done over and over for at least 60,000 years, they will move there. Global emigration disrupts and subtracts from the origin countries, while strengthening the target nations, primarily the Western democracies. At the same time the losing nations suffer a steady drain of ambitious, educated young people. This situation only makes it more complicated and more difficult to determine how best to proceed. A consequence is the natural reaction to ignore the broad, worldwide view and focus on a nation's own internal issues. One hundred years ago, where transportation, communication, and inhabitants could have been days or weeks apart, that might have been possible, though by 1939 at latest, that option was demonstrated to be a failure. [152]

---

151 Symbolically, the UN has long allowed its Human Rights Council to be a travesty with some of the worst offenders of the UN charter not merely ignored, but serving on the governing committee. Consequently, these less-than exemplary nations aggressively attack others as bullies do, to cover their own deficiencies by diverting attention and attempting to intimidate their detractors. Such actions, sadly not an isolated case, dismay the idealistic and turn the pragmatic away from the organization.

152 1939 marked the start of the Second World War; nearly every country eventually became involved directly or indirectly. As a result, individuals and countries desire to stay isolated and safe proved impossible.

The failure of UN members to fully utilize the opportunity and live up to the original founding principles only makes the necessary decisions for humanity's future more difficult – assuming that the will to make them even exists. In consequence, much of the real burden to humanity's lot and decision-making often falls to the United States. This heavy load of responsibility is often unwelcome and sometimes deeply resented.

It is easy to not only get depressed about our future, but also to play ostrich and put our collective heads in the sand. In periods when the international order has seemed chaotic – think of wars in Europe – in the U.S. this sentiment has periodically manifested itself as isolationism or has sometimes been called "America First." Current issues appear so immense that in general, they are avoided. Someone else should carry the burden and solve the problems. In other words, the summer soldiers and the sunshine patriots continue to be the ones at the head of our packs. Most Americans choose to accept that "leadership."

But the story continues; there is more to it. Plenty of reasons exist to be confident and optimistic. Today's United States – and the world – supports democracy and opportunity for the largest percentage of humanity in history. The percentage of countries with at least limited democracy is over 50% and encouragingly, is not limited to those from the wealthy democracies, but includes nations and people from all genders, all races, education levels, and economic backgrounds. It remains far from ideal and incurs setbacks. Yet across the board, most people live better and have the potential to raise their children in a more positive world than at any time in the past. And despite being bombarded with negative news, terrible tragedies happening daily, and conspiracies through social media, the world is healthier and more peaceful than any time previously.

Governments, either with and without UN assistance or approval, have worked collectively together to solve many issues. Individuals and small groups or businesses have developed positive solutions to elements of **all** the problems listed earlier. Even without central leadership, there is forward momentum. One could not make that statement in 1945 when the UN was established. Its formation, caused by the human and material losses of the war, represented hopes for a future where the UN could serve as a keystone for peace, sustainable development, and human rights. This recent march of history can give us confidence. It also gives reassurances that in the worst crises, great people have risen to the occasion to exert real change, real improvement like Washington, Lincoln, and Joan.

Where does that leave today's concerned American or World citizen?

One option is to change nothing. Have belief that we will take care of ourselves, whether due to faith in a Higher Being, through mankind's innovation in technology, or by market forces. Of course, the possibility also exists that all the research, measurements, and predictions of what may be occurring, as well as our perceptions, is plain wrong. That would mean that those not willing to investigate or compare old versus current situations were correct all along. Doing nothing remains an option.

However, that option is not common sense. Anyone willing to look with an open mind realizes that some or all of these issues are not sustainable in the long-term, if for no other reason than the earth is of finite size. Not just the aggression of rogue states, but the growth of populism are among the reactions to what many sense have begun to occur. Taking advantage of hard times, blaming others, and promising unrealistic fantasies remain typical responses of tyrants and demagogues ever since civilization began.

This still does not change the imperative that these debts must be paid within the lifetimes of those alive today. In his Second Inaugural Address, Lincoln made this very commitment to erase the institution of slavery; his solution was to offer reconciliation and unity. Our ability to reason is our greatest gift. We should apply reason – common sense – to take advantage of what has been done before to resolve our own debts, to be proactive, and make our country – and world – better places.

Paradoxically, the answers to these complex issues may actually be simple: assemble the best and the brightest of the country [153] and aspire to two goals:

- Reduce our physical footprint in our country, consequently the planet.

- Use our incredible available resources to assist, advise, and support ourselves and like-minded countries willing to help themselves.

There are two relevant precedents in recent 20th century American history where we gathered our greatest minds and most competent individuals – one wartime and technical, the other postwar and political.

In the mid-20th century, the United States faced massive challenges to our existence and the way we hoped to live with the rest of the world. America took action – and succeeded. One precedent involved a technical threat – the potential for development of an atomic bomb by Nazi Germany – that sparked a technological response. The U.S. answered by initiating the Manhattan Project in late 1939. The government organized a public-private partnership to catch up with and surpass the threat posed by the Nazis. Eventually, the U.S. led an international, unified project with Britain, Canada, and staffed with many émigré scientists from Europe. The group created the first atom bombs and ushered in the atomic age, hastening the end of World War II in the Pacific. The United States had become aware of a new challenge and turned what had been considered a science fiction idea into a practical tool – at a fraction of the cost and time needed to successfully invade the Japanese home islands. [154]

The Manhattan Project cost less than $2 billion U.S. in 1945 or equivalent to just over $20 billion today. That cost was equal to less than 10 days

---

153 The term "the Best and the Brightest" originated in the 18th century as satire. Over time, the phrase lost the irony evident in its earliest usage. In the early 1960s, it was used to describe the industry and academic eminences recruited to the administration by President Kennedy who remained to serve President Johnson. As the U.S. military footprint in Vietnam expanded, these intellectuals overruled career officials even as victory remained elusive. The disastrous results of their theoretically brilliant decisions dragged the country into a quagmire that came to define the '60s – and much of President Johnson's legacy. The phrase had inadvertently returned to its earliest, ironic meaning.

Nonetheless, the author believes that successes as the Manhattan Project, the Marshall Plan, or the 19th century Napoleonic Codes provide contrary examples. In a cooperative framework, teams of experts with imaginative leaders can achieve great successes.

154 The discovery of the process to split the nucleus of heavy elements from an atom was discovered by Germans Otto Hahn and Fritz Strassmann in December 1938. This splitting was shown to release untold magnitudes of energy – or destructive power.

of government spending during the Second World War. By comparison, the Afghanistan war has cost close to an estimated $2 trillion dollars with the simultaneous Iraq War costing another $1 - 2 trillion. Notably, these amounts exclude the ongoing costs for many veterans' lifelong care. The results for the Afghani and Iraqi people are somewhere between disappointing and destructive and do not come close to meeting the UN charter's principles.

In contrast, the Manhattan Project saved an estimated one million allied soldiers from death in 1945, as well as the lives of millions of Japanese soldiers and civilians, analysts estimated. The project proved that one could gather many of the world's top scientists, that a common purpose could be set, and that an achievable target could be attained in a reasonable period of time at a relatively reasonable price. And that cost, with imaginative government direction – and recruitment – is far, far less than fighting wars with ships, planes, and soldiers.

The second precedent originated after the Second World War and pertained to the utter devastation that encompassed nearly all of Europe, much of Asia, and parts of the rest of the world. Many nations had been reduced to extreme poverty and even starvation from the cataclysm of the war. The U.S. determined not to repeat the mistakes of the punitive Versailles Treaty that ended World War I and indirectly led to the growth of Nazism and World War II. A contributing factor was the Soviet Union's occupation of Eastern Europe. The idea targeted rebuilding the economies of Europe, Western *and* Eastern, in order for them to regain prosperity and self-sufficiency without American financial support or Soviet occupation.

The U.S. answered these circumstances with comprehensive economic and social efforts called the Marshall Plan and Operation Blacklist. The first covered Western Europe and the second Japan along with a lesser amount of assistance to what became South Korea in 1948. The Marshall Plan focused on ensuring grants went to locals – individuals, companies, and regional authorities. Requestors submitted the equivalent of a business case to secure investment funds for work to be carried out by the people who had the most to gain, the locals. Each country rebuilt themselves – by their own efforts, though with American funding, oversight, and support, *yet* within limited timelines. Deadlines ensured that the U.S. withdrew on schedule and prevented the establishment of U.S.-funded bureaucracies. It remains a classic example of free enterprise utilizing what amounted to a public-private partnership.

President Truman's actions to make the plan happen are worth reviewing. The 1946 Congressional elections returned a total Republican majority that had campaigned to restore fiscal responsibility, lowering taxes, and reducing involvement in world affairs. Truman was a Democrat, yet enlisted Republican support to overcome isolationism and make the Plan a true bipartisan project. Good leadership made the difference.

This framework stands in sharp contrast to recent aid for Afghanistan and Iraq, where much of the funding was granted to central government authorities without a coordinated strategy, without timelines, or processes to monitor proper use and progress. Funds did not flow down to the people who were willing to invest and rebuild. Accountability did not happen; however, many of the elites, who worked with the funding, amassed fortunes. Unfortunately, even with this assistance, these war-scarred lands have not gained prosperity, self-sufficiency, or even peace after far more years and expenditures than the post-war investments in Europe.

In less than four years, 1948 – 1952, the United States granted over $12 billion to 18 countries, all in Western Europe. That amount equates to over $120 billion of today's value. The Soviet Union declined to accept Marshall Plan's help for Eastern Europe due to their fear of losing control of their established puppet governments. But, within four years all 18 countries that accepted aid had not only returned to, but *surpassed* prewar economic levels – every one of them.

That jump-start allowed Western Europe to continue not only with economic successes, but uninterrupted peace. Between the two world wars, many European nations became dictatorships or one-party states – Germany, Italy, Spain, Portugal, Hungary, Austria, and Yugoslavia. Since the Marshall Plan was implemented, all Western European countries are mainstays of thriving democracy and opportunity in a region that has never known such a golden period. Friends *and* enemies turned into America's closest trading and international political partners. It proved the wisdom of the earlier mentioned Winston Churchill's statement quoted earlier, "in Victory: Magnanimity. in Peace: Good Will." There have been few "investments" that ever produced such a return for both donor and recipient. Though conducted in a different manner, Operation Blacklist's comparable investments in Japan and South Korea provided similar results.

Even further back in history, there shines another example of successful initiatives when the efforts of a country's best are properly channeled. Between 1800 and 1803, during a break in European wars lasting less than three years, Napoleon gathered distinguished experts throughout France to review every aspect of life – legal, economic, social, government, and religious. Their deliberations resulted in numerous comprehensive and long-lasting enhancements to French society. Their efforts, now called the Napoleonic Codes, not only continue to exist today in France, but in many other countries as well, which adopted all or parts. [155]

Napoleon intentionally followed in the footsteps of another ruler who had done something similar, Julius Caesar. Both are remembered today for their military prowess, but their true, permanent contributions were to their societies. Despite being the de facto ruler of France as First Consul, Napoleon personally presided over hundreds of these brainstorming sessions and always asked two questions: Is it Fair? Is it Useful? Napoleon demanded common sense with these questions and accepted nothing less as answers. [156]

Lest anyone think these types of successes are no longer possible, one need only consider the most recent, global success unfolding before us. After a short period of disruption to the global economy, the world has developed and is distributing Covid vaccines. Like the other plans, the vaccines resulted from a collaboration of government and private organizations on research, experimentation, testing, and production to deliver safe and life-protecting immunity. Without central direction, but in response to an emergency situation, dozens of companies and scientists cooperated with varying levels of government support. In less than a year, these efforts presented solutions to

---

155 A notable portion of Louisiana's state laws are based on the Napoleonic codes; it was part of France until 1803.

156 Between July 1800 and May 1803, Napoleon led wide-ranging civil efforts that produced a number of significant achievements. A partial list includes: concluding a Concordat with the Catholic Church that resolved some of the discord following the French Revolution, ensuring religious and civil toleration was enshrined in law, adopting a national standard of uniform weights and measures (the metric system), establishing a central currency, promulgating internal markets and commerce guidelines, guaranteeing centralized education based on merit with scholarships for the needy, reforms that made medical care widely available, nationwide infrastructure projects, and a financial system with protections from the unscrupulous.

the world – in such a short period of time that it would have been considered impossible when the virus hit. Mankind has the potential to do what is right when required.

These programs have proven that large, collective achievements can be reached when a goal is clearly defined. Although there is never a guarantee of success, the costs of these projects were a fraction of the prices of war and the likely economic and societal disorder. Why could the United States not do the same again today? If the U.S. leads by example, other nations that share its values will follow.

Recruit, entice, inspire the nation – and the world. Bring together the best and the brightest, our distinguished experts, to work on restoring the country. Continue to ask, is it fair? Is it useful? Beyond the United States, such efforts also benefit the entire planet, physically and at intellectual and emotional levels as examples of successful application of universal principles that all peoples aspire toward.

Paradoxically, success in these endeavors will dramatically lower the country's carbon footprint far faster than a government-mandated top-heavy set of rules to lower greenhouse emissions. Free enterprise, especially with coordinated assistance, will outperform a bureaucratic agreement like the Paris Accords that has little enforcement and allows the worst offenders to *increase* pollution. [157] A further benefit is that success will also stimulate our economy, provide jobs, and invigorate our technology sectors by sharpening our edge with the whetstone of competition.

The opportunity beckons to follow and improve upon these highly successful investment examples – the Manhattan Project and the Marshall Plan. A united effort could have two components. One element would focus on the scientific issues. It could consist of a multifaceted project to deal with biodiversity, energy and transportation, water, consumer usages, infrastructure, waste and pollution, and indirectly fulfill our commitments to the Paris Agreement by being proactive rather than adhering to reactive directives. It can follow in the footsteps of how the Manhattan Project was conceived, built, operated, and then succeeded. One could call it Project 2025 and use it to define a dated goal across and into a new election cycle.

---

157 Officially, the accords are the United Nations Framework Convention on Climate Change signed in 2016.

A short list of the concepts could include developing parallel and connecting interdisciplinary programs for each main subject. Increase biodiversity and decrease extinctions by coordinating the many successful programs already existing around the country and the globe by providing an operations center to extend, grow, and maintain at a national level. That program would necessarily cover terrestrial and aquatic wildlife.

If Americans can initiate and complete a program to develop a bomb with a new type of energy, a new assembly of distinguished experts should be able to do the same to develop an energy source(s) that is an economically viable replacement for fossil fuels. Part of the goal must also be to provide clean energy that can power vehicles and aircraft. Again, solutions must be commercially viable.

Many clever ways, currently and historically, have been devised to make the best use of limited sources of water. [158] Organize systems that maximize usage and minimize waste based on various environments. A harder ask is to convince citizens that a "circle economy" of consumer items, infrastructure, and garbage can be initiated and applied – closed-loop recycling. The U.S. operated scrap and recycling programs during the Second World War that incorporated much of this concept. With present-day technology and the small-scale enterprises that already exist, a managed effort with clear direction would be able to elevate that effort up to a far more comprehensive level.

Decades ago, as a field tester for an outdoor equipment manufacturer and retailer, this writer was reminded – as he had earlier learned during reconnaissance operations in the army – "one packs out what one packs in," that is – leave no trace of one's presence. As a nation, we have forgotten this formerly standard responsibility to make proper use of all resources and not waste or despoil them. Not only does America need to minimize waste for the future, but the country needs to do a massive retroactive clean-up of what we have not been packing out, our pollution on land, water, and air.

And rather than just a group of technocrats, established business captains, or military/ government officials in the fore of the effort, its leadership

---

158 Irrigation channels hundreds or even thousands of years old in desert areas of Mesopotamia, Egypt, Petra, and the American Southwest are several of many examples. Archaeologists have found examples of terraced fields and rice paddies going back to the dawn of civilizations. Both can compare to drip technology for some farming in today's world.

group needs to include youth and passion. Leaders, like the 17-year-old Greta Thunberg – the same age as Joan – can provide passion, energy, vision, and the certainty of belief to keep progress on track. Youth have a far stronger self-interest to right the ship than any other age group.

Project 2025, comprising technical and scientific goals, requires clear, objective targets that can be evaluated by time, cost, and effectiveness. The second program – mankind and quality of life – presents an even more complicated group of challenges. Actions to achieve these targets **must be decentralized**. Yet, like the scientific solutions the second, human, element also requires quantifiable goals. Despite the complexity, the Marshall Plan demonstrated that measurable results and decentralized execution are possible, indeed required for this effort.

Telling people what to do without widespread individual commitments seldom works, assuming one wants engaged contributors rather than resentful or compliant coworkers, much less those claiming their rights were unfairly seized. The second program's initial focus must be clear enough to inspire contributors, narrow enough to reach its targets, while broad enough to achieve real change.

The critical starting point is to accept that the status quo does not currently improve life for a broad-enough swath of American citizens. Enabling millions of Americans to simply "Get by," is too low an aim to be acceptable for the world's leading nation. Much of the idealism and opportunities that shaped this country are moribund or worse. A new Marshall Plan or Napoleonic Code project can put the United States on a trajectory to regain the status as the world's leader of hope, domestically and abroad.

Perhaps a separate name for this project, like the Eden Plan, can inspire people for these subjective challenges that concern people and the way we live. The name evokes an unspoiled paradise for three of the world's great religions and has parallels in other belief systems. Simultaneously, such an effort can ignite support from other nations that share our values and aspirations that choose to join with us. The world changes ever more quickly. America can update with change, as well as remember and hold onto the parts of the past that gave the country the moral leadership, which has guided the nation for over 200 years. Like Project 2025, leaders with different expertise would be asked to volunteer using the same criteria for selection – America's best.

Rather than trying to compile a comprehensive list of problems and potential solutions, the following challenges are nominated as focused start points for the Eden Plan. The list does not pretend to be all-encompassing, but to spark discussion. Further, the designated modus operandi needs to ensure flexibility; people are the intended beneficiaries of these actions. End goals must be specified, like the Marshall Plan, but the ways and means to achieve them need to be delegated to the diverse and accomplished working group(s). Targeted problem areas may include:

Population.
The United States has no plan for an optimal population. Is it 350 million, 400 million, 1 billion? Is the US better off with today's 330 million or at a lower number? Do any extra millions place too large a toll on all other services and our quality of life, much of which requires overdue maintenance, significant upkeep, and a lot of upgrading? Or can the country expand and improve?

Once a goal is selected, policies and processes must be established to meet the desired headcount, including immigration. Educate, encourage, incentivize, and give the means for families to maintain a birth rate that our nation – and individual families – can support adequately. Whether the amount set is higher or lower than present, part of the program has to include civic and community efforts to give children maximum opportunity and nurturing. At the same time, the plan should provide their parents a wider range of career options if they choose. Lastly, the country needs to invest in the infrastructure necessary to support the plan.

Accommodating religious observances and encouraging family cohesion also need to be part of this strategy. Education should start at kindergarten level through high school, including options and importance on being capable to achieve self-sufficiency. The goal should provide all the tools needed to enable everyone to contribute to society.

Internationally, the U.S can assist other nations develop control measures so they can support their own populations. Ensuring options for birth control, establishing minimum ages to marry, and instituting mandatory schooling for females, as well as males are the bare essentials, as it is in our country. To a degree, U.S. agencies and the UN aid in these areas now, but not anywhere close to a comprehensive level. See the section below on National Service.

Employment and the Economy.
The past generation has seen an incredible change in job patterns and oc-cupations as the United States has largely shifted from manufacturing to service. The notion of being employed in rewarding blue-collar lifelong vocations is nearly gone in many parts of the country. This change has fostered both significant inequalities and resentments, as well as significant impact on nuclear families.

Effective options to educate, retrain, or provide apprentice programs to workers of any age or background need to co-exist along with motivating businesses to situate in areas that have languished – as Europe did in the late 1940s. Rebuilding pride and engagement, across all geographies – urban, rural, reservations, low income, old center, and new location needs to be addressed in a methodical review, while ensuring flexibility.

The idea has to be that *all* Americans see they have the opportunity to find and thrive with stimulating work, which has a long-term future or op-tion to adjust as economic conditions continue to evolve. The concept also has to be capable adapting for full-time, part-time, or community service, as adults progress through life. Yet, welfare, unemployment compensation, retraining programs, and job support must still be provided by the govern-ment; disruptions and tragedies will still happen.

However, reform should make it easier to work than to receive benefits, both financially and practically. Government must invest in its citizens, short and long-term, but not provide them a way of life. Citizens need to see work as contributing to society as well as themselves. We are all in it together, including all races, genders, and people with disabilities.

Government.
The federal tax system has become inefficient and unequal. Even accoun-tants – those who earn a living from the complexity of tax laws – believe that it continues to be far too complicated. If the professionals cannot grasp it, no hope exists for the normal citizen. The special interests that have driven America to this plight need to be minimized. Simplify and ensure that

all Americans, especially those people and companies that evade their fair share, contribute. An overhaul can partially address economic inequality. Taxes should also be seen as a service and obligation to our democracy, not a blunt weapon or an enemy.

The same failures apply to the federal budget. The last balanced budget occurred in 2001; the country as of late 2020 flounders with over $27,000,000,000,000 (27 trillion) dollars in debt. That amount works out to nearly $85,000 per person – owed to those who have loaned money to the federal government. This is not only unsustainable, it starves the programs we need for today, while putting incredible hardships on our children and grandchildren – who will inherit the liability without having received the benefits.

A third crisis in government concerns elections. Donations and lobbyists are too uncontrolled and invisible to the public. Entering civic office must be regarded as achievable for any citizen, not only the wealthy or connected – and no office can be bought. Today, a candidate cannot win an election – with few exceptions – unless outspending the opposition. Our Founding Fathers did not intend for such a system. The existing one is not fair to the people they serve, the voting citizens; rather, it rewards donors who remain unaccountable to the public.

Education.
Teaching Civics and History are critical parts to unite – and develop – modern American citizens. Teachers should celebrate what our country has done well in the past, as well as face up to what we failed to do. They go together – successes and mistakes. Toleration and acceptance of diversity in our multicultural melting pot remains crucial for all Americans to be capable of contributing to society.

Outside of the family, schools serve as a crucial step to connecting us as a people, while preparing children for the future. Our national government cannot constitutionally mandate a curriculum. But federal education funding to states can and does incentivize states and school districts. Encouraging these subjects for elementary, intermediate, and high school levels provides much of the glue that holds our diverse citizenry as one people. Civics and history knowledge is required for an immigrant to become a citizen. It should also be required as part of university entrance exams to provide more stepping stones that link all to be part of our country, no matter how long or short they have been inhabitants.

Vocational training options were previously more common for those not academically inclined. Their disappearance as cost cutting decisions a generation ago have created both a shortage of men and women working in skilled trades and more importantly, eliminated a positive career path for a significant group of students. As new technologies continue to evolve, education must be available lifelong to ensure all have the opportunity to keep up with the changes in the workforce.

Professional educators need to make certain that knowledge critical for life be retained, while teaching students to grasp the need for continuing education in order to be prepared to adapt. Periodic reviews of curriculums at both state and national level can assist to identify what is working, and what is not.

The examples of self-educated students like Washington and Lincoln shine, as do more modern ones like Bill Gates and Greta Thunberg. Education should endeavor to instill an attitude of individual self-sufficiency rather than entitlement. Achievement should be celebrated, as should the willingness to risk failure. Dumbing down curriculums to allow all to pass does not prepare pupils to successfully enter the workforce or face life as a full adult. High goals and persistence can only serve to assist students and adults navigating the life paths ahead.

National Service.

Such a program, perhaps tailored as an updated post-Civil War Freedman's Bureau, can beckon to the youth of America to give service to their land. The intent is not to revive the military "draft" of yesteryear. Service can be organized by combining the organizational techniques of Selective Service and the successful Civilian Conservation Corps (CCC) of the Great Depression.

It is possible to construct a short program of 12 -15 months to provide assistance with public needs: National Parks, pollution cleanup, assisting in low-income areas, support with biodiversity/ water/ infrastructure projects, even harvesting crops, as well as expanding AmeriCorps for disaster relief and their other programs.

Make a concerted effort to encourage people who are retired or disabled to serve as instructors, mentors, and group leaders. Rejuvenate the Peace Corps and the non-government MBA Enterprise Corps to reach out to the rest of the world as originally intended. [159] Encourage Americans to consider joining them or coordinating with the United States Agency for International Development (USAID). Volunteers for any of these programs directly interface with the people and places receiving aid.

Such efforts can support our own disadvantaged citizens, give attention to neglected areas of the country, and show the world that we can assist them to make better places to live. Further, they can furnish an expanded range of options for other countries to develop their own homelands – with American help. Such results deliver a "Win-Win" for all.

As with military service, such an experience will provide the vast majority of teens a better appreciation of their fellow citizens, as well as supplying true experience of real toleration and diversities. Service unites us all. America has done it before. Appeal to Americans by reinvigorating the idealism that led President Kennedy to call out, "Ask not what your country can do for you, ask what you can do for your country." [160]

Public services.
Unlike most countries, the U.S. is highly decentralized in hiring, training, and operating many public services. Local police exist as a community organization providing service and protection to all. Militarizing them, as is recently evident, all too often leads to the opposite of service. Too many examples of brutal tactics inflamed not just neighborhoods, but worldwide opinion. America can do better. We have to do better. A good place to start

---

159 The MBA Enterprise Corps was formed in 1990 to assist the privatizing economies in Eastern Europe. Recent MBA graduates from a consortium of top U.S. business schools worked for a minimum of a year at recently privatized firms in former communist countries. Compensated only at Peace Corps level wages, they contributed management expertise in exchange for the opportunity to make historic contributions.

160 January 21, 1961 Inaugural Address.

would be to resurrect Sir Robert Peel's nine principles of policing, which are based on securing public consent and earning respect. [161]

The same applies to medical service. Of the world's democracies, the United States has the best services anywhere for research and many needs, as long as an individual has the means to pay. However, we too often fail to provide adequate services for those that do not. Utilizing the talents and expertise the country possesses should be obligatory. Combining the care and generosity that Americans have been noted for since Clara Barton served in the Civil War, as well as thousands still do today, remains a case of plain common sense.

It not only cries out as a requirement, but gives the opportunity to be another measure to unify one and all. National plans do work elsewhere without bankrupting their treasuries; the U.S. can draw on the best of what others already offer and augment our systems so that all have access to reasonable health care. Direction in upgrading our services and learning from others has to come from a central source with clear and workable parameters.

Immigration.

There is nothing wrong with new citizens joining the world's greatest melting pot, except like the earth, the country has only a finite amount of space and opportunity. If America adopts a national plan connected to the population, it must maintain it. The more America endeavors to aid other countries to make their own lands worthy of freedom, justice, and opportunity will assist both other nations and ourselves. This could be promptly possible with the help of our Peace Corps, MBA Corps, USAID, and Project 2025.

People illegally enter the United States because they do not have the basic rights and quality of life in their home countries that exist for Americans, that we in fact take for granted. Rather than trying to stop them at the border – a reaction – the U.S. should become proactive, helping migrants' home countries improve life choices within their borders.

---

161   Peel, as British Home Secretary in the 1820s, established and led the London police with a series of nine guidelines. He focused on the belief that police served as fellow citizens, were ethical, earned trust, and were accountable for their actions. Arrests were not the target; lack of crime was.

A feasible initiative could establish free trade zones in these developing countries. Parameters could include U.S. laws inside zones, tariff-free trade for a fixed, modest duration, bi-lateral treaties setting terms and approved by the Senate and host government, and incentivizing USA companies to invest – and train locals or previous American immigrants, including "Dreamers" to provide them a path to citizenship.

The direct benefits to the developing country are manifold – capital investment, a better trained workforce, retaining many of their ambitious people, the working example of a functional democracy inside their borders with USA-level infrastructure, and the certainty of return of this golden nest egg within one to two decades. It has worked in the past; Hong Kong and Singapore are the most prominent examples of free trade zones that retain the human capital and laws nurtured from abroad. Accepting American laws has worked well for decades in countries that host the U.S. military and its civilian workforce in dozens of nations worldwide.

Indirectly, encouraging people in developing countries with opportunities and exposing them to the best aspects of our society would give both individuals and governments an improved capability to transform their own lands, rather than having many of their best citizens flee elsewhere. Once the program demonstrates success, perhaps other G7 or G20 countries would be inspired to foster similar programs elsewhere. A skilled, expanding workforce in friendly nations close to the U.S. would also serve to reduce reliance on China – which becomes a foreign policy win.

Washington's Farewell Address, indirectly, encouraged similar ideas over 200 years ago. Commercially, vibrant neighbors are good for America. Paine has a term for this as well, it is pure common sense; an idea that should readily stimulate bi-partisan support.

Racism.
Black Lives matter. This statement should be a call for unification, not divisiveness or outrage, as has been the case in the past with other rallying calls attempting to confirm all Americans enjoy the same rights, administered impartially. The United States has a problem – a self-inflicted one. The country came close to reconciling races with the Declaration of Independence, but drew back in the final version – to ensure all 13 colonies joined the union.

Following the Civil War, the Freedman's Bureau and three Constitutional Amendments came close again. But much of that progress ended with the Compromise of 1877, which resolved the 1876 presidential election and ended the policies of Reconstruction.

The Civil Rights movement of the 1960s and 1970s, again, moved closer to full equality, resulting in laws and hiring statutes to guarantee opportunity. But the country's progress stagnated. The seemingly unending war in Vietnam, the protests and rioting the war provoked, and the assassinations of Martin Luther King and Robert F. Kennedy led a majority to yearn for the stability of earlier days. Further, some claim progress was undermined by opening up an overly generous entitlement and social welfare net. Others point to the persistence of unequal opportunities and education stymieing ambition.

Granted, those who are willing to seek opportunity and advancement can and do, despite hidden obstacles. America has tens of thousands of Black millionaires; however, their representation among higher income brackets is well below other ethnic groups. At the other end of the scale, measures of social-economic progress continue to show that far too high a percentage of too many minorities stay mired in poverty, drugs, crime, lower education levels, teenage pregnancy, and other social ills. Opportunity exists, but is not fully shared. The complicated question remains – how to break the chain of past injustices and inequality? The nation needs to develop a balance that assists individuals striving to achieve and advance themselves, while securing an even playing field for all citizens.

For the country to truly be united, as the protests following George Floyd's murder show all too clearly, efforts need to be redoubled. Employment and educational opportunities need to be nurtured to make diversity and tolerance the reality, rather than an aspiration. Further, these two markers, dignified work and practical learning, can/will provide the differences that fuels ambition and the willingness to seek the Great American Dream – a better life than our parents had, and even better than that for the next generation.

Washington and other Founding Fathers succeeded in changing America's *attitude* to support religious toleration, overcoming prevailing attitudes against other religions and sects. Americans can succeed – again.

Currently, these efforts have a huge groundswell of support and awareness. Now is the time for positive and practical leadership to seize that momentum to strengthen and intensify toleration and acceptance, the attitudes necessary to match America's laws – and our ideals. With that type of leadership, we can realize the goal envisioned by the Founding Fathers and Lincoln, yet fell short of achieving.

One step, relatively easy, but highly conspicuous, could follow the example of President Harry Truman. In 1948, he exercised his powers as Commander-in-Chief to remove institutional vestiges of racism by ordering the military to desegregate prior to any other public institution. Renaming military bases and ships that still commemorate Confederate generals would set a similar example. They could be replaced with names of the soldiers who led the "Greatest Generation" like Patton, MacArthur, Marshall, Eisenhower, and Benjamin Davis Jr, and earlier icons such as John Pershing and U.S. Grant. [162] Using the named convention employed on some sections of American highways and U.S. Navy warships, some bases and ships could also be named for enlisted Medal of Honor recipients – from a mix of America's diverse backgrounds and regions. This symbolic act, combined with initiating others in this secondary group, can build momentum, and the results of groups working together can make other problems far more easy to resolve – the basis of unity.

Foreign Affairs.

Turn back the clock to 1796 and look again at George Washington's Farewell Address. Washington recommended that we resolve our own internal affairs, set an example, and stay vigilant against foreign interference. He suggested that we maximize commerce and minimize involvement in foreign politics.

---

162 In 1936, Benjamin Davis Jr. graduated from West Point as the fourth Black cadet, commanded a Tuskegee air group in World War II, flying and surviving 60 missions, and was promoted to four-star general after retirement. "Black Jack" John Pershing made an early name for himself in the Army by successfully commanding Native American Sioux scouts and Black "Buffalo Soldiers." As military governor of the Philippines' second-largest island, he governed while working with Christian, Muslim, and Chinese Filipinos to mitigate a local civil war. His career culminated in leading all U.S. troops to victory in Europe during World War 1. He later became U.S. Army Chief of Staff and was promoted to the rank of General of the Armies.

If so, others will follow our lead. Those same admonitions are equally valid today.

Trying to solve others' civil wars or rebuild nations as we want them has too often resulted in failure. Additionally, our national treasure has been wasted with little results – except lost and broken lives and a growing national debt; our attention has been focused on the wrong priorities. We could have supplied social assistance and political, economic, and military advisers to assist those lands in solving their own problems. When necessary, our military could have aided local forces in targeting terrorist groups that threatened legitimate governments.

During the three decades since the end of the Soviet Union, America has curtailed our collaboration with other states that try to follow laws, liberty, equality, and justice. There have been some exceptions; one positive example of UN supported international collaboration that the United States initiated and led, was Desert Storm between 1990 – 1991 to liberate the recently conquered Kuwait from Iraq. However, in general, we have neglected to be vigilant enough against rogue states. These nations have pursued overt and covert aggression against other states, including the U.S. Unfortunately, though the list of these rogues is short, their ongoing actions continue to disrupt and distract attention from what should be more pressing problems. America needs to give time and effort to remedy long, overlooked inattention.

In a world of increasing globalization, a Project 2025 and an Eden Plan can make the concept not just a national effort, but involve other nations that are willing to participate.

Reclaim America's moral leadership, as expressed in Emma Lazarus' words on the Statue of Liberty – and the hope it has given worldwide. Encourage any country that aspires to the Rule of Law to engage with us as participants in Project 2025 and an Eden Plan. While these countries assist in solving our mutual problems, their involvement will also strengthen their ability to return to their home countries and do the same there. Improvement for both means gains for both, while at the same time building trust, cooperation, reestablishing values, and principles of conduct.

Such a coordinated partnership reinforces basic democratic standards, not only for partner nations, but this country as well. In the meantime, nations that practice belligerence, while disregarding the UN charter – which they have signed – are best marginalized. Stop trade with them and make an effort to ensure others do not as well. Beat them on the merchant lanes and the playing fields, not battlefields – ground, air, water, or cyber. And safeguard democracies, via trade and security alliances, so rogue states do not export havoc.

Due to globalization, it is not possible for any isolated nation to fully prosper. However, if an embargoed nation accepts it has to change its un-principled actions, agrees to honor the UN charter, resumes international commerce, and therefore regains national wellbeing, UN membership will carry a moral weight that is currently lacking. Additionally, it will give confidence to states abiding by the charter to continue cooperating by the charter in the future.

George Washington and John Adams avoided war in the early years of independence by ignoring provocations from the more powerful English and French during the 1790s. Lincoln acted the same towards the British Empire during the Civil War. More recently, the Cold War became a victory for democracies without outright war due to winning the economic contest. A simple rule of thumb: Nations that treat America the way we want to be treated are the ones that merit our commerce.

China exists in a different category from any other foreign power. Like the U.S., it stands as a true Great Power with political, economic, and military influence worldwide. Additionally, it has a 5000-year history of culture, learning, and pride. Their ruling class retains a belief that their predecessors have held for millennia – China is the Middle Kingdom, the center of Earth. It holds the Mandate of Heaven while other people are traditionally viewed as something less – barbarians.

Beginning in 1949, China's Communist Party Chairman was considered the First among Equals of those in the Politburo, the senior governing group. Because of the fiascos of the Great Leap Forward and Cultural Revolution,

[163] China established and maintained a version of succession that prevented recurrence of the type of leadership abuses that occurred prior to 1980.

That system changed in 2012; succession no longer occurs unless the current leader wills it. Recent events have shown Chairman Xi Jinping holds little regard for China's minorities in Tibet and Xinjiang. Hong Kong residents have seen their rights as citizens restricted or abolished. Political and religious protestors inside China and Hong Kong are dealt with harshly, without due process, and outside their judicial system. All this occurs despite rights guaranteed to citizens in the Chinese Constitution. Further, the 1984 Sino-British Joint Declaration, whereby China guaranteed that Hong Kong's economic and political systems would remain unchanged until 2047, has proved to be worthless.

Outside China's borders, the nation displays the same disregard for others and their basic rights. Among the many examples are violating Taiwan's territorial boundaries, border clashes with India, support for North Korea in violation of UN trade and nuclear embargoes, international wildlife trafficking, and usurping fishing rights. However, the most brazen example takes place in the South China Sea. China has seized islets and built military bases hundreds of miles outside their 200-mile exclusive economic zone border (EEZ) committing repeated violations of the UN guaranteed right of Freedom of the Seas. [164] In addition, China continues to sponsor frequent state-level hacking and industrial theft of countries' cyber and proprietary commercial rights.

Ignoring China or failing to trade with them is neither practical nor sound judgement. Diplomatic and economic measures can be exerted to *gently* remind China about its international obligations. Publicizing illegal acts in the UN – ironically, using the partisan Human Rights Council – might

163 The Great Leap Forward marked an attempt by China between 1958 - 1962 to convert from an agrarian economy to an industrialized nation. It failed – between 20 and 45 million people starved to death. The Cultural Revolution, between 1965 - 1976, was the name given the effort to eliminate all vestiges of China's noncommunist history, as well as any influences from outside peoples. Millions more of those who questioned state policies died between re-education camps, starvation, and executions.

164 The UN Convention on the Law of the Sea approved in 1982 guarantees both territorial rights and freedom of the seas for navigation of commerce. It also outlines rules concerning countries' EEZs.

address two issues with one action. Concurrent efforts through bilateral diplomatic channels could be another avenue. During the Cold War, a presidential hotline was utilized between the U.S. and the USSR in moments of crisis – and kept a prompt communication channel open and was used. A hotline exists with China, but has seldom been utilized or emphasized.

Joining and supporting regional economic associations, that are in accord with UN agreements, provides another method to highlight good global citizenship, while reducing other nations' reliance on trade with China. Another option that may assist would be to encourage others not to accept preferential trade treatment with China through either exports or imports. Non-confrontational peaceful and economic measures can deliver success whereas neither ignoring transgressions nor direct confrontation have worked.

It is essential to convince China to abide by the UN charter. Expecting it to trust the United States or treat America – or the UN – with the same dignity the Chinese government expects to be treated, will not happen under an autocrat. This will require a deft hand to ensure that China's security and legitimate resource concerns are met, while ending its expansionist and belligerent actions. Persuading Xi that our country, their former ally in the Second World War, is not a military or political threat, just a commercial competitor, is a foreign policy challenge every bit as daunting as those faced by Washington as president.

Perhaps, the efforts outlined above will convince China to honor its signatures and commitments.

More likely though, a unified international effort, preferably through a revitalized UN, that uniformly applies carrots – trade – and sticks – sanctions – for actions outside the charter and law, has the most potential for peaceful resolution. That international effort cannot simply be the United States or even the English-speaking nations, but must be composed of the G-20 nations at a minimum. Such an effort will only prove effective when China respects rules of international law, justice, the UN Charter agreement and treaties it has signed, including the Hong Kong Declaration and the UN Law of the Sea. At the same time, the U.S. has to maintain vigilance in case peaceful efforts fail. The ancient Romans stated it precisely: if you want peace, prepare for war. [165]

The ideas above outline one method, a proposed sketch, to start reviewing the concepts of what could result with an American Project 2025 and an Eden Plan. One could easily add plenty of details to flesh them out, as well as drop or revise other sections, in order to produce workable solutions. The reality, though, is that this long list of problems, challenges, and impossibilities is seen by most as insurmountable – mere pipedreams. Then again, so were the Manhattan Project, the Marshall Plan, or the accomplishments described in the first nine chapters.

If the president of the United States agrees that the current situation is not acceptable and embraces the belief that we can better ourselves by facing these challenges, he can encourage and lead all Americans, citizens and Congress, to surmount them. President Biden can seize these ideas, inspire individuals to volunteer their service, and then have them organize, plan, recruit, and unify participants with stated goals. George, Abe, or Joan could do it – and would do it. They would confront these adversities by setting a clear goal, thoroughly prepare, get to work, gain support, build momentum, and achieve results. The challenges would not overwhelm them; the opportunities would provide their motivation.

The gauntlet lies on the ground, like a challenge from the duels of yesteryear. Will Americans continue to pretend all looks well and hide behind past triumphs? Or, can the nation step up? Can we come to grips with the challenges? And can America lead by example again – in a time of relative peace and prosperity? Do we or will we have a president keen to lead against and with this set of challenges – that can also serve as opportunities?

Let us look at what is possible now based on the office that President Biden has assumed. He steps into the role to lead a bitterly divided country. His predecessor claims the electoral process failed him, and that fraud has been committed. Congress remains divided along strict party lines with significant opposition to most legislative proposals. The Supreme Court leans to a conservative view and may be ideologically oriented against his policies. A pandemic has affected the entire country – and world – and changed the

---

165   There are similar adages in classical Greek and Chinese writings, but the Latin *Si vis pacem, para bellum* is the most widely known version.

way all live. Whether the nation is immersed in the worst economic situation of the last 100 years – or it has received a sharp wake-up call to consider new ways to develop American prosperity – is immaterial. Economic challenges as well as other challenges await leadership. Yet, there is one item that is the most important: the country's population holds a significant percentage that neither trusts the president or his platform. Can he unify America?

The president has the opportunity to look directly at these troubles and address them with integrity and the resolve of his forebears. He has incredible resources at his disposal; however, he cannot succeed as a one-person operation. With help, he can utilize the skill of a Lincoln to carry Congress along, the example of a Washington to convince the public he stands alongside them, and the passion of a Joan to support him and the vision of a better America that he defines. That vision has to include re-unifying the country – and Congress – across party lines. [166] It should also include a comprehensive economic development program, gaining control

---

166 The author has attempted to balance the line between positive critique and partisan comments. However, one area could use a push, and he believes mainstream America recognizes the issue as well. It is the inability of recent presidents and Congress to work together. Going back to a military view, if the mission is bi-partisan support, a short list of suggestions representing "tactics" are worthy of consideration if President Biden is serious about his stated, primary goal, national unity:

- Veto any legislation that does not have at least 25% of each party vote for it.
- State he will freeze federal spending unless 25% of each party supports future budgets.
- Halt efforts that may require Constitutional challenges – Supreme Court size, states' right power, and making Washington D.C. a state are examples.
- Submit all foreign agreements to the Senate for ratification rather than using executive decrees. The failure to get Senate ratification can result in changes with each incoming president. U.S. policy changed between the Obama-Trump and Trump-Biden administrations for the Paris Climate agreement and the Iran nuclear deal. Without treaties ratified by the Senate – per the Constitution – expect more of the same.
- Introduce an agreement that previously had bi-partisan support, like the Trans-Pacific-Partnership (TPP – signed by the U.S. in 2016 and withdrew in 2017) that can build trade along the Pacific Rim and re-engage with former friends and allies. Use it or something similar to begin momentum and build trust.
- Other likely options could be to counter China's Belt and Road Initiative (BRI) by assisting nations financially crippled by infrastructure loans or accelerating global Covid vaccine distribution – growing respect, herd immunity, and opening borders/ trade again.

If the president can succeed in convincing Congress to work as a bi-partisan organization and in conjunction with the president, he will have overcome both his hardest challenge and his easiest – working with the people he has spent his career alongside.

Strategy (or big-picture ideas) would be implementing a Project 2025 and an Eden Plan.

of the pandemic, and convincing fellow citizens he can lead them forward as one people. If President Biden can master these immediate objectives, he will have earned the latitude to expand his focus to the many other problems that already loom ahead casting a dark shadow, and those yet unforeseen.

To summarize, President Biden assumes a responsibility that provides incredible opportunities – if he can ensure that the country works together. Due to the lack of an external foe, as was the situation in previous crises, the president – and nation – have an extra challenge as well. A medieval European term for chivalry, "Noblese Oblige," meant privilege entails responsibility. [167] A person of authority had obligations for their position, which included duty, honor, service, and generosity, and they were compelled to act accordingly. Washington, Lincoln, and Joan epitomize these characteristics. They knew how to bring others together for a common purpose, no matter how difficult the conditions, to fulfill the responsibilities they assumed.

America needs that concept. That moment is now, not after some future election. Thomas Paine would call this American crisis a time requiring common sense. The president has many superb examples from the nation's past to look at to assist in guiding him and his fellow citizens. Just as importantly, the United States has the resources in ideas, industries, organizations, and especially people that he can call on to serve the country. What matters is that President Biden steps up to his role and leads a unified effort to master today's adversities. May President Biden prove capable of leading all of America onward as a unified nation.

---

167 The chivalric code was never formally structured. However, a number of characteristics were considered the norm and expected throughout Europe's aristocratic class. They included military bravery, individual self-training, service to others, loyalty, self-control, knightly piety, and courtly manners to establish honor and nobility. Piety represented the ruling passion of the ethic of chivalry, ranking above courage.

14. AN EXCERPT FROM A SPEECH TEDDY ROOSEVELT DELIVERED IN A LECTURE AT SORBONNE UNIVERSITY, PARIS ON APRIL 23, 1910, TITLED *CITIZENSHIP IN A REPUBLIC*. IN IT, TR CONSIDERED CRITICS AND CONTRASTED THEM WITH ACHIEVERS.

It is not the critic who counts; not the man who points out
how the strong man stumbles or where the doer of deeds
could have done them better.
The credit belongs to the man who is actually in the arena,
whose face is marred by dust and sweat and blood;
who strives valiantly; who errs, who comes short again and again,
because there is no effort without error and shortcoming;
but who does actually strive to do the deeds;
who knows the great enthusiasms, the great devotions;
who spends himself in a worthy cause; who at the best knows in the end
the triumph of high achievement, and who at the worst, if he
fails, at least fails while daring greatly, so that his place shall
never be with those cold and timid souls who know neither
victory nor defeat.

COMMON SENSE
- ACKNOWLEDGEMENTS

My primary purpose in writing this book was to leave a written record for my grown children, Celine and Ian, on how good people have overcome monumental challenges. Life and its situations have been terrible many times in the past. Yet, good people did not accept things as they were. They rejected acquiescence and incompetence to confront and solve major problems head-on. And they were innovative thinkers – well "outside the box" of what was accepted. Their leadership and the inspiration they provided are worthy of remembering – again, especially in this day and age.

My secondary purpose was the hope that someone in a national position of responsibility might be inspired enough by this narrative to become a catalyst for decisive leadership. The challenges America faces now are terrible because the underlying problems have festered since long before Celine's and Ian's births. It is only so because no "good folks" have stood up long enough to lead change, real change.

Frankly, I also wrote the book for myself. I have been collecting notes on George Washington, Abraham Lincoln, and Joan of Arc - among others - for decades. Gathering my thoughts on these inspirational leaders and their accomplishments is something I have always wanted to do. But I did not take the first step until a physician, Dr. Nat Anglem, examining a chronic leg injury, suggested I do something mentally stimulating. He stated that connecting my latest period of physical rehabilitation with a positive mental activity would be more likely to heal these chronic leg problems than anything else. And he provided examples from my own past illustrating the connection. That was November 2019, and I started organizing a plan for this book. By late January 2020, I had assembled what I wanted and prepared an outline. [168]

That's when I began writing the Prelude. I enjoyed it; in fact much more so than I expected. To my surprise the words came reasonably easily – my subjects and their actions write their own stories.

I wish to acknowledge the assistance of two former roommates from the West Point class of 1979. My friend and fellow military history buff, Timothy Deady, and I enjoyed a busman's holiday in Spring 2019 traveling and visiting historical sites across Alsace-Lorraine in France and adjoining lands. Afterwards, we prepared individual travel notes and collaborated on preparing a joint account for our friends. The process of doing so fed each other's creativity and writing skills.

To my great relief -- and enjoyment – Tim agreed to review this book as well. By mid-February 2020, he was looking at the Prelude and in the following months continuing to comment on following chapters. Although reviewing was part of what he has done, so was editing and critiquing my explanations from history. Both have provided indispensable support for me. I also wish to acknowledge the assistance of his wife, Kristin Merrigan, regarding the Catholic Church's beliefs and practices.

By mid-June, I was wrapping up the body of the book, chapters 1-10, and mentioned to our friend, Gary Patton, what I was doing. To my surprise and enjoyment, he also offered to comment and then edit. As our exchanges unfolded, Gary's detailed editing and creative rewrites involving the Prelude and most chapters contributed greatly to the coherence and language of the final composition. I was grateful to accept a third pair of eyes for these sections, particularly given his education and experience as an editor – and commander of soldiers in battle. His efforts have required me to focus on clarity and seek better ways express my ideas.

Both of their thorough sets of comments from chapter to chapter have improved the book's readability. Their critical questions have helped ensure historical accuracy and well-reasoned viewpoints, as well as ensuring I stayed focused on leadership and history, not politics. There is no doubt their assistance has not only produced a far better book, but made it more

---

168 Dr. Anglem was right about the leg too.

satisfying for me as well - despite my grumbling through the editing and feedback process.

My daughter, Celine, a recent university graduate, also stepped up as an editor. She read sections and looked at the material through a modern day lens – a very different way than those of us from an earlier generation who grew up during the Vietnam War and entered the military during the Cold War. She challenged references and conclusions, forcefully reminding me of the essential need to appeal to all Americans today. Accordingly, I have attempted to present a more thoroughly researched product and to address concerns of today's youth in order to relate to and inspire all generations with the work.

Additionally, a number of others provided specific assistance and encouragement.

First and foremost is my mother's cousin, Jim Packard. Jim has been a lifelong mentor, a constant source of inspiration, and the one who has always encouraged me to look beyond the boundaries of the status quo. Secondly, Scott Easton, another long ago roommate and friend, provided encouragement and confidence that my project was not only possible, but something I was made to do. Thanks Scottie.

Additionally, a number of other individuals were critical at various points to push my work forward. Most important, was Richard Malloch, who took a hodgepodge of sketch maps and ideas to make practical representations of locations described. Rich Killblane and Bob Sweetman, both West Point graduates, former Army officers, and published writers, provided key tips that assisted me to continue to move forward. Noted writers, Jeff Shaara and Bernard Cornwell, freely gave advice and answers to questions that enabled me to begin to navigate the perils of the publishing world, as well as to back my own work. Further, a number of others contributed encouragement and help along the way. They included, Paul Menzel, Janet Beam Smith, Lynn and Kevin Berner, Bob Collins, Fred Schwien, and Brian Walsh. Lastly, the Christchurch, New Zealand Park Run group were a constant set of positive support and uplifting reassurance week in and week out throughout these many months.

Yet, thankful as I am for all their assistance, I am the person responsible for the book and its contents. While I have endeavoured to report history as recorded by many of the most respected authors and authorities on my subjects, and had my work reviewed by trusted, knowledgeable colleagues, any errors that remain are my responsibility.

While I had hoped to have the book in print in time to encourage political debate before the 2020 U.S. Presidential election, it became clear that I began the writing process too far into the election cycle. Further, my unfamiliarity and lack of contacts with the publishing business were not conducive to the aggressive schedule I had in mind. Yet the crises facing our country remain, and with them the book's relevance.

I have spent decades working with people in the military and manufacturing firms in dozens of countries around the world. My experience and observations have convinced me that character is what defines one as a person and is the most powerful force for accomplishing good.

With that in mind, I would particularly like to thank the book's three subjects. Their lives and accomplishments have inspired me to attempt to live my life on a higher plane. It is my fervent hope that the vignettes of their lives and observations on their character, statesmanship, and faith captured herein provide much needed inspiration to our nation and my fellow citizens.

BIBLIOGRAPHY

Main sources based on subjects beginning with George Washington.

George Washington
Though researching and consulting all of these sources, the main reference for confirming fact, dates, and individuals has been James Thomas Flexner and his four-volume biography of George Washington. As the primary source, it will be listed first with other nonfiction references alphabetically following.

Nonfiction:
Flexner, James Thomas, G*eorge Washington, the Forge of Experience, 1732 – 1775* (Boston, 1965)
Flexner, James Thomas, *George Washington, In the American Revolution, 1775 -1783* (Boston, 1967)
Flexner, James Thomas, *George Washington, And the New Nation, 1783 – 1793* (Boston, 1969)
Flexner, James Thomas, *George Washington, Anguish and Farewell, 1793 – 1799* (Boston, 1972)
Clark, George Rogers, *Clark's Memoir* (New York, 1966 reprint)
Clary, David A., *George Washington's First War* (New York, 2011)
Cook, Fred, *The Golden Book of the American Revolution* (New York, 1966, 5th edition)
Cook, Jacob E., *Alexander Hamilton* (New York, 1982)
Dann, John C., ed, *The Revolution Remembered, Eyewitness Accounts of the War for Independence* (Chicago, 1980)
Dupuy, R. Ernest and Depuy, Trevor N., *The Encyclopedia of Military History* (New York, 1970)
Ewald, Johann, *Diary of the American War, a Hessian Journal*, Joseph P. Tustin editor and translator (Westford, 1979)
Franklin, Benjamin, *The Autobiography of Benjamin Franklin* (New York, 1994 reprint)

Hibbert, Christopher, *Redcoats and Rebels* (London, 2006)

Isaacson, Walter, *Benjamin Franklin, an American Life* (New York, 2003)

Ketchum, Richard M., *The Battle for Bunker Hill* (Garden City, 1972, 2nd edition)

Ketchum, Richard M., *The Winter Soldiers* (Garden City, 1973)

McCullough, David, *John Adams* (New York, 2001)

McCullough, David, *1776* (New York, 2005)

Martin, James Kirby and Lender, Mark Edward, *A Respectable Army, the Military Origins of the Republic, 1763 – 1789* (Wheeling, 1982)

Martin, J. P., *Private Yankee Doodle* (New York, 2006 reprint)

Nell, William Cooper, *The Colored Patriots of the American Revolution* (Boston,1855)

Paine, Thomas, *The Life and Major Writings of Thomas Paine*, ed Phillip S Foner (Binghamton, 1945)

Paine, Thomas, *The Rights of Man* (London, 1979 reprint)

Smith, William, *Expedition against the Ohio Indians* (New York, 1966 reprint)

Stryker, James W., Major, *Evolution of US Military Policy, 1783 – 1860* (West Point, late 1970s)

Thwaites, Reuben Gold, *How George Rogers Clark won the Northwest and other Essays in Western History* (Freeport, 1968 reprint)

Tuchman, Barbara, *The First Salute* (New York, 1988)

Washington, George, "Address to Officers of the Army," Headquarters Continental Army, Newburgh, New York, 15 March 1783, Newburgh Address

Washington, George, "Farewell to his French and Indian War Officers," from Flexner, J, *George Washington the Forge of Experience*, 1965 edition, Appendix A

Washington, George, *The Journal of Major George Washington* (New York, 1966 reprint)

Washington, George, *To the PEOPLE of the United States Friends and fellow citizens*, American Daily Advertiser, Philadelphia, 19 September 1796, Farewell Address

Weigley, Russell F., *History of the United States Army* (New York, 1974, 4th edition)

Whitney, David C., *The American Presidents* (New York, 1967)

Willis, Garry, *Cincinnatus, George Washington & the Enlightenment* (Garden City, 1984)
Film Documentary:
Wise, Robert M., director, *Washington the Warrior*, the History Channel (2006)

Abraham Lincoln
A much broader range of general subject matter is available on the Civil War which I have also researched. Many capture the atmosphere of the times and the altitudes of many on the interconnected concepts of slavery and state's rights/ national unity. The listings below tie directly into Lincoln's life and events with the support, or lack of, for him during his life. Carl Sandburg stands as the primary reference for fact, dates, and individuals, though plenty of cross-checking details are available with other references. Nonfiction:
Sandburg, Carl, *Abraham Lincoln Illustrated Edition, The Prairie Years and the War Years* (New York, 1970, 14th edition)
Burchard, Peter, *Glory, One Gallant Rush* (New York, 1965)
Carnegie, Dale, *Lincoln the Unknown* (Garden City, 1968, 7th edition)
Catton, Bruce, *The Army of the Potomac, Mr. Lincoln's Army, vol 1* (Garden City, 1962, 2nd edition)
Catton, Bruce, *The Army of the Potomac, Glory Road, vol 2* (Garden City, 1952)
Catton, Bruce, *The Army of the Potomac, A Stillness at Appomattox, vol 3* (Garden City, 1953)
Catton, Bruce, *This Hallowed Ground* (New York, 1956)
Catton, Bruce, *The Coming Fury, vol 1* (Garden City, 1961)
Catton, Bruce, *Terrible Swift Sword, vol 2* (Garden City, 1963)
Catton, Bruce, *Never Call Retreat, vol 3* (Garden City, 1965)
Donovan, Timothy H., Flint, Roy K., Grant, Arthur V. Jr., and Stadler, Gerald P., *The American Civil War* (West Point, 1978)
Duncan, Russell, ed, *Blue-Eyed Child of Fortune, The Civil War Letters of Colonel Robert Gould Shaw* (Athens, 1992)
Goodheart, Adam, *A Quiet Man's Arrival* article (NY Times, 2010)
Goodheart, Adam, *The Narrowest of Loopholes* article (NY Times, 2010)

Goodheart, Adam, *The Night Escape* article (NY Times, 2010)

Goodheart, Adam, *Two Communiques, and a Commander's Dilemma* article (NY Times, 2010)

Goodheart, Adam, *Loose Lips (Almost) Sink Ships* article (NY Times, 2011)

Grafton, John, ed, *Abraham Lincoln Great Speeches* (Mineola, 1991)

Grant, U. S., *Personal Memoirs of U. S. Grant* (New York, 1982 reprint)

Kerner, Fred, ed, *A Treasury of Lincoln Quotations* (Chicago, 1996, 2nd edition)

Lincoln, Abraham, "First Inaugural Address," the Capitol, Washington D.C., 4 March 1861

Lincoln, Abraham, "Gettysburg Address" at dedication of the Soldiers National Cemetery, Gettysburg, Pennsylvania, 19 November 1863, Bliss copy

Lincoln, Abraham, "Last Public Address" in response to the surrender of the Confederate Army of Northern Virgina, the White House, Washington D.C., 11 April 1865, limited enfranchisement

McClure, J. B., ed, *Anecdotes & Stories of Abraham Lincoln* (Mechanicsburg, 2006 reprint)

McGrath, Charles, *Looking at Lincoln through a Prism of War* article (NY Times, 2008)

Malanowski, Jamie, *The Choice is Charybdis* article (NY Times, 2011)

Malanowski, Jamie, *War in the Cabinet* article (NY Times, 2011)

Nicolay, Helen, ed, *Personal Traits of Abraham Lincoln* (Mechanicsburg, 2006 reprint)

Film Documentary:

Burns, Ken, director, *The Civil War*, PBS (1990)

Joan of Arc

Benedictow, O, *The Black Death, 1346 – 1353, The Complete History* (Woodbridge, UK, 2004)

Harrison, Kathryn, *Joan of Arc: A Life Transfigured* (New York, 2014)

Hitchcock, J, *History of the Catholic Church from the Apostolic Era to the Third Millennium* (San Francisco, 2012)

Jehanne la Pucelle, "letter to King Henry VI and the Duke of Bedford" from Sackville-West, V, *St Joan of Arc,* 2nd edition, Appendix D in medieval French

Manchester, William, *A World Lit Only by Fire* (Boston, 1992)

Pernoud, Regine, *The Maid of Orleans, Expanding Horizons* (New York, 1974, 2nd edition)

Sackville-West, V., *St Joan of Arc* (London, 1948, 2nd edition)

University of Canterbury, class outline/ notes for: *Henry VI, The Dauphin, and Joan of Arc* (Christchurch, New Zealand, 2008)

Warner, Marina, *Joan of Arc, The Image of Female Heroism* (New York, 1981)

Miscellaneous

Biden, Joe, "Inaugural Address," the Capitol, Washington D.C., 20 January 2021

Chang, Jung and Halliday, Jon, *Mao, the Unknown Story* (London, 2005)

Gilbert, Martin, *Descent into Barbarism, a history of the 20th century, 1933 – 1951* (London, 1998)

Howard, Roger, *Mao Tse-Tung and the Chinese People* (New York, 1977)

Humes, James C., *The Wit & Wisdom of Winston Churchill* (New York, 1995 edition)

Hunt, John Gabriel, ed, *The Essential Theodore Roosevelt* (New York, 1994)

Kipling, Rudyard, *Rewards and Fairies* (London, 1910), first publication of the poem, *If*

Morgan, Richard, *Decade of Crisis, 11, Milestones of History* (New York, 1975 edition)

Patten, Chris, *East and West* (London, 1998)

Roosevelt, Theodore, *Citizenship in a Republic*, Sorbonne University, Paris, France 23 April 1910, speech on Critics and Achievers

Tuchman, Barbara, *Notes from China* (New York, 1972)

Documentary: *Living with the Enemy, 1945 - 1949* (Germany, 2010)

A number of outstanding historical fiction writings concerning these three eras capture as much historical fact as is known, but also add a personal characterization of Washington, Lincoln, and Joan. The author encourages the reader to back up factual historical readings with good historical fiction. These readings can portray a wider view of the atmosphere of the period described and also help give a better understanding of the why such accomplishments could be done by these three exemplary individuals.

ABOUT THE AUTHOR

Dave Evans is a retired businessman and an American idealist who began serious study of history at West Point. Living abroad for most of the next forty years, he developed a perspective on the roots of American greatness influenced by his travels, the nation's reflection across the globe, and his remove from daily political struggles. Dave shares the disappointment of many Americans with the country's political direction and the increasing partisan divide. This volume offers observations on three transformative leaders – George Washington, Abraham Lincoln, and Joan of Arc – and suggests how their leadership examples can inspire a renewal of the United States. Much as Thomas Paine stirred Americans to seize and hold independence, the author endeavors to persuade and embolden his fellow citizens to restore American unity. It is simply Common Sense.

CPSIA information can be obtained
at www.ICGtesting.com
Printed in the USA
BVHW050243110323
660178BV00013B/1478